Stories of Success:

Bound to Rise
and
Risen from the Ranks
(Illustrated)

Stories of Success:

Bound to Rise
and
Risen from the Ranks
(Illustrated)

Horatio Alger, Jr.

Sumner Books
Hermosa Beach, CA

FIRST EDITION
Sumner Books
737 3rd St
Hermosa Beach, California 90254
310-337-7003
ISBN 978-1-939104-26-7
CREATORS PUBLISHING

TABLE OF CONTENTS

BOOK I: BOUND TO RISE

BOOK II: RISEN FROM THE RANKS

A NOTE FROM THE PUBLISHER

Horatio Alger helped form the American character, yet he is largely forgotten today. Those who are familiar with him think of the phrase, "rags to riches," but that's about it. Most young people have never even heard of him, even though at one time he was described as "America's most influential writer."

What an opportunity! More than a hundred years before our contemporary self-help movement, Horatio Alger paved the way with his vivid illustrations of the keys to success and happiness. Today, Sumner Books is excited to introduce a new generation of Americans to some of the most inspirational stories ever written, what we call "Stories of Success." Regardless of your age, you simply cannot read a Horatio Alger book without coming away with a good feeling.

These books initially sold in the millions and then the tens of millions and finally the hundreds of millions. In fact, the Chicago Daily News once called Horatio Alger "America's best selling author of all time."

Sumner Books is committed to bringing to life this best selling collection in the form of audiobooks and e-books. For the first time ever, these "Stories of Success" will be bundled together as e-books when appropriate. Many times Horatio Alger wrote a novel that was well received, then he wrote three or four more novels over the next few years, and then came back to write Part II to the original novel. So we have taken the two novels that follow the same characters and interwoven plots and published them as a single e-book.

All of the "Stories of Success" e-books offer a detailed table of contents, colored illustrations, commentary and a teacher's guide. They are professionally edited, including the occasional updating of phrases to make the books as easy to read today as they were when they were first published between 1865 and 1900.

Long after his death in 1899, the magazine Publishers Weekly wrote: "To call Horatio Alger Jr. America's most influential writer may seem like an overstatement ... but ... only Benjamin Franklin meant as much to the formation of the American popular mind."

Our goal is to bring back some of the influence that Alger exerted on millions of young people in America. Yes, it's retro; it's counterintuitive and totally contrary to the cynicism that has become a part of American culture. But we are proud to be leading a movement that is as positive and uplifting as the last pages of a Horatio Alger story.

Rick Newcombe
President
Sumner Books

Stories of Success

"Lucky can often mean simply taking advantage of a situation at the right moment. It is possible to 'make' your luck by being always prepared."
Michael Korda

Stories of Success:

Bound To Rise
(Illustrated)

CHAPTER I

BOUND TO RISE

"Sit up to the table, children, breakfast's ready."

The speaker was a woman of middle age, not good-looking in the ordinary acceptation of the term, but nevertheless she looked good. She was dressed with extreme plainness, in a cheap calico; but though cheap, the dress was neat. The children she addressed were six in number, varying in age from twelve to four. The oldest, Harry, the hero of the present story, was a broad-shouldered, sturdy boy, with a frank, open face, resolute, though good-natured.

"Father isn't here," said Fanny, the second child.

"He'll be in directly. He went to the store, and he may stop as he comes back to milk."

The table was set in the center of the room, covered with a coarse tablecloth. The breakfast provided was hardly of a kind to tempt an epicure. There was a loaf of bread cut into slices, and a dish of boiled potatoes. There was no butter and no meat, for the family was very poor.

The children sat up to the table and began to eat. They were blessed with good appetites, and did not grumble, as the majority of my readers would have done, at the scanty fare. They had not been accustomed to anything better, and their appetites were not pampered by indulgence.

They had scarcely commenced the meal when the father entered. Like his wife, he was coarsely dressed. In personal appearance he resembled his oldest boy. His wife looking up as he entered perceived that he looked troubled.

**Boiled potatoes: the modest meal we see the
Walton family eating at the beginning of the story.**

"What is the matter, Hiram?" she asked. "You look as if something had happened."

"Nothing has happened yet," he answered; "but I am afraid we are going to lose the cow."

"Going to lose the cow!" repeated Mrs. Walton in dismay.

"She is sick. I don't know what's the matter with her."

"Perhaps it is only a trifle. She may get over it during the day."

"She may, but I'm afraid she won't. Farmer Henderson's cow was taken just that way last fall, and he couldn't save her."

"What are you going to do?"

"I have been to Elihu Perkins, and he's coming over to see what he can do for her. He can save her if anybody can."

The children listened to this conversation, and, young as they were, the elder ones understood the calamity involved in the possible loss of the cow. They had but one, and that was relied upon to furnish milk for the family, and, besides a small amount of butter and cheese, not for home consumption, but for sale at the store in exchange for necessary groceries. The Waltons were too poor to indulge in these luxuries.

The father was a farmer on a small scale; that is, he cultivated ten acres of poor land, out of which he extorted a living for his family, or rather a partial living. Besides this he worked for his neighbors by the day, sometimes as a farm laborer, sometimes at odd jobs of different kinds, for he was a sort of a Jack at all trades. But his income, all told, was miserably small, and required the utmost economy and good management on the part of his wife to make it equal to the necessity of a growing family of children.

Hiram Walton was a man of good natural abilities, though of not much education, and after half an hour's conversation with him one would say, unhesitatingly, that he deserved a better fate than his hand-to-hand struggle with poverty. But he was one of those men who, for some unaccountable reason, never get on in the world. They can do a great many things creditably, but do not have the knack of conquering fortune. So Hiram had always been a poor man, and probably always would be poor. He was discontented at times, and often felt the disadvantages of his lot, but he was lacking in energy and ambition, and perhaps this was the chief reason why he did not succeed better.

After breakfast Elihu Perkins, the "cow doctor," came to the door. He was an old man with iron-gray hair, and always wore steel-bowed spectacles; at least for twenty years nobody in the town could remember ever having seen him without them. It was the general opinion that he wore them during the night. Once when questioned on the subject, he laughingly said that he "couldn't see to go to sleep without his specs".

"Well, neighbor Walton, so the cow's sick?" he said, opening the outer door without ceremony.

"Yes, Elihu, she looks down in the mouth. I hope you can save her."

"I kin tell better when I've seen the critter. When you've got through breakfast, we'll go out to the barn."

"I've got through now," said Mr. Walton, whose anxiety for the cow had diminished his appetite.

"May I go, too, father?" asked Harry, rising from the table.

"Yes, if you want to."

The three went out to the small, weather-beaten building which served as a barn for the want of a better. It was small, but still large enough to contain all the crops, which Mr. Walton could raise. Probably he could have got more out of the land if he had had means to develop its resources; but it was naturally barren, and needed much more manure than he was able to spread over it.

So the yield to an acre was correspondingly small, and likely, from year to year, to grow smaller rather than larger.

They opened the small barn door, which led to the part occupied by the cow's stall. The cow was lying down, breathing with difficulty. Elihu Perkins looked at her sharply through his specs.

"What do you think of her, neighbor Perkins?" asked the owner, anxiously.

The cow doctor shifted a piece of tobacco from one cheek to the other, and looked wise.

"I think the critter's nigh her end," he said, at last.

"Is she so bad as that?"

"Pears like it. She looks like Farmer Henderson's that died a while ago. I couldn't save her."

"Save my cow, if you can. I don't know what I should do without her."

"I'll do my best, but you mustn't blame me if I can't bring her round. You see there's this about dumb critters that makes 'em harder to cure than human bein's. They can't tell their symptoms, nor how they feel; and that's why it's harder to be a cow doctor than a doctor for humans. You've got to go by the looks, and looks is deceivin'. If I could only ask the critter how she feels, and where she feels worst, I might have some guide to go by. Not but I've had my luck. There's more'n one of 'em I've saved, if I do say it myself."

"I know you can save her if anyone can, Elihu," said Mr. Walton, who appreciated the danger of the cow, and was anxious to have the doctor begin.

"Yes, I guess I know about as much about them critters as anybody," said the garrulous old man, who had a proper appreciation of his dignity and attainments as a cow doctor. "I've had as good success as anyone I know on. If I can't cure her, you may call her a gone case. Have you got any hot water in the house?"

"I'll go in and see."

"I'll go, father," said Harry.

"Well, come right back. We have no time to lose."

Harry appreciated the need of haste as well as his father, and speedily reappeared with a pail of hot water.

"That's right, Harry," said his father. "Now you'd better go into the house and do your chores, so as not to be late for school."

Harry would have liked to remain and watch the steps, which were being taken for the recovery of the cow; but he knew he had barely time to do the "chores" referred to before school, and he was far from wishing to be late there. He had an ardent thirst for learning, and, young as he was, ranked first in the district school, which he attended. I am not about to present my young hero as a marvel of learning, for he was not so. He had improved what opportunities he had enjoyed, but these were very limited. Since he was nine years of age, his schooling had been for the most part limited to eleven weeks in the year. There was a summer as well as a winter school; but in the summer he only attended irregularly, being needed to work at home. His father could not afford to hire help, and there were many ways in which Harry, though young, could help him. So it happened that Harry, though a tolerably good scholar, was deficient in many respects, on account of the limited nature of his opportunities.

He set to work at once at the chores. First he went to the woodpile and sawed and split a quantity of wood, enough to keep the kitchen stove supplied till he came home again from school in the afternoon. This duty was regularly required of him. His father never touched the saw or the ax, but placed upon Harry the general charge of the fuel department.

After sawing and splitting what he thought to be sufficient, he carried it into the house by armfuls, and piled it up near the kitchen stove. He next drew several buckets of water from the well, for it was washing day, brought up some vegetables from the cellar to boil for lunch, and then got ready for school.

CHAPTER II

A CALAMITY

Efforts for the recovery of the cow went on. Elihu Perkins exhausted all his science in her behalf. I do not propose to detail his treatment, because I am not sure whether it was the best, and possibly some of my readers might adopt it under similar circumstances, and then blame me for its unfortunate issue. It is enough to say that the cow grew rapidly worse in spite of the hot-water treatment, and about eleven o'clock breathed her last. Elihu, who first perceived it, announced the sad intelligence.

"The critter's gone," he said. "'Tain't no use doin' anything more."

"The cow's dead!" repeated Mr. Walton, sorrowfully. He had known for an hour that this would be the probable termination of the disease. Still while there was life there was hope. Now both went out together.

"Yes, the critter's dead!" said Elihu, philosophically, for he lost nothing by her. "It was so to be, and there wa'n't no help for it. That's what I thought from the fust, but I was willin' to try."

"Wasn't there anything that could have saved her?"

Elihu shook his head decidedly.

"If she could a-been saved, I could 'ave done it," he said. "What I don't know about cow diseases ain't wuth knowin'."

Everyone is more or less conceited. Elihu's conceit was as to his scientific knowledge on the subject of cows and horses and their diseases. He spoke so confidently that Mr. Walton did not venture to dispute him.

"I s'pose you're right, Elihu," he said; "but it's hard on me."

"Yes, neighbor, it's hard on you, that's a fact. What was she wuth?"

"I wouldn't have taken forty dollars for her yesterday."

"Forty dollars is a good sum."

"It is to me. I haven't got five dollars in the world outside of my farm."

"I wish I could help you, neighbor Walton, but I'm a poor man myself."

"I know you are, Elihu. Somehow it doesn't seem fair that my only cow should be taken, when Squire Green has got ten, and

—

6

they're all alive and well. If all his cows should die, he could buy as many more and not feel the loss."

"Squire Green's a close man."

"He's mean enough, if he is rich."

"Sometimes the richest are the meanest."

"In his case it is true."

"He could give you a cow just as well as not. If I was as rich as he, I'd do it."

"I believe you would, Elihu; but there's some difference between you and him."

"Maybe the squire would lend you money to buy a cow. He always keeps money to lend on high interest."

Mr. Walton reflected a moment, then said slowly, "I must have a cow, and I don't know of any other way, but I hate to go to him."

"He's the only man that's likely to have money to lend in town."

"Well, I'll go."

"Good luck to you, neighbor Walton."

"I need it enough," said Hiram Walton, soberly. "If it comes, it'll be the first time for a good many years."

"Well, I'll be goin', as I can't do no more good."

Hiram Walton went into the house, and a look at his face told his wife the news he brought before his lips uttered it.

"Is she dead, Hiram?"

"Yes, the cow's dead. Forty dollars clean gone," he said, rather bitterly.

"Don't be discouraged, Hiram. It's bad luck, but worse things might happen."

"Such as what?"

"Why, the house might burn down, or—or some of us might fall sick and die. It's better that it should be the cow."

"You're right there; but though it's pleasant to have so many children round, we shan't like to see them starving."

"They are not starving yet, and please God they won't yet awhile. Some help will come to us."

Mrs. Walton sometimes felt despondent herself, but when she saw her husband affected, like a good wife she assumed cheerfulness, in order to raise his spirits. So now, things looked a little more hopeful to him, after he had talked to his wife. He soon took his hat, and approached the door.

"Where are you going, Hiram?" she asked.

"Going to see if Squire Green will lend me money; enough to buy another cow."

"That's right, Hiram. Don't sit down discouraged, but see what you can do to repair the loss."

"I wish there was anybody else to go to. Squire Green is a very mean man, and he will try to take advantage of any need."

"It is better to have a poor resource than none at all."

"Well, I'll go and see what can be done."

Squire Green was the rich man of the town. He had inherited from his father, just as he came of age, a farm of a hundred and fifty acres, and a few hundred dollars.

A large New Hampshire farm, much like the one that Squire Green owns.

The land was not good, and far from productive; but he had scrimped and saved and pinched and denied himself, spending almost nothing, till the little money which the farm annually yielded him had accumulated to a considerable sum. Then, too, as there were no banks near at hand to accommodate borrowers, the squire used to lend money to his poorer neighbors. He took care not to exact more than six percent openly, but it was generally understood that the borrower must pay a bonus besides to secure a loan, which, added to the legal interest, gave him a very handsome consideration for the use of his spare funds. So his money rapidly increased, doubling every five or six years through his shrewd mode of management, and every year he grew more economical. His wife had died ten years before. She had worked hard for very poor pay, for the squire's table was proverbially meager, and her bills for dress, judging from her appearance, must have been uncommonly small.

The squire had one son, now in the neighborhood of thirty, but he had not been at home for several years. As soon as he attained his majority he left the homestead, and set out to seek his fortune elsewhere. He vowed he wouldn't any longer submit to the penurious ways of the squire. So the old man was left alone, but he did not feel the solitude. He had his gold, and that was company enough. A time was coming when the two must part company, for when death should come he must leave the gold behind; but he did not like to think of that, putting away the idea as men will unpleasant subjects. This was the man to whom Hiram Walton applied for help in his misfortune.

"Is the squire at home?" he asked, at the back door. In that household the front door was never used. There was a parlor, but it had not been opened since Mrs. Green's funeral.

"He's out to the barn," said Hannah Green, a niece of the old man, who acted as maid of all work.

"I'll go out there."

The barn was a few rods northeast of the house, and thither Mr. Walton directed his steps.

Entering, he found the old man engaged in some light work.

"Good morning, Squire Green."

"Good morning, Mr. Walton," returned the squire.

He was a small man, with a thin figure, and a face deep seamed with wrinkles, more so than might have been expected in a man of his age, for he was only just turned of sixty; but hard work, poor and scanty food and sharp calculation, were responsible for them.

"How are you gettin' on?" asked the squire.

This was rather a favorite question of his, it being so much the custom for his neighbors to apply to him when in difficulties, so that their misfortune he had come to regard as his harvests.

"I've met with a loss," answered Hiram Walton.

"You don't say so," returned the squire, with instant attention. "What's happened?"

My cow is dead."

"When did she die?"

"This morning."

"What was the matter?"

"I don't know. I didn't notice but that she was welt enough last night; but this morning when I went out to the barn, she was lying down breathing heavily."

"What did you do?"

"I called in Elihu Perkins, and we worked over her for three hours; but it wasn't of any use; she died half an hour ago."

"I hope it isn't any disease that's catchin'," said the squire in alarm, thinking of his ten. "It would be a bad job if it should get among mine."

"It's a bad job for me, squire. I hadn't but one cow, and she's gone."

"Just so, just so. I s'pose you'll buy another."

"Yes, I must have a cow. My children live on bread and milk mostly. Then there's the butter and cheese, that I trade off at the store for groceries."

"Just so, just so. Come into the house, neighbor Walton."

The squire guessed his visitor's business in advance, and wanted to take time to talk it over. He would first find out how great his neighbor's necessity was, and then he accommodated him, would charge him accordingly.

CHAPTER III

HIRAM'S MOTTO

There was a little room just off the kitchen, where the squire had an old-fashioned desk. Here it was that he transacted his business, and in the desk he kept his papers. It was into this room that he introduced Mr. Walton.

"Set down, set down, neighbor Walton," he said. "We'll talk this thing over. So you've got to have a cow?"

"Yes, I must have one."

The squire fixed his eyes cunningly on his intended victim, and said, "Goin' to buy one in town?"

"I don't know of any that's for sale."

"How much do you calc'late to pay?"

"I suppose I'll have to pay thirty dollars."

Squire Green shook his head.

"More'n that, neighbor Walton. You can't get a decent cow for thirty dollars. I hain't got one that isn't wuth more, though I've got ten in my barn."

"Thirty dollars is all I can afford to pay, squire."

"Take my advice, and get a good cow while you're about it. It don't pay to get a poor one."

"I'm a poor man, squire. I must take what I can get."

"I ain't sure but I've got a cow that will suit you, a red with white spots. She's a fust-rate milker."

"How old is she?"

"She's turned of five."

"How much do you ask for her?"

"Are you going to pay cash down?" asked the squire, half shutting his eyes, and looking into the face of his visitor.

"I can't do that. I'm very short of money."

"So am I," chimed in the squire. He had two hundred dollars in his desk at that moment waiting for profitable investment; but then he didn't call it exactly a lie to misrepresent for a purpose. "So am I. Money's tight, neighbor."

"Money's always tight with me, squire," returned Hiram Walton, with a sigh.

"Was you a-meanin' to pay anything down?" inquired the squire.

"I don't see how I can."

"That alters the case, you know. I might as well keep the cow, as to sell her without the money down."

"I am willing to pay interest on the money."

"Of course that's fair. Wall, neighbor, what do you say to goin' out to see the cow?"

"Is she in the barn?"

"No, she's in the pastur'. 'Tain't fur."

"I'll go along with you."

They made their way by a short cut across a cornfield to the pasture—a large ten-acre lot, covered with scanty vegetation. The squire's cows could not be said to live in clover.

"That's the critter," he said, pointing out one of the cows which was grazing near by. "Ain't she a beauty?"

"She looks pretty well," said Mr. Walton, dubiously, by no means sure that she would equal his lost cow.

"She's one of the best I've got. I wouldn't sell ef it wasn't to oblige. I ain't at all partic'lar, but I suppose you've got to hev a cow."

"What do you ask for her, squire?"

"She's wuth all of forty dollars," answered the squire, who knew perfectly well that a fair price would be about thirty. But then his neighbor must have a cow, and had no money to pay, and so was at his mercy.

"That seems high," said Hiram.

"She's wuth every cent of it; but I ain't nowise partic'lar about sellin' her."

"Couldn't you say thirty-seven?"

"I couldn't take a dollar less. I'd rather keep her. Maybe I'd take thirty-eight, cash down."

Hiram Walton shook his head.

"I have no cash," he said. "I must buy on credit."

"Wall, then, there's a bargain for you. I'll let you have her for forty dollars, giving you six months to pay it, at reg'lar interest, six percent. Of course I expect a little bonus for the accommodation."

"I hope you'll be easy with me—I'm a poor man, squire."

"Of course, neighbor; I'm always easy."

"That isn't your reputation," thought Hiram; but he knew that this was a thought to which he must not give expression.

"All I want is a fair price for my time and trouble. We'll say three dollars extra for the accommodation—three dollars down."

Hiram Walton felt that it was a hard bargain the squire was driving with him, but there seemed no help for it.

He must submit to the imposition, or do without a cow. There was no one else to whom he could look for help on any terms. As to the three dollars, his whole available cash amounted to but four dollars, and it was for three quarters of this sum that the squire called. But the sacrifice must be made.

"Well, Squire Green, if that is your lowest price, I suppose I must come to it," he answered, at last.

"You can't do no better," said the squire, with alacrity.

"If so be as you've made up your mind, we'll make out the papers."

"Very well."

"Come back to the house. When do you want to take the cow?"

"I'll drive her along now, if you are willing."

"Why, you see," said the squire, hesitating, while a mean thought entered his, mind, "she's been feedin' in my pastur' all the mornin', and I calc'late I'm entitled to the next milkin', you'd better come 'round tonight, just after milkin', and then you can take her."

"I didn't think he was quite so mean," passed through Hiram Walton's mind, and his lip curved slightly in scorn, but he knew that this feeling must be concealed.

"Just as you say," he answered. "I'll come round tonight, or send Harry."

"How old is Harry now?"

"About fourteen."

"He's got to be quite a sizable lad—ought to earn concid'able. Is he industrious?"

"Yes, Harry is a good worker—always ready to lend a hand."

"That's good. Does he go to school?"

"Yes, he's been going to school all the term."

"Seems to me he's old enough to give up larnin' altogether. Don't he know how to read and write and cipher?"

"Yes, he's about the best scholar in school."

"Then, neighbor Walton, take my advice and don't send him any more. You need him at home, and he knows enough to get along in the world."

"I want him to learn as much as he can. I'd like to send him to school till he is sixteen."

"He's had as much schoolin' now as ever I had," said the squire, "and I've got along pooty well. I've been seleckman, and school committy, and filled about every town office, and I never wanted no more schoolin'. My father took me away from school when I was thirteen."

"It wouldn't hurt you if you knew a little more," thought Hiram, who remembered very well the squire's deficiencies when serving on the town school committee.

"I believe in learning," he said. "My father used to say, 'Live and learn.' That's a good motto, to my thinking."

"It may be carried too far. When a boy's got to be of the age of your boy, he'd ought to be thinking of workin.' His time is too valuable to spend in the schoolroom."

"I can't agree with you, squire. I think no time is better spent than the time that's spent in learning. I wish I could afford to send my boy to college."

"It would cost a mint of money; and wouldn't pay. Better put him to some good business."

That was the way he treated his own son, and for this and other reasons, as soon as he arrived at man's estate, he left home, which had never had any pleasant associations with him. His father wanted to convert him into a money-making machine—a mere drudge, working him hard, and denying him, as long as he could, even the common recreations of boyhood—for the squire had an idea that the time devoted in play was foolishly spent, inasmuch as it brought him in no pecuniary return. He was willfully blind to the faults and defects of his system, and their utter failure in the case of his own son, and would, if could, have all the boys in town brought up after severely practical method. But, fortunately for Harry, Mr. Walton had very different notions. He was compelled to keep his son home the greater part of the summer, but it was against his desire.

"No wonder he's a poor man," thought the squire, after his visitor returned home. "He ain't got no practical idees. Live and learn! that's all nonsense. His boy looks strong and able to work, and it's foolish sendin' him school any longer. That wa'n't my way, and see where I am," he concluded, with complacent remembrance of bonds and mortgages and money out at interest. "That was a pooty good cow trade," he concluded. "I didn't calc' late for to get more'n thirty-five dollars for the critter; but then neighbor Walton had to have a cow, and had to pay my price."

14

Now for Hiram Walton's reflections.

"I'm a poor man," he said to himself, as he walked slowly homeward, "but I wouldn't be as mean as Tom Green for all the money he's worth. He's made a hard bargain with me, but there was no help for it."

CHAPTER IV

A SUM IN ARITHMETIC

Harry kept on his way to school, and arrived just the bell rang. Many of my readers have seen a country schoolhouse, and will not be surprised to learn that the one in which our hero obtained his education was far from stately or ornamental, architecturally speaking. It was a one-story structure, about thirty feet square, showing traces of having been painted once, but standing greatly in need of another coat. Within were sixty desks, ranged in pairs, with aisles running between them. On one side sat the girls, on the other the boys. These were of all ages from five to sixteen. The boys' desks had suffered bad usage, having been whittled and hacked, and marked with the initials of the temporary occupants, with scarcely an exception. I never knew a Yankee boy who was not the possessor of a knife of some kind, nor one who could resist the temptation of using it for such unlawful purposes. Even our hero shared the common weakness, and "H. W." rudely carved in a conspicuous place distinguished his desk from the rest.

The teacher of the school for the present session was Nathan Burbank, a country teacher of good repute, who usually taught six months in a year, and devoted the balance of the year to surveying land, whenever he could get employment in that line, and the cultivation of half a dozen acres of land, which kept him in vegetables, and enabled him to keep a cow. Altogether he succeeded in making a fair living, though his entire income would seem very small to many of my readers. He was not deeply learned, but his education was sufficient to meet the limited requirements of a country school.

This was the summer term, and it is the usual custom in New England that the summer schools should be taught by females. But in this particular school the experiment had been tried, and didn't work. It was found that the scholars were too unruly to be kept in subjection by a woman, and the school committee had therefore engaged Mr. Burbank, though, by so doing, the school term was shortened, as he asked fifty percent higher wages than a female teacher would have done. However, it was better to have a short school than an unruly school, and so the district acquiesced.

Eight weeks had not yet passed since the term commenced, and yet this was the last day but one. Tomorrow would be examination day. To this Mr. Burbank made reference in a few remarks which he made at the commencement of the exercises.

He was rather a tall, spare man, and had a habit of brushing his hair upward, thus making the most of a moderate forehead. Probably he thought it made him look more intellectual.

"Boys and girls," he said, "tomorrow is our examination day. I've tried to bring you along as far as possible toward the temple of learning, but some of you have held back, and have not done as well as I should like—John Plympton, if you don't stop whispering I'll keep you after school—I want you all to remember that knowledge is better than land or gold. What would you think of a man who was worth a great fortune, and couldn't spell his name?—Mary Jones, can't you sit still till I get through?—It will be well for you to improve your opportunities while you are young, for by and by you will grow up, and have families to support, and will have no chance to learn—Jane Quimby, I wish you would stop giggling, I see nothing to laugh at—There are some of you who have studied well this term, and done the best you could. At the beginning of the term I determined to give a book to the most deserving scholar at the end of the term. I have picked out the boy, who, in my opinion, deserves it—Ephraim Higgins, you needn't move round in your seat. You are not the one."

There was a general laugh here, for Ephraim was distinguished chiefly for his laziness.

The teacher proceeded:

"I do not mean to tell you today who it is. Tomorrow I shall call out his name before the school committee, and present him the prize. I want you to do as well as you can tomorrow. I want you to do yourselves credit, and to do me credit, for I do not want to be ashamed of you. Peter Shelby, put back that knife into your pocket, and keep it there till I call up the class in whittling."

There was another laugh here at the teacher's joke, and Peter himself displayed a broad grin on his large, good-humored face.

"We will now proceed to the regular lessons," said Mr. Burbank, in conclusion. "First class in arithmetic will take their places."

The first class ranked as the highest class, and in it was Harry Walton.

"What was your lesson today?" asked the teacher.

"Square root," answered Harry.

"I will give you out a very simple sum to begin with. Now, attention all! Find the square root of 625. Whoever gets the answer first may hold up his hand."

The first to hold up his hand was Ephraim Higgins.

"Have you got the answer?" asked Mr. Burbank in some surprise. "Yes, sir."

"State it."

"Forty-five."

"How did you get it?"

Ephraim scratched his head, and looked confused. The fact was, he was entirely ignorant of the method of extracting the square root, but had slyly looked at the slate of his neighbor, Harry Walton, and mistaken the 25 for 45, and hurriedly announced the answer, in the hope of obtaining credit for the same.

"How did you get it?" asked the teacher again.

Ephraim looked foolish.

"Bring me your slate."

Ephraim reluctantly left his place, and went up to Mr. Burbank.

"What have we here?" said the teacher. "Why, you have got down the 625, and nothing else, except 45. Where did you get that answer?"

"I guessed at it," answered Ephraim, hard pressed for an answer, and not liking to confess the truth—namely, that he had copied from Harry Walton.

"So I supposed. The next time you'd better guess a little nearer right, or else give up guessing altogether. Harry Walton, I see your hand up. What is your answer?"

"Twenty-five, sir."

"That is right."

Ephraim looked up suddenly. He now saw the explanation of his mistake.

"Will you explain how you did it? You may go to the blackboard, and perform the operation once more, explaining as you go along, for the benefit of Ephraim Higgins, and any others who guessed at the answer. Ephraim, I want you to give particular attention, so that you can do yourself more credit next time. Now Harry, proceed."

Our hero explained the sum in a plain, straightforward way, for he thoroughly understood it.

"Very well," said the schoolmaster, for this, rather than teacher, is the country name of the office. "Now, Ephraim, do you think you can explain it?"

"I don't know, sir," said Ephraim, dubiously.

"Suppose you try. You may take the same sum."

Ephraim advanced to the board with reluctance, for he was not ambitious, and had strong doubts about his competence for the task.

"Put down 625."

Ephraim did so.

"Now extract the square root. What do you do first?"

"Divide it into two figures each."

"Divide it into periods of two figures each, I suppose you mean. Well, what will be the first period?"

"Sixty-two," answered Ephraim.

"And what will be the second?"

"I don't see but one other figure."

"Nor I. You have made a mistake. Harry, show to point it off."

Harry Walton did so.

"Now what do you do next?"

"Divide the first figure by three."

"What do you do that for?"

Ephraim didn't know. It was only a guess of his, because he knew that the first figure of the answer was two, and this would result from dividing the first figure by three.

"To bring the answer," he replied.

"And I suppose you divide the next period by five, for the same reason, don't you?"

"Yes, sir."

"You may take your seat, sir. You are an ornament to the class, and you may become a great mathematician, if you live to the age of Methuselah. I rather think it will take about nine hundred years for you to reach that, point."

The boys laughed. They always relish a joke at the expense of a companion, especially when perpetrated by the teacher.

"Your method of extracting the square root is very original. You didn't find it in any arithmetic, did you?"

"No, sir."

"So I thought. You'd better take out a patent for it. The next boy may go to the board."

I have given a specimen of Mr. Burbank's method of conducting the school, but do not propose to enter into further details at present. It will doubtless recall to some of my readers experiences of their own, as the school I am describing is very similar to hundreds of country schools now in existence, and Mr. Burbank is the representative of a large class.

CHAPTER V

THE PRIZE WINNER

"Are you going to the examination today, mother?" asked Harry, at breakfast.

"I should like to go," said Mrs. Walton, "but I don't see how I can. Today's my bakin' day, and somehow my work has got behindhand during the week."

"I think Harry'll get the prize," said Tom, a boy of ten, not heretofore mentioned. He also attended the school, but was not as promising as his oldest brother.

"What prize?" asked Mrs. Walton, looking up with interest.

"The master offered a prize, at the beginning of the term, to the scholar that was most faithful to his studies."

"What is the prize?"

"A book."

"Do you think you will get it, Harry?" asked his mother.

"I don't know," said Harry, modestly. "I think I have some chance of getting it."

"When will it be given?"

"Toward the close of the afternoon."

"Maybe I can get time to come in then; I'll try."

"I wish you would come, mother," said Harry earnestly. "Only don't be disappointed if I don't get it. I've been trying, but there are some other good scholars."

"You're the best, Harry," said Tom.

"I don't know about that. I shan't count my chickens before they are hatched. Only if I am to get the prize I should like to have mother there."

"I know you're a good scholar, and have improved your time," said Mrs. Walton. "I wish your father was rich enough to send you to college."

"I should like that very much," said Harry, his eyes sparkling at merely the suggestion.

"But it isn't much use hoping," continued his mother, with a sigh. "It doesn't seem clear whether we can get a decent living, much less send our boy to college. The cow is a great loss to us."

Just then Mr. Walton came in from the barn.

"How do you like the new cow, father?" asked Harry.

"She isn't equal to our old one. She doesn't give as much milk within two quarts, if this morning's milking is a fair sample."

"You paid enough for her," said Mrs. Walton.

"I paid too much for her," answered her husband, "but it was the best I could do. I had to buy on credit, and Squire Green knew I must pay his price, or go without."

"Forty-three dollars is a great deal of money to pay for a cow."

"Not for some cows. Some are worth more; but this one isn't."

"What do you think she is really worth?"

"Thirty-three dollars is the most I would give if I had the cash to pay."

"I think it's mean in Squire Green to take such advantage of you," said Harry.

"You mustn't say so, Harry, for it won't do for me to get the squire's ill will. I am owing him money. I've agreed to pay for the cow in six months."

"Can you do it?"

"I don't see how; but the money's on interest, and it maybe the squire'll let it stay. I forgot to say, though, that last evening when I went to get the cow he made me agree to forfeit ten dollars if I was not ready with the money and interest in six months. I am afraid he will insist on that if I can't keep my agreement."

"It will be better for you to pay, and have done with it."

"Of course. I shall try to do it, if I have to borrow the money. I suppose I shall have to do that."

Meantime Harry was busy thinking. "Wouldn't it be possible for me to earn money enough to pay for the cow in six months? I wish I could do it, and relieve father."

He began to think over all the possible ways of earning money, but there was nothing in particular to do in the town except to work for the farmers, and there was very little money to earn ill that way. Money is a scarce commodity with farmers everywhere. Most of their income is in the shape of farm produce, and used in the family. Only a small surplus is converted into money, and a dollar, therefore, seems more to them than to a mechanic, whose substantial income is perhaps less. This is the reason, probably, why farmers are generally loath to spend money. Harry knew that if he should hire out to a farmer for the six months the utmost he could expect would be a dollar a week, and it was not certain he could earn that. Besides, he would probably be worth as much to his father as anyone, and his labor in neither case provide money to pay for the cow. Obviously, that would not answer. He must think of some other way, but at present none seemed open. He sensibly deferred thinking till after the examination.

"Are you going to the school examination, father?" asked our hero.

"I can't spare time, Harry. I should like to, for I want to know how far you have progressed. 'Live and learn,' my boy. That's a good motto, though Squire Green thinks that 'Live and earn' is a better."

"That's the rule he acts on," said Mrs. Walton. "He isn't troubled with learning."

"No, he isn't as good a scholar probably as Tom, here."

"Isn't he?" said Tom, rather complacently.

"Don't feel too much flattered, Tom," said his mother.

"You don't know enough to hurt you."

"He never will," said his sister, Jane, laughing.

"I don't want to know enough to hurt me," returned Tom, good humoredly. He was rather used to such compliments, and didn't mind them.

"No," said Mr. Walton; "I am afraid I can't spare time to come to the examination. Are you going, mother?"

It is quite common in the country for husbands to address wives in this manner.

"I shall try to go in the last of the afternoon," said Mrs. Walton.

"If you will come, mother," said Harry, "we'll all help you afterwards, so you won't lose anything by it."

"I think I will contrive to come."

The examination took place in the afternoon. Mr. Burbank preferred to have it so, for two reasons. It allowed time to submit the pupils to a previous private examination in the morning, thus insuring a better appearance in the afternoon. Besides, in the second place, the parents were more likely to be at liberty to attend in the afternoon, and he naturally liked to have as many visitors as possible. He was really a good teacher, though his qualifications were limited; but as far as his knowledge went, he was quite successful in imparting it to others.

In the afternoon there was quite a fair attendance of parents and friends of the scholars, though some did not come in till late, like Mrs. Walton. It is not my intention to speak of the examination in detail. My readers know too little of the scholars to make that interesting. Ephraim Higgins made some amusing mistakes, but that didn't excite any surprise, for his scholarship was correctly estimated in the village. Tom Walton did passably well, but was not likely to make his parents proud of his performances. Harry, however, eclipsed himself. His ambition had been stirred by the offer of a prize, and he was resolved to deserve it. His recitations were prompt and correct, and his answers were given with confidence. But perhaps he did himself most credit in declamation. He had always been very fond of that, and though he had never received and scientific instruction in it, he possessed a natural grace and a deep feeling of earnestness which made success easy. He had selected an extract from Webster—the reply to the Hayne—and this was the showpiece of the afternoon. The rest of the declamation was crude enough, but Harry's impressed even the most ignorant of his listeners as superior for a boy of his age. When he uttered his last sentence, and made a parting bow, there was subdued applause, and brought a flush of gratification to the cheek of our young hero.

"This is the last exercise," said the teacher "except one. At the commencement of the term, I offered a prize to the scholar that would do the best from that time till the close of the school. I will now award the prize. Harry Walton, come forward."

Harry rose from his seat, his cheeks flushed again with gratification, and advanced to where the teacher was standing.

"Harry," said Mr. Burbank, "I have no hesitation in giving you the prize. You have excelled all the other scholars, and it is fairly yours. The book is not of much value, but I think you will find it interesting and instructive. It is the life of the great American philosopher and statesman, Benjamin Franklin. I hope you will read and profit by it, and try like him to make your life a credit to yourself and a blessing to mankind."

Benjamin Franklin is the inspiration for Harry Walton.

"Thank you, sir," said Harry, bowing low. "I will try to do so." There was a speech by the chairman of the school committee, in which allusion was made to Harry and the prize, and the exercises were over. Harry received the congratulations of his schoolmates and others with modest satisfaction, but he was most pleased by the evident pride and pleasure which his mother exhibited, when she, too, was congratulated on his success. His worldly prospects were very uncertain, but he had achieved the success for which he had been laboring, and he was happy.

CHAPTER VI

LOOKING OUT ON THE WORLD

It was not until evening that Harry had a chance to look at his prize. It was a cheap book, costing probably not over a dollar; but except his schoolbooks, and a ragged copy of "Robinson Crusoe," it was the only book that our hero possessed. His father found it difficult enough to buy him the necessary books for use in school, and could not afford to buy any less necessary. So our young hero, who was found of reading, though seldom able to gratify his taste, looked forward with great joy to the pleasure of reading his new book. He did not know much about Benjamin Franklin, but had a vague idea that he was a great man.

After his evening chores were done, he sat down by the table on which was burning a solitary tallow candle, and began to read. His mother was darning stockings, and his father had gone to the village store on an errand.

So he began the story, and the more he read the more interesting he found it. Great as he afterwards became, he was surprised to find that Franklin was a poor boy, and had to work for a living. He started out in life on his own account, and through industry, frugality, perseverance, and a fixed determination to rise in life, he became a distinguished an in the end, and a wise man also, though his early opportunities were very limited. It seemed to Harry that there was a great similarity between his own circumstances and position in life and those of the great man about whom he was reading, and this made the biography the more fascinating. The hope came to him that, by following Franklin's example, he, too, might become a successful man.

His mother, looking up at intervals from the stockings which had been so repeatedly darned that the original texture was almost wholly lost of sight of, noticed how absorbed he was.

"Is your book interesting, Harry?" she asked.

"It's the most interesting book I ever read," said Harry, with a sigh of intense enjoyment.

"It's about Benjamin Franklin, isn't it?"

"Yes. Do you know, mother, he was a poor boy, and he worked his way up?"

"Yes, I have heard so, but I never read his life."

"You'd better read this when I have finished it. I've been thinking that there's a chance for me, mother."

"A chance to do what?"

"A chance to be somebody when I get bigger. I'm poor now, but so was Franklin. He worked hard, and tried to learn all he could. That's the way he succeeded. I'm going to do the same."

"We can't all be Franklins, my son," said Mrs. Walton, not wishing her son to form high hopes which might be disappointed in the end.

"I know that, mother, and I don't expect to be a great man like him. But if I try hard I think I can rise in the world, and be worth a little money."

"I hope you wont' be as poor as your father, Harry," said Mrs. Walton, sighing, as she thought of the years of pain privation and pinching poverty reaching back to the time of their marriage. They had got through it somehow, but she hoped that their children would have a brighter lot.

"I hope not," said Harry. "If I ever get rich, you shan't have to work any more."

Mrs. Walton smiled faintly. She was not hopeful, and thought it probable that before Harry became rich, both she and her husband would be resting from their labor in the village churchyard. But she would not dampen Harry's youthful enthusiasm by the utterance of such a thought.

"I am sure you won't let your father and mother want, if you have the means to prevent it," she said aloud.

"We can't any of us tell what's coming, but I hope you may be well off some time."

"I read in the country paper the other day that many of the richest men in Boston and New York were once poor boys," said Harry, in a hopeful tone.

"So I have heard," said his mother.

"If they succeeded I don't see why I can't."

"You must try to be something more than a rich man. I shouldn't want you to be like Squire Green."

"He is rich, but he is mean and ignorant. I don't think I shall be like him. He has cheated father about the cow."

"Yes, he drove a sharp trade with him, taking advantage of his necessities. I am afraid your father won't be able to pay for the cow six months from now."

"I am afraid so, too."

"I don't see how we can possibly save up forty dollars. We are economical now as we can be."

"That is what I have been thinking of, mother. There is no chance of father's paying the money."

"Then it won't be paid, and we shall be worse off when the note comes due, than now."

"Do you think," said Harry, laying down the book on the table, and looking up earnestly, "do you think, mother, I could any way earn the forty dollars before it is to be paid?"

"You, Harry?" repeated his mother, in surprise, "what could you do to earn the money?"

"I don't know, yet," answered Harry; "but there are a great many things to be done."

"I don't know what you can do, except to hire out to a farmer, and they pay very little. Besides, I don't know of any farmer in the town that wants a boy. Most of them have boys of their own, or men."

"I wasn't thinking of that," said Harry. "There isn't much chance there."

"I don't know of any work to do here."

"Nor I, mother. But I wasn't thinking of staying in town."

"Not thinking of staying in town!" repeated Mrs. Walton, in surprise. "You don't want to leave home, do you?"

"No, mother, I don't want to leave home, or I wouldn't want to, if there was anything to do here. But you know there isn't. Farm work wont' help me along, and I don't' like it as well as some other kinds of work. I must leave home if I want to rise in the world."

"But your are too young, Harry."

This was touching Harry on a tender spot. No boy of fourteen likes to be considered very young. By that time he generally begins to feel a degree of self-confidence and self-reliance, and fancies he is almost on the threshold of manhood. I know boys of fourteen who look in the glass daily for signs of a coming mustache, and fancy they can see plainly what is not yet visible. Harry had not got as far as that, but he no longer looked upon himself as a young boy. He was stout and strong, and of very good height for his age, and began to feel manly. So he drew himself up, upon this remark of his mother's, and said proudly: "I am going on fifteen"—that sounds older than fourteen—"and I don't call that very young."

28

"It seems but a little while since you were a baby," said his mother, meditatively.

"I hope you don't think me anything like a baby now, mother," said Harry, straightening up, and looking as large as possible.

"No, you're quite a large boy, now. How quick the years have passed!"

"And I am strong for my age, too, mother. I am sure I am old enough to take care of myself."

"But you are young to go out into the world."

"I don't believe Franklin was much older than I, and he got along. There are plenty of boys who leave home before they are as old as I am."

"Suppose you are sick, Harry?"

"If I am I'll come home. But you know I am very healthy, mother, and if I am away from home I shall be very careful."

"But you would not be sure of getting anything to do."

"I'll risk that, mother," said Harry, in a confident tone.

"Did you think of this before you read that book?"

"Yes, I've been thinking of it for about a month; but the book put it into my head tonight. I seem to see my way clearer than I did. I want most of all, to earn money enough to pay for the cow in six months. You know yourself, mother, there isn't any chance of father doing it himself, and I can't earn anything if I stay at home."

"Have you mentioned the matter to your father yet, Harry?"

"No, I haven't. I wish you would speak about it tonight, mother. You can tell him first what makes me want to go."

"I'll tell him that you want to go; but I won't promise to say I think it a good plan."

"Just mention it, mother, and then I'll talk with him about it tomorrow."

To this Mrs. Walton agreed, and Harry, after reading a few pages more in the "Life of Franklin," went up to bed; but it was some time before he slept. His mind was full of the new scheme on which he had set his heart.

CHAPTER VII

IN FRANKLIN'S FOOTSTEPS

"Father," said Harry, the next morning, as Mr. Walton was about to leave the house, "there's something I want to say to you."

"What is it?" asked his father, imagining it was some trifle.

"I'll go out with you, and tell you outside."

"Very well, my son."

Harry put on his cap, and followed his father into the open air.

"Now, my son, what is it?"

"I want to go away from home."

"Away from home! Where?" asked Mr. Walton, in surprise.

"I don't know where; but somewhere where I can earn my own living."

"But you can do that here. You can give me your help on the farm, as you always have done."

"I don't like farming, father."

"You never told me that before. Is it because of the hard work?"

"No," said Harry, earnestly. "I am not afraid of hard work; but you know how it is, father. This isn't a very good farm, and it's all you can do to make a living for the rest of us out of it. If I could go somewhere, where I could work at something else, I could send you home my wages."

"I am afraid a boy like you couldn't earn very large wages."

"I don't see why not, father. I'm strong and stout, and willing to work."

"People don't give much for boys' work."

"I don't expect much; but I know I can get something, and by and by it will lead to more. I want to help you to pay for that cow you've just bought of Squire Green."

"I don't see how I'm going to pay for it," said Mr. Walton, with a sigh. "Hard money's pretty scarce, and we farmers don't get much of it."

"That's just what I'm saying, father. There isn't much money to be got in farming. That's why I want to try something else."

"How long have you been thinking of this plan, Harry?"

"Only since last night."

"What put it into your head?"

"That book I got as a prize."

"It is the life of Franklin, isn't it?"

"Yes."

"Did he go away from home when he was a boy?"

"Yes, and he succeeded, too."

"I know he did. He became a famous man. But it isn't every boy that is like Franklin."

"I know that. I never expect to become a great man like him; but I can make something."

Harry spoke those words in a firm, resolute tone, which seemed to indicate a consciousness of power. Looking in his son's face, the elder Walton, though by no means a sanguine man, was inclined to think favorably of the scheme, But he was cautious, and he did not want Harry to be too confident of success.

"It's a new idea to me," he said. "Suppose you fail?"

"I don't mean to."

"But suppose you do—suppose you get sick?"

"Then I'll come home. But I want to try. There must be something for me to do in the world."

"There's another thing, Harry. It takes money to travel round, and I haven't got any means to give you."

"I don't want any, father. I mean to work my way. I've got twenty-five cents to start with. Now, father, what do you say?"

"I'll speak to your mother about it."

"Today?"

"Yes, as soon as I go in."

With this Harry was content. He had a good deal of confidence that he could carry his point with both parents. He went into the house, and said to his mother:

"Mother, father's going to speak to you about my going away from home. Now don't you oppose it."

"Do you really think it would be a good plan, Harry?"

"Yes, mother."

"And if you're sick will you promise to come right home?"

"Yes, I'll promise that."

"Then I won't oppose your notion, though I ain't clear about its being wise."

"We'll talk about that in a few months, mother."

"Has Harry spoken to you about his plan of going away from home?" asked the farmer, when he re-entered the house.

"Yes," said Mrs. Walton.

"What do you think?"

"Perhaps we'd better let the lad have his way. He's promised to come home if he's taken sick."

"So let it be, then, Harry. When do you want to go?"

"As soon as I can."

"You'll have to wait till Monday. It'll take a day or two to fix up your clothes," said his mother.

"All right, mother."

"I don't know but you ought to have some new shirts. You haven't got but two except the one you have on."

"I can get along, mother. Father hasn't got any money to spend for me. By the time I want some new shirts, I'll buy them myself."

"Where do you think of going, Harry? Have you any idea?"

"No, mother. I'm going to trust to luck. I shan't go very far. When I've got fixed anywhere I'll write, and let you know."

In the evening Harry resumed the "Life of Franklin," and before he was ready to go to bed he had got two-thirds through with it. It possessed for him a singular fascination. To Harry it was not only the "Life of Benjamin Franklin." It was the chart by which he meant to steer in the unknown career which stretched before him. He knew so little of the world that he trusted implicitly to that as a guide, and he silently stored away the wise precepts in conformity with which the great practical philosopher had shaped and molded his life.

During that evening, however, another chance was offered to Harry, as I shall now describe.

As the family were sitting around the kitchen table, on which was placed the humble tallow candle by which the room was lighted, there was heard a scraping at the door, and presently a knock. Mr. Walton answered it in person, and admitted the thin figure and sharp, calculating face of Squire Green.

"How are you, neighbor?" he said, looking about him with his parrot like glance. "I thought I'd just run in a minute to see you as I was goin' by."

"Sit down, Squire Green. Take the rocking-chair."

"Thank you, neighbor. How's the cow a-doin'?"

"Middling well. She don't give as much milk as the one I lost."

"She'll do better bymeby. She's a good bargain to you, neighbor."

"I don't know," said Hiram Walton, dubiously. "She ought to be a good cow for the price you asked."

"And she is a good cow," said the squire, emphatically; "and you're lucky to get her so cheap, buyin' on time. What are you doin' there, Harry? School through, ain't it?"

"Yes, sir."

"I hear you're a good scholar. Got the prize, didn't you?"

"Yes," said Mr. Walton; "Harry was always good at his books."

"I guess he knows enough now. You'd ought to set him to work."

"He is ready enough to work," said Mr. Walton. "He never was lazy."

"That's good. There's a sight of lazy, shiftless boys about in these days. Seems as if they expected to earn their bread 'n butter a-doin' nothin'. I've been a thinkin', neighbor Walton, that you'll find it hard to pay for that cow in six months."

"I am afraid I shall," said the farmer, thinking in surprise, "Can he be going to reduce the price?"

"So I thought mebbe we might make an arrangement to make it easier."

"I should be glad to have it made easier, squire. It was hard on me, losing that cow by disease."

"Of course. Well, what I was thinkin' was, you might hire out your boy to work for me. I'd allow him two dollars a month and board, and the wages would help pay for the cow."

Harry looked up in dismay at this proposition. He knew very well the meanness of the board which the squire provided, how inferior it was even to the scanty, but well-cooked meals which he got at home; he knew, also that the squire had the knack of getting more work out of his men than any other farmer in the town; and the prospect of being six months in his employ was enough to terrify him. He looked from Squire Green's mean, crafty face to his father's in anxiety and apprehension. Were all his bright dreams of future success to terminate in this?

CHAPTER VIII

HARRY'S DECISION

Squire Green rubbed his hands as if he had been proposing a plan with special reference to the interest of the Waltons. Really he conceived that it would save him a considerable sum of money. He had in his employ a young man of eighteen, named Abner Kimball, to whom he was compelled to pay ten dollars a month. Harry, he reckoned, could be made to do about as much, though on account of his youth he had offered him but two dollars, and that not to be paid in cash.

Mr. Walton paused before replying to his proposal.

"You're a little too late," he said, at last, to Harry's great relief.

"Too late!" repeated the squire, hastily. "Why, you hain't hired out your boy to anybody else, have you?"

"No; but he has asked me to let him leave home, and I've agreed to it."

"Leave home? Where's he goin'?"

"He has not fully decided. He wants to go out and seek his fortune."

"He'll fetch up at the poorhouse," growled the squire.

"If he does not succeed, he will come home again."

"It's a foolish plan, neighbor Walton. Take my word for't. You'd better keep him here, and let him work for me."

"If he stayed at home, I should find work for him on my farm."

Mr. Walton would not have been willing to have Harry work for the squire, knowing well his meanness, and how poorly he paid his hired men.

"I wanted to help you pay for that cow," said the squire, crossly. "If you can't pay for't when the time comes you mustn't blame me."

"I shall blame no one. I can't foresee the future; but I hope to get together the money somehow."

"You mustn't ask for more time. Six months is a long time to give."

"I believe I haven't said anything about more time yet, Squire Green," said Hiram Walton, stiffly. "I don't see that you need warn me."

"I thought we might as well have an understandin' about it," said the squire. "So you won't hire out the boy?"

"No, I cannot, under the circumstances. If I did, I should consider his services worth more than two dollars a month."

"I might give him two'n a half," said the squire, fancying it was merely a question of money.

"How much do you pay Abner Kimball?"

"Wal, rather more than that," answered the squire, slowly.

"You pay him ten dollars a month, don't you?"

"Wal, somewheres about that; but it's more'n he earns."

"If he is worth ten dollars, Harry would be worth four or six."

"I'll give three," said the squire, who reflected that even at that rate he would be saving considerable.

"I will leave it to Harry himself," said his father.

"Harry, you hear Squire Green's offer. What do you say? Will you go to work for him at three dollars a month?"

"I'd rather go away, as you told me I might, father."

"You hear the boy's decision, squire."

"Wal, wal," said the squire, a good deal disappointed—for, to tell the truth, he had told Abner he should not want him, having felt confident of obtaining Harry. "I hope you won't neither of ye regret it."

His tone clearly indicated that he really hoped and expected they would. "I bid ye good night."

"I'll hev the cow back ag'in," said the squire to himself. "He needn't hope no massy. If he don't hev the money ready for me when the time is up, he shan't keep her."

The next morning he was under the unpleasant necessity of re-engaging Abner.

"Come to think on't, Abner," he said, "I guess I'd like to hev you stay longer. There's more work than I reckoned, and I guess I'll hev to have somebody."

This was at the breakfast table. Abner looked around him, and after making sure that there was nothing eatable left, put down his knife and fork with the air of one who could have eaten more, and answered, deliberately: "Ef I stay I'll hev to hev more wages."

"More wages?" repeated Squire Green, in dismay. "More'n ten dollars?"

"Yes, a fellow of my age orter hey more'n that."

"Ten dollars is a good deal of money."

"I can't lay up a cent off'n it."

"Then you're extravagant."

"No I ain't. I ain't no chance to be. My cousin, Paul Bickford, is gettin' fifteen dollars, and he ain't no better worker'n I am."

"Fifteen dollars!" exclaimed, the squire, as if he were naming some extraordinary sum. "I never heerd of such a thing."

"I'll work for twelve'n a half," said Abner, "and I won't work for no less."

"It's too much," said the squire. "Besides, you agreed to come for ten."

"I know I did; but this is a new engagement."

Finally Abner reduced his terms to twelve dollars, an advance of two dollars a month, to which the squire was forced to agree, though very reluctantly. He thought, with an inward groan, that but for his hasty dismissal of Abner the night before, on the supposition that he could obtain Harry in his place, he would not have been compelled to raise Abner's wages. This again resulted indirectly from selling the cow, which had put the new plan into his head. When the squire reckoned up this item, amounting in six months to twelve dollars, he began to doubt whether his cow trade had been quite so good after all.

"I'll get it out of Hiram Walton some way," he muttered. "He's a great fool to let that boy have his own way. I thought to be sure he'd oblige me arter the favor I done him in sellin' him the cow. There's gratitude for you!"

The squire's ideas about gratitude, and the manner in which he had earned it, were slightly mixed, it must be acknowledged. But, though he knew very well that he had been influenced only by the consideration of his own interest, he had a vague idea that he was entitled to some credit for his kindness in consenting to sell his neighbor a cow at an extortionate price.

Harry breathed a deep sigh of relief after Squire Green left the room.

"I was afraid you were going to hire me out to the squire, father," he said.

"You didn't enjoy the prospect, did you?" said his father, smiling.

"Not much."

"Shouldn't think he would," said his brother Tom.

"The squire's awful stingy. Abner Kimball told me he had the meanest breakfast he ever ate anywhere."

"I don't think any of his household are in danger of contracting the gout from luxurious living."

"I guess not," said Tom.

"I think," said Jane, slyly, "you'd better hire out Tom to the squire."

"The squire would have the worst of the bargain," said his father, with a good-natured hit at Tom's sluggishness.

"He wouldn't earn his board, however poor it might be."

"The squire didn't seem to like it very well," said Mrs. Walton, looking up from her mending.

"No, he fully expected to get Harry for little or nothing. It was ridiculous to offer two dollars a month for a boy of his age."

"I am afraid he will be more disposed to be hard on you, when the time comes to pay for the cow. He told you he wouldn't extend the time."

"He is not likely to after this; but, wife, we won't borrow trouble. Something may turn up to help us."

"I am sure I shall be able to help you about it, father," said Harry.

"I hope so, my son, but don't feel too certain. You may not succeed as well as you anticipate."

"I know that, but I mean to try at any rate."

"If you don't, Tom will," said his sister.

"Quit teasin' a feller, Jane," said Tom. "I ain't any lazier'n you are. If I am, I'll eat my head."

"Then you'll have to eat it, Tom," retorted Jane; "and it won't be much loss to you, either."

"Don't dispute, children," said Mrs. Walton. "I expect you both will turn over a new leaf by and by."

Meanwhile, Harry was busily reading the "Life of Franklin." The more he read, the more hopeful he became as to the future.

CHAPTER IX

LEAVING HOME

Monday morning came, and the whole family stood on the grass plat in front of the house, ready to bid Harry good-bye. He was encumbered by no trunk, but carried his scanty supply of clothing wrapped in a red cotton handkerchief, and not a very heavy bundle at that. He had cut a stout stick in the woods near by, and from the end of this suspended over his back bore the bundle which contained all his worldly fortune except the twenty-five cents which was in his vest pocket.

"I don't like to have you go," said his mother, anxiously. "Suppose you don't get work?"

"Don't worry about me, mother," said Harry, brightly. "I'll get along somehow."

"Remember you've got a home here, Harry, whatever happens," said his father.

"I shan't forget, father."

"I wish I was going with you," said Tom, for the first time fired with the spirit of adventure.

"What could you do, Tom?" said Jane, teasingly.

"Work, of course."

"I never saw you do it yet."

"I'm no more lazy than you," retorted Tom, offended.

"Don't dispute, children, just as your brother is leaving us," said Mrs. Walton.

"Good-bye, mother," said Harry, feeling an unwonted moistening of the eyes, as he reflected that he was about to leave the house in which he had lived since infancy.

"Good-bye, my dear child," said his mother, kissing him.

"Be sure to write."

"Yes, I will."

So with farewell greetings Harry walked out into the world. He had all at once assumed a man's responsibilities, and his face grew serious, as he began to realize that he must now look out for himself.

His native village was situated in the northern part of New Hampshire. Not far away could be seen, indistinct in the distance, the towering summits of the White Mountain range, but his back was turned to them. In the south were larger and more thriving villages,

—

and the wealth was greater. Harry felt that his chances would be greater there. Not that he had any particular place in view. Wherever there was an opening, he meant to stop.

"I won't come back till I am better off," he said to himself. "If I don't succeed it won't be for want of trying."

He walked five miles without stopping. This brought him to the middle of the next town. He was yet on familiar ground, for he had been here more than once. He felt tired, and sat down by the roadside to rest before going farther. While he sat there the doctor from his own village rode by, and chanced to espy Harry, whom he recognized.

"What brings you here, Harry?" he asked, stopping his chaise.

"I'm going to seek my fortune," said Harry.

"What, away from home?"

"Yes, sir."

"I hadn't heard of that," said the doctor, surprised.

"You haven't run away from home?" he asked, with momentary suspicion.

"No, indeed!" said Harry, half indignantly. "Father's given his permission for me to go."

"Where do you expect to go?"

"South," said Harry, vaguely.

"And what do you expect to find to do?"

"I don't know—anything that'll bring me a living."

"I like your spunk," said the doctor, after a pause. "If you're going my way, as I suppose you are, I can carry you a couple of miles. That's better than walking, isn't it?"

"I guess it is," said Harry, jumping to his feet with alacrity.

In a minute he was sitting beside Dr. Dunham in his old-fashioned chaise. "I might have known that you were not running away," said the doctor. "I should be more likely to suspect your Brother Tom."

"Tom's too lazy to run away to earn his own living," said Harry, laughing, "as long as he can get it at home."

The doctor smiled.

"And what put it into your head to start out in this way?" he asked.

"The first thing, was reading the' Life of Franklin.'"

"To be sure. I remember his story."

"And the next thing was, because my father is so poor. He finds it hard work to support us all. The farm is small, and the land is poor. I want to help him if I can."

"Very commendable, Harry," said the doctor, kindly.

"You owe a debt of gratitude to your good father, who has not succeeded so well in life as he deserves."

"That's true, sir. He has always been a hard-working man."

"If you start out with such a good object, I think you will succeed. Have you any plans at all, or any idea what you would like to do?"

"I thought I should like to work in a shoe shop, if I got a chance," said Harry.

"You like that better than working on a farm, then?"

"Yes, sir, There isn't much money to be earned by working on a farm. I had a chance to do that before I came away."

"You mean working on your father's land, I suppose?"

"No, Squire Green wanted to hire me."

"What wages did he offer?"

"Two dollars a month, at first. Afterwards he got up to three."

The doctor smiled.

"How could you decline such a magnificent offer?" he asked.

"I don't think I should like boarding at the squire's."

A dollar is twice as large at least in his eyes as in those of anyone else."

By this time they had reached a place where a road turned at right angles.

"I am going down here, Harry," said the doctor. "I should like to have you ride farther, but I suppose it would only be taking you out of your course."

"Yes, doctor. I'd better get out."

"I'll tell your father I saw you."

"Tell him I was in good spirits," said Harry, earnestly. "Mother'll be glad to know that."

"I will certainly. Good-bye!"

"Good-bye, doctor. Thank you for the ride."

"You are quite welcome to that, Harry."

Harry followed with his eyes the doctor's chaise. It seemed like severing the last link that bound him to his native village. He was very glad to have fallen in with the doctor, but it seemed all the more lonesome that he had left him.

Harry walked six miles farther, and then decided that it was time to rest again. He was not only somewhat fatigued, but decidedly hungry, although it was but eleven o'clock in the morning. However, it must be considered that he had walked eleven miles, and this was enough to give anyone an appetite.

He sat down again beside the road, and untying the handkerchief which contained his worldly possessions, he drew therefrom a large slice of bread and began to eat with evident relish. There was a slice of cold meat also, which he found tasted particularly good.

"I wonder whether they are thinking of me at home," he said to himself.

They were thinking about him, and when an hour later the family gathered around the table, no one seemed to have much appetite. All looked sober, for all were thinking of the absent son and brother.

"I wish Harry was here," said Jane, at length, giving voice to the general feeling.

"Poor boy," sighed his mother. "I'm afraid he'll have a hard time. I wish he had stayed at home, or even have gone to Squire Green's to work. Then we could have seen him every day."

"I should have pitied him more if he had gone there than I do now," said his father. "Depend upon it, it; will be better for him in the end."

"I hope so," said his mother, dubiously.

"But you don't feel sure? Well, time will show. We shall hear from him before long."

We go back to Harry.

He rested for a couple of hours, sheltered from the sun by the foliage of the oak beneath which he had stretched himself. He whiled away the time by reading for the second time some parts of the "Life of Franklin," which he had brought away in his bundle, with his few other possessions. It seemed even more interesting to him now that he, too, like Franklin, had started out in quest for fortune.

He resumed walking, but we will not dwell upon the details of his journey. At six o'clock he was twenty-five miles from home. He had not walked much in the afternoon when, all at once, he was alarmed by the darkening of the sky. It was evident that a storm was approaching. He looked about him for shelter from the shower, and a place where he could pass the night.

41

**Gathering storm clouds drive Harry to
seek shelter at a stranger's house.**

CHAPTER X

THE GENERAL

The clouds were darkening, and the shower was evidently not far off. It was a solitary place, and no houses were to be seen near by. But nearly a quarter of a mile back Harry caught sight of a small house, and jumping over the fence directed his steps toward it. Five minutes brought him to it. It was small, painted red, originally, but the color had mostly been washed away. It was not upon a public road, but there was a narrow lane leading to it from the highway. Probably a poor family occupied it, Harry thought. Still it would shelter him from the storm which had even now commenced.

He knocked at the door.

Immediately it was opened and a face peered out—the face of a man advanced in years. It was thin, wrinkled, and haggard. The thin white hair, uncombed, gave a wild appearance to the owner, who, in a thin, shrill voice, demanded, "Who are you?"

"My name is Harry Walton."

"What do you want?"

"Shelter from the storm. It is going to rain."

"Come in," said the old man, and opening the door wider, he admitted our hero.

Harry found himself in a room very bare of furniture, but there was a log fire in the fireplace, and this looked comfortable and pleasant. He laid down his bundle, and drawing up a chair sat down by it, his host meanwhile watching him closely.

"Does he live alone, I wonder?" thought Harry.

He saw no other person about, and no traces of a woman's presence. The floor looked as if it had not been swept for a month, and probably it had not.

The old man sat down opposite Harry, and stared at him, till our hero felt somewhat embarrassed and uncomfortable.

"Why don't he say something?" thought Harry.

"He is a very queer old man."

After a while his host spoke.

"Do you know who I am?" he asked.

"No," said Harry, looking at him.

"You've heard of me often," pursued the old man.

"I didn't know it," answered Harry, beginning to feel curious.

—
43

"In history," added the other.

"In history?"

"Yes."

Harry began to look at him in increased surprise.

"Will you tell me your name, if it is not too much trouble," he asked, politely.

"I gained the victory of New Orleans," said the old man.

"I thought General Jackson did that," said Harry.

"You're right," said the old man, complacently. "I am General Jackson."

"But General Jackson is dead."

"That's a mistake," said the old man, quietly. "That's what they say in all the books, but it isn't true."

Andrew Jackson at the Battle of New Orleans. Did the old man really serve under Jackson at this battle? We never find out.

This was amusing, but it was also startling. Harry knew now that the old man was crazy, or at least a monomaniac, and, though he seemed harmless enough, it was of course possible that he might be dangerous. He was almost sorry that he had sought shelter here. Better have encountered the storm in its full fury than place himself in the power of a maniac. The rain was now falling in thick drops, and he decided at any rate to remain a while longer. He knew that it would not be well to dispute the old man, and resolved to humor his delusion.

"You were President once, I believe?" he asked.

"Yes," said the old man; "and you won't tell anybody, will you?"

"No."

"I mean to be again," said the old man in a low voice, half in a whisper. "But you mustn't say anything about it. They'd try to kill me, if they knew it."

"Who would?"

"Mr. Henry Clay, and the rest of them."

"Doesn't Henry Clay want you to be President again?"

"Of course not. He wants to be President himself. That's why I'm hiding. They don't any of them know where I am. You won't tell, will you?"

"No."

"You might meet Henry Clay, you know."

Harry smiled to himself. It didn't seem very likely that he would ever find himself in such distinguished company, for Henry Clay was at that time living, and a United States Senator.

"What made you come here, General Jackson?" he inquired.

The old man brightened, on being called by this name.

"Because it was quiet. They can't find me here."

"When do you expect to be President again?"

"Next year," said the old man. "I've got it all arranged. My friends are to blow up the capitol, and I shall ride into Washington on a white horse. Do you want an office?"

"I don't know, but I should like one," said Harry, amused.

"I'll see what I can do for you," said the old man, seriously. "I can't put you in my Cabinet. That's all arranged. If you would like to be Minister to England or to France, you can go."

"I should like to go to France. Benjamin Franklin was Minister to France."

"Do you know him?"

"No; but I have read his life."

"I'll put your name down in my book. What is it?"

"Harry Walton."

The old man went to the table, on which was a common account book. He took a pen, and, with a serious look, made this entry:

"I promise to make Harry Walton Minister to France, as soon as I take my place in the White House.

"GENERAL ANDREW JACKSON"

45

"It's all right now," he said.

"Thank you, general. You are very kind," said our hero.

"Were you ever a soldier?" asked his host.

"I never was."

"I thought you might have been in the battle of New Orleans. Our men fought splendidly, sir."

"I have no doubt of it."

"You'll read all about it in history. We fought behind cotton bales. It was glorious!"

"General," said Harry, "if you'll excuse me, I'll take out my dinner from this bundle."

"No, no," said the old man; "you must take dinner with me."

"I wonder whether he has anything fit to eat," thought Harry. "Thank you," he said aloud. "If you wish it."

The old man had arisen, and, taking a teakettle, suspended it over the fire. A monomaniac though he was on the subject of his identity with General Jackson, he knew how to make tea. Presently he took from the cupboard a baker's roll and some cold meat, and when the tea was ready, invited Harry to be seated at the table. Our hero did so willingly. He had lost his apprehensions, perceiving that his companion's lunacy was of a very harmless character.

"What if mother could see me now!" he thought.

Still the rain poured down. It showed no signs of slackening. He saw that it would be necessary to remain where he was through the night.

"General, can you accommodate me till morning?" he asked.

"Certainly," said the old man. "I shall be glad to have you stay here. Do you go to France tomorrow?"

"I have not received my appointment yet."

"True, true; but it won't be long. I will write your instructions tonight."

"Very well."

The dinner was plain enough, but our young traveler, whose long walk had stimulated a naturally good appetite, relished it.

"Eat heartily, my son," said the old man. "A long journey is before you."

After the meal was over, the old man began to write.

—

Harry surmised that it was his instructions. He paid little heed, but fixed his eyes upon the fire, listening to the rain that continued to beat against the window panes, and began to speculate about the future. Was he to be successful or not? He was not without solicitude, but he felt no small measure of hope. At nine o'clock he began to feel drowsy, and intimated as much to his host. The old man conducted him to an upper chamber, where there was a bed upon the floor.

"You can sleep there," he said.

"Where do you sleep?" asked Harry.

"Down below; but I shall not go to bed till late. I must get ready your instructions."

"Very well," said Harry. "Good night."

"Good night."

"I am glad he is not in the room with me," thought Harry. "I don't think there is any danger, but it isn't comfortable to be too near a crazy man."

CHAPTER XI

IN SEARCH OF WORK

When Harry awoke the next morning, after a sound and refreshing sleep, the sun was shining brightly in at the window. He rubbed his eyes, and stared about him, not at first remembering where he was. But almost immediately recollection came to his aid, and he smiled as he thought of the eccentric old man whose guest he was. He leaped out of bed, and quickly dressing himself, went downstairs. The fire was burning, and breakfast was already on the table. It was precisely similar to the dinner of the night previous. The old man sat at the fireside smoking a pipe.

"Good morning, general," said Harry. "I am up late."

"It is no matter. You have a long journey before you, and it is well to rest before starting."

"Where does he think I am going?" thought our hero.

"Breakfast is ready," said the old man, hospitably. "I can't entertain you now as I could have done when I was President. You must come and see me at the White House next year."

"I should like to."

Harry ate a hearty breakfast. When it was over, he rose to go.

"I must be going, general," he said. "Thank you for your kind entertainment. If you would allow me to pay you."

"General Jackson does not keep an inn," said the old man, with dignity. "You are his guest. I have your instructions ready."

He opened a drawer in the table, and took a roll of foolscap, tied with a string.

"Put it in your bundle," he said. "Let no one see it. Above all, don't let it fall into the hands of Henry Clay, or my life will be in peril."

Harry solemnly assured him that Henry Clay should never see it, and shaking the old man by the hand, made his way across the fields to the main road. Looking back from time to time, he saw the old man watching him from his place in the doorway, his eyes shaded by his hand.

"He is the strangest man I ever saw," thought Harry. "Still he treated me kindly. I should like to find out some more about him."

When he reached the road he saw, just in front of him, a boy of about his own age driving half a dozen cows before him.

—

48

"Perhaps he can tell me something about the old man."

"Hello!" he cried, by way of salutation.

"Hello!" returned the country boy. "Where are you going?"

"I don't know. Wherever I can find work," answered our hero.

The boy laughed. "Dad finds enough for me to do. I don't have to go after it. Haven't you got a father?"

"Yes."

"Why don't you work for him?"

"I want to work for pay."

"On a farm?"

"No. I'll work in a shoe shop if I get a chance or in a printing office."

"Do you understand the shoe business?"

"No; but I can learn."

"Where did you come from?"

"Granton."

"You didn't come from there this morning?"

"No, I guess not, as it's over twenty miles. Last night I stopped at General Jackson's."

The boy whistled.

"What, at the old crazy man's that lives down here a piece?"

"Yes."

"What made you go there?"

"It began, to rain, and I had no other place to go."

"What did he say?" asked the new boy with curiosity.

"Did he cut up?"

"Cut up? No, unless you mean the bread. He cut up that."

"I mean, how did he act?"

"All right, except when he was talking about being General Jackson."

"Did you sleep there?"

"Yes."

"I wouldn't."

"Why not?"

"I wouldn't sleep in a crazy man's house."

"He wouldn't hurt you."

"I don't know about that. He chases us boys often, and threatens to kill us."

"You plague him, don't you?"

"I guess we do. We call him 'Old Crazy,' and that makes him mad. He says Henry Clay puts us up to it—ho, ho, ho!"

"He thinks Clay is his enemy. He told me so."

"What did you say?"

"Oh, I didn't contradict him. I called him general. He treated me tip-top. He is going to make me Minister of France, when he is President again."

"Maybe that was the best way to get along."

"How long has he lived here? What made him crazy?"

"I don't know. Folks say he was disappointed."

"Did he ever see Jackson?"

"Yes; he fit at New Orleans under him."

"Has he lived long around here?"

"Ever since I can remember. He gets a pension, I've heard father say. That's what keeps him."

Here the boy reached the pasture to which he was driving the cows, and Harry, bidding him "good-bye," went on his way. He felt fresh and vigorous, and walked ten miles before he felt the need of rest. When this distance was accomplished, he found himself in the center of a good-sized village. He felt hungry, and the provision which he brought from home was nearly gone. There was a grocery store close at hand, and he went in, thinking that he would find something to help his meal. On the counter he saw some rolls, and there was an open barrel of apples not far off.

"What do you charge for your rolls?" he asked.

"Two cents."

"I'll take one. How do you sell your apples?"

"A cent apiece."

"I'll take two."

Thus for four cents Harry made quite a substantial addition to his meal. As he left the store, and walked up the road, with the roll in his hand, eating an apple, he called to mind Benjamin Franklin's entrance of Philadelphia with a roll under each arm.

"I hope I shall have as good luck as Franklin had," he thought.

Walking slowly, he saw, on a small building which he I had just reached, the sign, "Post Office."

"Perhaps the postmaster will know if anybody about here wants a boy," Harry said to himself. "At any rate, it won't do any harm to inquire."

—

50

He entered, finding himself in a small room, with one part partitioned off as a repository for mail matter. He stepped up to a little window, and presently the postmaster, an elderly man, presented himself.

"What name," he asked.

"I haven't come for a letter," said Harry.

"What do you want, then?" asked the official, but not roughly.

"Do you know of anyone that wants to hire a boy?"

"Who's the boy?"

"I am. I want to get a chance to work."

"What kind of work?"

"Any kind that'll pay my board and a little over."

"I don't know of any place," said the postmaster, after a little thought.

"Isn't there any shoe shop where I could get in?"

"That reminds me—James Leavitt told me this morning that his boy was going to Boston to go into a store in a couple of months. He's been pegging for his father and I guess they'll have to get somebody in his place."

Harry's face brightened at this intelligence.

"That's just the kind of place I'd like to get," he said. "Where does Mr. Leavitt live?"

"A quarter of a mile from here—over the bridge. You'll know it well enough. It's a cottage house, with a shoe shop in the backyard."

"Thank you, sir," said Harry. "I'll go there and try my luck."

"Wait a minute," said the postmaster. "There's a letter here for Mr. Leavitt. If you're going there, you may as well carry it along. It's from Boston. I shouldn't wonder if it's about the place Bob Leavitt wants."

"I'll take it with pleasure," said Harry.

It occurred to him that it would be a good introduction for him, and pave the way for his application.

"I hope I may get a chance to work for this Mr. Leavitt," he said to himself. "I like the looks of this village. I should like to live here for a while."

He walked up the street, crossing the bridge referred to by the postmaster, and looked carefully on each side of him for the cottage

---

and shop. At length he came to a place which answered the description, and entered the yard. As he neared the shop he heard a noise which indicated that work was going on inside. He opened the door, and entered.

CHAPTER XII

THE NEW BOARDER

Harry found himself in a room about twenty-five feet by twenty. The floor was covered with scraps of leather. Here stood a deep wooden box containing a case of shoes ready to send off. There was a stove in the center, in which, however, as it was a warm day, no fire was burning. There were three persons present. One, a man of middle age, was Mr. James Leavitt, the proprietor of the shop. His son Robert, about seventeen, worked at an adjoining bench. Tom Gavitt, a journeyman, a short, thick-set man of thirty, employed by Mr. Leavitt, was the third.

The three looked up as Harry entered the shop.

"I have a letter for Mr. Leavitt," said our hero.

"That is my name," said the eldest of the party.

Harry advanced, and placed it in his hands.

"Where did you get this letter?"

"At the post office."

"I can't call you by name. Do you live about here?"

"No, I came from Granton."

No further questions were asked just then, as Mr. Leavitt, suspending work, opened the letter.

"It's from your Uncle Benjamin," he said, addressing Robert. "Let us see what he has to say."

He read the letter in silence.

"What does he say, father?" asked Robert.

"He says he shall be ready to take you the first of September. That's in six weeks—a little sooner than we calculated. I wish it were a little later, as work is brisk, and I may find it difficult to fill your place without paying more than I want to."

"I guess you can pick up somebody," said Robert, who was anxious to go to Boston as soon as possible.

"Won't you hire me?" asked Harry, who felt that the time had come for him to announce his business.

Mr. Leavitt looked at him more attentively.

"Have you ever worked in a shop?"

"No, sir."

"It will take you some time to learn pegging."

"I'll work for my board till I've learned."

—

"But you won't be able to do all I want at first."

"Suppose I begin now," said Harry, "and work for my board till your son goes away. By that time I can do considerable."

"I don't know but that's a good idea," said Mr. Leavitt. "What do you think, Bob?"

"Better take him, father," said Robert, who felt that it would facilitate his own plans.

"How much would you want after you have learned?" asked the father.

"I don't know; what would be a fair price," said Harry.

"I'll give you three dollars a week and board," said Mr. Leavitt, after a little consideration—"that is, if I am satisfied with you."

"I'll come," said Harry, promptly. He rapidly calculated that there would be about twenty weeks for which he would receive pay before the six months expired, at the end of which the cow must be paid for. This would give him sixty dollars, of which he thought he should be able to save forty to send or carry to his father.

"How did you happen to come to me?" asked Mr. Leavitt, with some curiosity.

"I heard at the post office that your son was going to the city to work, and I thought I could get in here."

"Is your father living?"

"Yes, my father and mother both."

"What business is he in?"

"He is a farmer; but his farm is small, and not very profitable."

"So you thought you would leave home and try something else?"

"Yes, sir."

"Well, we will try you at shoemaking. Robert, you can teach him what you know about pegging."

"Come here," said Robert. "What is your name?"

"Harry Walton."

"How old are you?"

"Fifteen."

"Did you ever work much?"

"Yes, on a farm."

"Do you think you'll like shoemaking better?"

"I don't know yet, but I think I shall. I like almost anything better than farming."

———

54

"And I like almost anything better than pegging. I began when I was only twelve years old, and I'm sick of it."

"What kind of store is it you are going into?"

"Dry goods. My uncle, Benjamin Streeter, mother's brother, keeps a dry goods store on Washington Street. It'll be jolly living in the city."

"I don't know," said Harry thoughtfully. "I think I like a village just as well."

"What sort of a place is Granton, where you come from?"

"It's a farming town. There isn't any village at all."

"There isn't much going on here."

"There'll be more than in Granton. There's nothing to do there but to work on a farm."

"I shouldn't like that myself; but the city's the best of all."

"Can you make more money in a store than working in a shoe shop?"

"Not so much at first, but after you've got learned there's better chances. There's a clerk, that went from here ten years ago, that gets fifty dollars a week."

"Does he?" asked Harry, to whose rustic inexperience this seemed like an immense salary. "I didn't think any clerk ever got so much."

"They get it often if they are smart," said Robert.

Here he was wrong, however. Such cases are exceptional, and a city fry goods clerk, considering his higher rate of expense, is no better off than many country mechanics. But country boys are apt to form wrong ideas on this subject, and are in too great haste to forsake good country homes for long hours of toil behind a city counter, and a poor home in a dingy, third-class city boarding house. It is only in the wholesale houses, for the most part, that high salaries are paid, and then, of course, only to those who have shown superior energy and capacity. Of course some do achieve success and become rich; but of the tens of thousand who come from the country to seek clerkships, but a very small proportion rise above a small income.

"I shall have a start," Robert proceeded, "for I go into my uncle's store. I am to board at his house, and get three dollars a week."

"That's what your father offers me," said Harry.

55

"Yes; you'll earn more after a while, and I can now; but I'd rather live in the city. There's lots to see in the city—theaters, circuses and all kinds of amusements."

"You won't have much money to spend on theaters," said Harry, prudently.

"Not at first, but I'll get raised soon."

"I think I should try to save as much as I could."

"Out of three dollars a week?"

"Yes."

"What can you save out of that?"

"I expect to save half of it, perhaps more."

"I couldn't do that. I want a little fun."

"You see my father's poor. I want to help him all I can."

"That's good advice for you, Bob," said Mr. Leavitt.

"Save up money, and help me."

Robert laughed.

"You'll have to wait till I get bigger pay," he said.

"Your father's better off than mine," said Harry.

"Of course, if he don't need it, that makes a difference."

Here the sound of a bell was heard, proceeding from the house.

"Robert," said his father "go in and tell your mother to put an extra seat at the table. She doesn't know that we've got a new boarder."

He took off his apron, and washed his hands. Tom Gavitt followed his example, but didn't go into the house of his employer. He lived in a house of his own about five minutes' walk distant, but left the shop at the same time. In a country village the general lunch hour is twelve o'clock—a very unfashionably early hour—but I presume any of my readers who had been at work from seven o'clock would have no difficulty in getting up a good appetite at noon.

Robert went in and informed his mother of the new boarder. It made no difference, for the table was always well supplied.

"This is Harry Walton, mother," said Mr. Leavitt, "our new apprentice. He will take Bob's place when he goes."

"I am glad to see you," said Mrs. Leavitt, hospitably.

"You may sit here, next to Robert."

"What have you got for us today, mother?" asked her husband.

"A picked-up lunch. There's some cold beef left over from yesterday, and I've made an apple pudding."

"That's good. We don't want anything better."

So Harry thought. Accustomed to the painful frugality of the table at home, he regarded this as a splendid lunch, and did full justice to it.

In the afternoon he resumed work in the shop under Robert's guidance. He was in excellent spirits. He felt that he was very fortunate to have gained a place so soon, and determined to write home that same evening.

CHAPTER XIII

AN INVITATION DECLINED

The summer passed quickly, and the time arrived for Robert Leavitt to go to the city. By this time Harry was well qualified to take his place. It had not been difficult, for he had only been required to peg, and that is learned in a short time. Harry, however, proved to be a quick workman, quicker, if anything, than Robert, though the latter had been accustomed to the work for several years. Mr. Leavitt was well satisfied with his new apprentice, and quite content to pay him the three dollars a week agreed upon. In fact, it diminished the amount of cash he was called upon to pay.

"Good-bye, Harry," said Robert, as he saw the coach coming up the road, to take him to the railroad station.

"Good-bye, and good luck!" said Harry.

"When you come to the city, come and see me."

"I don't think I shall be going very soon. I can't afford it."

"You must save up your wages, and you'll have enough soon."

"I've got another use for my wages, Bob."

"To buy cigars?"

Harry shook his head. "I shall save it up to carry home."

"Well, you must try to make my place good in the shop."

"He can do that," said Mr. Leavitt, slyly; "but there's one place where he can't equal you."

"Where is that?"

"At the lunch table."

"You've got me there, father," said Bob, good-naturedly. "Well, good-bye, all, here's the stage."

In a minute more he was gone. Harry felt rather lonely, for he had grown used to working beside him. But his spirits rose as he reflected that the time had now come when he should be in receipt of an income. Three dollars a week made him feel rich in anticipation. He looked forward already with satisfaction to the time when he might go home with money enough to pay off his father's debt to Squire Green. But he was not permitted to carry out his economical purpose without a struggle.

On Saturday evening, after he had received his week's pay, Luke Harrison, who worked in a shop near by, met him at the post office.

58

"Come along, Harry," he said. "Let us play a game of billiards."

"You must excuse me," said Harry.

"Oh, come along," said Luke, taking him by the arm; "it's only twenty-five cents."

"I can't afford it."

"Can't afford it! Now that's nonsense. You just changed a two-dollar note for those postage stamps."

"I know that; but I must save that money for another purpose."

"What's the use of being stingy, Harry? Try one game."

"You can get somebody else to play with you, Luke."

"Oh, hang it, if you care so much for a quarter, I'll pay for the game myself. Only come and play."

Harry shook his head.

"I don't want to amuse myself at your expense."

"You are a miser," said Luke, angrily.

"You can call me so, if you like," said Harry, firmly; "but that won't make it so."

"I don't see how you can call yourself anything else, if you are so afraid to spend your money."

"I have good reasons."

"What are they?"

"I told you once that I had another use for the money."

"To hoard away in an old stocking," said Luke, sneering.

"You may say so, if you like," said Harry, turning away.

He knew he was right, but it was disagreeable to be called a miser. He was too proud to justify himself to Luke, who spent all his money foolishly, though earning considerably larger wages than he.

There was one thing that Harry had not yet been able to do to any great extent, though it was something he had at heart. He had not forgotten his motto, "Live and Learn," and now that he was in a fair way to make a living, he felt that he had made no advance in learning during the few weeks since he arrived in Glenville.

The day previous he had heard, for the first time, that there was a public library in another part of the town, which was open evenings. Though it was two miles distant, and he had been at work all day, he determined to walk up there and get a book. He felt that he was very ignorant, and that his advance in the world depended upon his improving all opportunities that might present themselves for extending his limited knowledge. This was evidently one.

After his unsatisfactory interview with Luke, he set out for the upper village, as it was called. Forty minutes' walk brought him to the building in which the library was kept. An elderly man had charge of it—a Mr. Parmenter.

"Can I take out a book?" asked Harry.

"Do you live in town?"

"Yes, sir."

"I don't remember seeing you before. You don't live in this village, do you?"

"No, sir. I live in the lower village."

"What is your name?"

"Harry Walton."

"I don't remember any Walton family."

"My father lives in Granton. I am working for Mr. James Leavitt."

"I have no doubt this is quite correct, but I shall have to have Mr. Leavitt's certificate to that effect, before I can put your name down, and trust you with books."

"Then can't I take any book tonight?" asked Harry, disappointed.

"I am afraid not."

So it seemed his two-mile walk was for nothing. He must retrace his steps and come again Monday night.

He was turning away disappointed when Dr. Townley, of the lower village, who lived near Mr. Leavitt, entered the library.

"My wife wants a book in exchange for this, Mr. Parmenter," he said. "Have you got anything new in? Ah, Harry Walton, how came you here? Do you take books out of the library?"

"That's is what I came up for, but the librarian says I must bring a line from Mr. Leavitt, telling who I am."

"If Dr. Townley knows you, that is sufficient," said the librarian.

"He is all right, Mr. Parmenter. He is a young neighbor of mine."

"That is enough. He can select a book."

Harry was quite relieved at this fortunate meeting, and after a little reflection selected the first volume of "Rollin's Universal History," a book better known to our fathers than the present generation.

"That's a good, solid book, Harry," said the doctor.

"Most of our young people select stories."

"I like stories very much," said Harry; "but I have only a little time to read, and I must try to learn something."

"You are a sensible boy," said the doctor, emphatically.

"I'm afraid there are few of our young people who take such wise views of what is best for them. Most care only for present enjoyment."

"I have got my own way to make," said Harry, "and I suppose that is what influences me. My father is poor and cannot help me, and I want to rise in the world."

"You are going the right way to work. Do you intend to take out books often from the library?"

"Yes, sir."

"It will be a long walk from the lower village."

"I would walk farther rather than do without the books."

"I can save you at any rate from walking back. My chaise is outside, and, if you will jump in, I will carry you home."

"Thank you, doctor. I shall be very glad to ride."

On the way, Dr. Townley said: "I have a few miscellaneous books in my medical library, which I will lend to you with pleasure, if you will come in. It may save you an occasional walk to the library."

Harry thanked him, and not long afterwards availed himself of the considerate proposal. Dr Townley was liberally educated, and as far as his professional engagements would permit kept up with general literature. He gave Harry some valuable directions as to the books which it would benefit him to read, and more than once took him up on the road to the library.

Once a week regularly, Harry wrote home. He knew that his letters would give pleasure to the family, and he never allowed anything to interfere with his duty.

His father wrote: "We are getting on about as usual. The cow does tolerably well, but is not as good as the one I lost. I have not yet succeeded in laying up anything toward paying for her. Somehow, whenever I have a few dollars laid aside Tom wants shoes, or your sister wants a dress, or some other expense swallows it up."

Harry wrote in reply: "Don't trouble yourself, father, about your debt to Squire Green. If I have steady work, and keep my health, I shall have enough to pay it by the time it comes due."

CHAPTER XIV

THE TAILOR'S CUSTOMER

At the end of six weeks from the date of Robert's departure, Harry had been paid eighteen dollars. Of this sum he had spent but one dollar, and kept the balance in his pocketbook. He did not care to send it home until he had enough to meet Squire Green's demand, knowing that his father would be able to meet his ordinary expenses. Chiefly through the reports of Luke Harrison he was acquiring the reputation of meanness, though, as we know, he was far from deserving it.

"See how the fellow dresses," said Luke, contemptuously, to two of his companions one evening. "His clothes are shabby enough, and he hasn't got an overcoat at all. He hoards his money, and is too stingy to buy one. See, there he comes, buttoned to the chin to keep warm, and I suppose he has more money in his pocketbook than the whole of us together. I wouldn't be as mean as he is for a hundred dollars."

"You'd rather get trusted for your clothes than do without them," said Frank Heath, slyly; for he happened to know that Luke had run up a bill with the tailor, about which the latter was getting anxious.

"What if I do," said Luke, sharply, "as long as I am going to pay for them?"

"Oh, nothing," said Frank. "I didn't say anything against it, did I? I suppose you are as able to owe the tailor as anyone."

By this time, Harry had come up.

"Where are you going, Walton?" asked Luke. "You look cold."

"Yes, it's a cold day."

"Left your overcoat at home, didn't you?"

Harry colored. The fact was, he felt the need of an overcoat, but didn't know how to manage getting one. At the lowest calculation, it would cost all the money he had saved up for one, and the purchase would defeat all his plans. The one he had worn at home during the previous winter was too small for him, and had been given to his brother.

"If I only could get through the winter without one," he thought, "I should be all right." But a New England winter is not to be braved with impunity, useless protected by adequate clothing. Luke's sneer was therefore not without effect. But he answered, quietly: "I did not leave it at home, for I have none to leave."

"I suppose you are bound to the tailor's to order one."

"What makes you think so?" asked Harry.

"You are not such a fool as to go without one when you have money in your pocket, are you?"

"You seem very curious about my private affairs," said Harry, rather provoked.

"He's only drumming up customers for the tailor," said Frank Heath. "He gets a commission on all he brings."

"That's the way he pays his bill," said Sam Anderson.

"Quit fooling, boys," said Luke, irritated. "I ain't a drummer. I pay my bills, like a gentleman."

"By keeping the tailor waiting," said Frank.

"Quit that!"

So attention was diverted from Harry by this opportune attack upon Luke, much to our hero's relief. Nevertheless, he saw, that in order to preserve his health, he must have some outer garment, and in order the better to decide what to do, he concluded to step into the tailor's, and inquire his prices.

The tailor, Merrill by name, had a shop over the dry goods store, and thither Harry directed his steps. There was one other person in the shop, a young fellow but little larger than Harry, though two years older, who was on a visit to an aunt in the neighborhood, but lived in Boston. He belonged to a rich family, and had command of considerable money. His name was Maurice Tudor. He had gone into the shop to leave a coat to be repaired.

"How are you, Walton?" he said, for he knew our hero slightly.

"Pretty well. Thank you."

"It's pretty cold for October."

"Yes, unusually so."

"Mr. Merrill," said Harry, "I should like to inquire the price of an overcoat. I may want to order one by and by."

"What sort of one do you want—pretty nice?"

"No, I can't afford anything nice—something as cheap as possible."

63

"This is the cheapest goods I have," said the tailor, pointing to some coarse cloth near by.

"I can make you up a coat from that for eighteen dollars."

"Eighteen dollars!" exclaimed Harry, in dismay. "Is that the cheapest you have?"

"The very cheapest."

After a minute's pause he added, "I might take off a dollar for cash. I've got enough of running up bills. There's Luke Harrison owes me over thirty dollars, and I don't believe he means to pay it al all."

"If I buy, I shall pay cash," said Harry, quietly.

"You can't get anything cheaper than this." said the tailor.

"Very likely not," said Harry, soberly. "I'll think about it, and let you know if I decide to take it."

Maurice Tudor was a silent listener to this dialogue. He saw Harry's sober expression, and he noticed the tone in which he repeated "eighteen dollars," and he guessed the truth. He lingered after Harry went out, and said:

"That's a good fellow."

"Harry Walton?" repeated the tailor. "Yes, he's worth a dozen Luke Harrisons."

"Has he been in the village long?"

"No, not more than two or three months. He works for Mr. Leavitt."

"He is rather poor, I suppose."

"Yes. The boys call him mean; but Leavitt tells me he is saving up every cent to send to his father, who is a poor farmer."

"That's a good thing in him."

"Yes, I wish I could afford to give him and overcoat. He needs one, but I suppose seventeen dollars will come rather hard on him to pay. If it was Luke Harrison, it wouldn't trouble him much."

"You mean he would get it on tick."

"Yes, if he found anybody fool enough to trust him. I've done it as long as I'm going to. He won't get a dollar more credit out of me till he pays his bill."

"You're perfectly right, there."

"So I think. He earns a good deal more than Walton, but spends what he earns on billiards, drinks and cigars."

"There he comes up the stairs, now."

In fact, Luke with his two companions directly afterwards entered the shop.

"Merrill," said he, "have you got in any new goods? I must have a new pair of pants."

"Yes, I've got some new goods. There's a piece open before you."

"It's a pretty thing, Merrill," said Luke, struck by it; "what's your price for a pair off of it?"

"Ten dollars."

"Isn't that rather steep?"

"No; the cloth is superior quality."

"Well, darn the expense. I like it, and must have it. Just measure me, will you?"

"Are you ready to pay the account I have against you?"

"How much is it?"

The tailor referred to his books.

"Thirty-two dollars and fifty cents," he answered.

"All right, Merrill. Wait till the pants are done, and I'll pay the whole at once."

"Ain't my credit good?" blustered Luke.

"You can make it good," said the tailor, significantly.

"I didn't think you'd make such a fuss about a small bill."

"I didn't think you'd find is so difficult to pay a small bill," returned the tailor.

Luke looked discomfited. He was silent a moment, and then changed his tactics.

"Come, Merrill," he said, persuasively; "don't be alarmed. I'm good for it, I guess. I haven't got the money convenient today. I lent fifty dollars. I shall have it back next week and then I will pay you."

"I am glad to hear it," said Merrill.

"So just measure me and hurry up the pants."

"I'm sorry but I can't till you settle the bill."

"Look here, has Walton been talking against me?"

"No; what makes you think so?"

"He don't like me, because I twitted him with his meanness."

"I don't consider him mean."

"Has he ever bought anything of you?"

"No."

"I knew it. He prefers to go ragged and save his money."

"He's too honorable to run up a bill without paying it."

"Do you mean me?" demanded Luke, angrily.

"I hope not. I presume you intend to pay your bills."

Luke Harrison left the shop. He saw that he exhausted his credit with Merrill. As to paying the bill, there was not much chance of that at present, as he had but one dollar and a half in his pocket.

CHAPTER XV

"BY EXPRESS"

"There's a model for you," said the tailor to Maurice Tudor. "He won't pay his bills."

"How did you come to trust him in the first place?"

"I didn't know him then as well as I do now. I make it a practice to accommodate my customers by trusting them for a month or two, if they want it. But Luke Harrison isn't one to be trusted."

"I should say not."

"If young Walton wants to get an overcoat on credit, I shan't object. I judge something by looks, and I am sure he is honest."

"Well, good night, Mr. Merrill. You'll have my coat done soon?"

"Yes, Mr. Tudor. It shall be ready for you tomorrow."

Maurice Tudor left the tailor's shop, revolving a new idea which had just entered his mind. Now he remembered that he had at home and excellent overcoat which he had worn the previous winter, but which was now too small for him. He had no younger brother to wear it, nor in his circumstances was such economy necessary. As well as he could judge by observing Harry's figure, it would be an excellent fit for him. Why should he not give it to him?

The opportunity came. On his way home he overtook our hero, plunged in thought. In fact, he was still occupied with the problem of the needed overcoat.

"Good evening, Harry," said young Tudor.

"Good evening, Mr. Tudor," answered Harry. "Are you going back to the city soon?"

"In the course of a week or two. Mr. Leavitt's son is in a store in Boston, is he not?"

"Yes. I have taken his place in the shop."

"By the way, I saw you in Merrill's this evening."

"Yes; I was pricing an overcoat."

"I bought this one in Boston just before I came away. I have a very good one left from last winter but it is too small for me. It is of no use to me. If I thought you would accept it, I would offer it to you."

Harry's heart gave a joyful bound.

"Accept it!" he repeated. "Indeed I will and thank you for your great kindness."

"Then I will write home at once to have it sent to me. I also have a suit which I have outgrown; if you wouldn't be too proud to take it."

"I am not so foolish. It will be a great favor."

"I thought you would take it right," said Maurice, well pleased. "I will also send for the suit. I will get my mother to forward them by express."

"They will be as good as money to me," said Harry; "and that is not very plenty with me."

"Will you tell me something of your circumstances? Perhaps I may have it in my power to help you."

Harry, assured of his friendly interest, did not hesitate to give him a full account of his plans in life, and especially of his desire to relieve his father of the burden of poverty. His straightforward narrative made a very favorable impression upon Maurice, who could not help reflecting: "How far superior this boy is to Luke Harrison and his tribe!"

"Thank you for telling me all this," he said. "It was not from mere curiosity that I asked."

"I am sure of that," said Harry. "Thanks to your generosity, I shall present a much more respectable appearance, besides being made more comfortable."

Three days later a large bundle was brought by the village express man to Mr. Leavitt's door.

"A bundle for you, Walton," said the express man, seeing Harry in the yard.

"What is there to pay?" he asked.

"Nothing. It was prepaid in the city?"

Harry took it up to his room and opened it eagerly. First came the promised overcoat. It was of very handsome French cloth, with a velvet collar, and rich silk facings, far higher in cost than any Mr. Merrill would have made for him. It fitted as if it had been made for him. Next came, not one, but two complete suits embracing coat, vest and pants. One of pepper-and-salt cloth, the other a dark blue. These, also, so similar was he in figure to Maurice, fitted him equally well. The clothes which he brought with him from Granton were not only of coarse material but were far from stylish in cut,

---

68

whereas these garments had been made by a fashionable Boston tailor and set off his figure to much greater advantage.

"I wonder what Luke Harrison will say?" said our hero to himself, smiling, as he thought of the surprise of Luke at witnessing his transformation.

"I've a great mind to keep these on tonight," he said.
"Perhaps I shall meet Luke. He won't have anything more to say about my going without an overcoat."

After dinner Harry, arrayed in his best suit and wearing the overcoat, walked down to the center of the village.

Luke was standing on the piazza of the tavern.

"Luke, see how Walton is dressed up!" exclaimed Frank Heath, who was the first to see our hero.

"Dressed up!" repeated Luke, who was rather shortsighted. "That would be a good joke."

"He's got a splendid overcoat," continued Frank.

"Where'd he get it? Merrill hasn't been making him one."

"It's none of Merrill's work. It's too stylish for him."

By this time Harry had come within Luke's range of vision. The latter surveyed him with astonishment and it must be confessed, with disappointment; for he had been fond of sneering at Harry's clothes, and now the latter was far better dressed than himself.

"Where did you get that coat, Walton?" asked Luke, the instant Harry came up.

"Honestly," said Harry, shortly.

"Have you got anything else new?"

Harry opened his coat and displayed the suit.

"Well, you are coming out, Walton, that's a fact," said Frank Heath. "That's a splendid suit."

"I thought you couldn't afford to buy a coat," said Luke.

"You see I've got one," answered Harry.

"How much did it cost?"

"That's a secret."

Here he left Luke and Frank.

"Well, Luke, what do you say to that?" said Frank Heath.

Luke said nothing. He was astonished and unhappy. He had a fondness for dress and spent a good share of his earnings upon it, paying where he must, and getting credit besides where he could. But he had never had so stylish a suit as this and it depressed him.

CHAPTER XVI

ASKING A FAVOR

There was one other tailor in the village, James Hayden, and to him Luke Harrison determined to transfer his custom, hoping to be allowed to run up a bill with him. He did not like his style of cut as well as Merrill's, but from the latter he was cut off unless he would pay the old bill, and this would be inconvenient.

He strolled into James Hayden's shop and asked to look at some cloth for pants.

Hayden was a shrewd man and, knowing that Luke was a customer of his neighbor, suspected the reason of his transfer. However, he showed the cloth, and, a selection having been made, measured him.

"When will you have them done?" asked Luke.

"In three days."

"I want them by that time sure."

"Of course you pay cash."

"Why," said Luke, hesitating, "I suppose you won't mind giving me a month's credit."

Mr. Hayden shook his head.

"I couldn't do it. My goods are already paid for, and I have to pay for the work. I must have cash."

"Merrill always trusted me," pleaded Luke.

"Then why did you leave him?"

"Why," said Luke, a little taken aback, "he didn't cut the last clothes exactly to suit me."

"Didn't suit you? I thought you young people preferred his cut to mine. I am old-fashioned. Hadn't you better go back to Merrill?"

"I've got tired of him," said Luke. "I'll get a pair of pants of you, and see how I like them."

"I'll make them but I can't trust."

"All right. I'll bring the money," said Luke, who yet thought that he might get off by paying part down when he took the pants.

"The old fellow's deuced disobliging," said he to Frank Heath, when they got into the street.

"I don't know as I blame him," said Frank.

"I wish Merrill wasn't so stiff about it. He's terribly afraid of losing his bill."

70

"That's where he's right," said Frank, laughing. "I'd be the same if I were in his place."

"Do you always pay your bills right off?" said Luke.

"Yes, I do. I don't pretend to be a model boy. I'm afraid I keep bad company," he continued, "but I don't owe a cent to anybody except for board and that I pay up at the end of every week."

Luke dropped the subject, not finding it to his taste.

On Saturday night he went round to the tailor's.

"Have you got my pants done, Mr. Hayden?"

"Yes—here they are."

"Let me see," he said, "how much are they?"

"Nine dollars."

"I'll pay you three dollars tonight and the rest at the end of next week," he said.

"Very well; then you may have them at the end of next week."

"Why not now? They are done, ain't they?"

"Yes," said Mr. Hayden; "but not paid for."

"Didn't I tell you I'd pay three dollars now?"

"Our terms are cash down."

"You ain't afraid of me, are you?" blustered Luke.

"You understood when you ordered the pants that they were to be paid for when they were taken."

"I hate to see people so afraid of losing their money."

"Do you? Was that why you left Merrill?"

Luke colored. He suspected that the fact of his unpaid bill at the other tailor's was known to Mr. Hayden.

"I've a great mind to leave them on your hands."

"I prefer to keep them on my hands, rather than to let them go out of the shop without being paid for."

"Frank," said Luke, turning to his companion, "lend me five dollars, can't you?"

"I'm the wrong fellow to ask," said he; "I've got to pay my board and another bill tonight."

"Oh, let your bills wait."

"And lend you the money? Thank you, I ain't so green. When should I get the money again?"

"Next week."

"In a horn. No; I want to wear the pants tomorrow. I'm going out to ride."

"I don't see, unless you fork over the spondulies."

71

"I can't. I haven't got enough money."

"See Harry Walton."

"I don't believe he has got any. He bought a lot of clothes last week. They must have cost a pile."

"Can't help it. I saw him open his pocketbook last night and in it was a roll of bills."

Turning to the tailor, Luke said: "Just lay aside the pants and I'll come back for them pretty soon."

Mr. Hayden smiled to himself.

"There's nothing like fetching up these fellows with a round turn," he said. "'No money, no clothes'—that's my motto. Merrill told me all about that little bill that sent Luke Harrison over here. He don't run up any bill with me, if I know myself."

Luke went round to the village store. Harry Walton usually spent a part of every evening in instructive reading and study; but after a hard day's work he felt it necessary to pass an hour or so in the open air, so he came down to the center of center of the village.

"Hello, Walton!" said Luke, accosting him with unusual cordiality. "You are just the fellow I want to see."

"Am I?" inquired Harry in surprise, for there was no particular friendship or intimacy between them.

"Yes; I'm going to ask a little favor of you—a mere trifle. Lend me five or ten dollars for a week. Five will do it, you can't spare more."

Harry shook his head.

"I can't do that, Luke."

"Why not? Haven't you got as much?"

"Yes, I've got it."

"Then why won't you lend it to me?"

"I have little money and I can't run any risk."

"Do you think I won't pay you back?"

"Why do you need to borrow of me? You get much higher wages than I do."

"I want to pay a bill tonight. I didn't think you'd be so unaccommodating."

"I shouldn't be willing to lend to anyone," said Harry.

"The money isn't mine. I am going to send it home."

"A great sight you are!" sneered Luke. "I wanted to see just how mean you were. You've got the money in your pocket but you won't lend it."

This taunt did not particularly disturb Harry. There is a large class like Luke, who offended at being refused a loan, though quite aware that they are never likely to repay it. My young readers will be sure to meet specimens of this class, against whom the only protection is a very firm and decided "No."

CHAPTER XVII

THE NIGHT SCHOLARS

Immediately after Thanksgiving Day, the winter schools commenced. That in the center district was kept by a student of Dartmouth college, who had leave of absence from the college authorities for twelve weeks, in order by teaching to earn something to help defray his college expenses. Leonard Morgan, now a junior, was a tall, strongly made young man of twenty-two, whose stalwart frame had not been reduced by his diligent study. There were several shoe shops in the village, each employing from one to three boys, varying in age from fifteen to nineteen. Why could he not form a private class, to meet in the evening, to be instructed in advanced arithmetic, or, if desired, in Latin and Greek? He broached the idea to Stephen Bates, the prudential committeeman.

"I don't know," said Mr. Bates, "what our boys will think of it. I've got a boy that I'll send, but whether you'll get enough to make it pay I don't know."

"I suppose I can have the schoolhouse, Mr. Bates?"

"Yes, there won't be no objection. Won't it be too much for you after teachin' in the daytime?"

"It would take a good deal to break me down."

"Then you'd better draw up a notice and put it up in the store and tavern," suggested the committeeman.

In accordance with this advice, the young teacher posted up in the two places the following notice:

"EVENING SCHOOL

"I propose to start an evening school for those who are occupied during the day, and unable to attend the district school. Instruction will be given in such English branches as may be desired, and also in Latin and Greek, if any are desirous of pursuing a classical course. The school will commence next Monday evening at the schoolhouse, beginning at seven o'clock. Terms: Seventy cents a week, or five dollars for the term of ten weeks.

"LEONARD MORGAN."

"Are you going to join the class, Walton?" asked Frank Heath.

"Yes," said Harry, promptly.

"Where'll you get the money?" asked Luke Harrison, in a jeering tone.

"I shan't have to go far for it."

"I don't see how you can spend so much money."

"I am willing to spend money when I can get my money's worth," said our hero. "Are you going?"

"To school? No, I guess not. I've got through my schooling."

"You don't know enough to hurt you, do you, Luke?" inquired Frank Heath, slyly.

"Nor I don't want to. I know enough to get along."

"I don't and never expect to," said Harry.

"Do you mean to go to school when you're a gray-headed old veteran?" asked Frank, jocosely.

"I may not go to school then but I shan't give up learning then," said Harry, smiling. "One can learn without going to school. But while I'm young, I mean to go to school as much as I can."

"I guess you're right," said Frank; "I'd go myself, only I'm too lazy. It's hard on a feller to worry his brain with study after he's been at work all day. I don't believe I was cut out for a great scholar."

"I don't believe you were, Frank," said Joe Bates.

"You always used to stand pretty well down toward the foot of the class when you went to school."

"A feller can't be smart as well as handsome. As long as I'm good-looking, I won't complain because I wasn't born with the genius of a Bates."

"Thank you for the compliment, Frank, though I suppose it means that I am homely. I haven't got any genius or education to spare."

A small country schoolhouse like the one where Harry and his classmates attend school.

When Monday evening arrived, ten pupils presented themselves, of whom six were boys, or young men, and four were girls. Leonard Morgan felt encouraged. A class of ten, though paying but five dollars each, would give him fifty dollars, which would be quite an acceptable addition to his scanty means.

"I am glad to see so many," he said. "I think our evening class will be a success. I will take your names and ascertain what studies you wish to pursue."

When he came to Harry; he asked, "What do you propose to study?"

"I should like to take up algebra and Latin, if you are willing," answered our hero.

"Have you studied either at all?"

"No, sir; I have not had an opportunity."

"How far have you been in arithmetic?"

"Through the square and cube root?"

"If you have been so far, you will have no difficulty with algebra. As to Latin, one of the girls wishes to take up that and I will put you in the class with her."

It will be seen that Harry was growing ambitious. He didn't expect to go to college, though nothing would have pleased him better; but he felt that some knowledge of a foreign language could do him no harm. Franklin, whom he had taken as his great exemplar, didn't go to college; yet he made himself one of the foremost scientific men of the age and acquired enduring reputation, not only as a statesman and a patriot, but chiefly as a philosopher.

A little later, Leonard Morgan came round to the desk at which Harry was sitting.

"I brought a Latin grammar with me," he said, "thinking it probable some one might like to begin that language. You can use it until yours comes."

"Thank you," said Harry; and he eagerly took the book, and asked to have a lesson set, which was done.

"I can get more than that," he said.

"How much more?"

"Twice as much."

Still later he recited the double lesson, and so correctly that the teacher's attention was drawn to him.

76

"That's a smart boy," he said. "I mean to take pains with him. What a pity he can't go to college!"

CHAPTER XVIII

LOST OR STOLEN

Harry learned rapidly. At the end of four weeks he had completed the Latin grammar, or that part of it which his teacher, thought necessary for a beginner to be familiar with, and commenced translating the easy sentences in "Andrews' Latin Reader."

"You are getting on famously, Harry," said his teacher. "I never had a scholar who advanced so."

"I wish I knew as much as you."

"Don't give me too much credit. When I compare myself with our professors, I feel dissatisfied."

"But you know so much more than I do," said Harry.

"I ought to; I am seven years older."

"What are you going to study, Mr. Morgan?"

"I intend to study law."

"I should like to be an editor," said Harry; "but I don't see much prospect of it."

"Why not?"

"An editor must know a good deal."

"There are some who don't," said Leonard Morgan, with a smile. "However, you would like to do credit to the profession and it is certainly in these modern days a very important profession."

"How can I prepare myself?"

"By doing your best to acquire a good education; not only by study but by reading extensively. An editor should be a man of large information. Have you ever practiced writing compositions?"

"A little; not much."

"If you get time to write anything, and will submit it to me, I will point out such faults as I may notice."

"I should like to do that," said Harry, promptly.

"What subject shall I take?"

"You may choose your own subject. Don't be too ambitious but select something upon which you have some ideas of your own."

"Suppose I take my motto? 'Live and learn.'"

"Do so, by all means. That is a subject upon which you may fairly be said to have some ideas of your own."

In due time Harry presented a composition on this subject. The thoughts were good, but, as might be expected, the expression was somewhat crude, and of course the teacher found errors to correct and suggestions to make. These Harry eagerly welcomed and voluntarily proposed to rewrite the composition. The result was a very much improved draft. He sent a copy home and received in reply a letter from his father, expressing surprise and gratification at the excellence of his essay.

"I am glad, Harry," the letter concluded, "that you have formed just views of the importance of learning. I have never ceased to regret that my own opportunities for education were so limited and that my time has been so much absorbed by the effort to make a living, that I have been able to do so little toward supplying my deficiencies. Even in a pecuniary way, an education will open to you a more prosperous career, and lead, I hope, to competence, instead of the narrow poverty which has been my lot. I will not complain of my own want of success, if I can see my children prosper."

But while intent upon cultivating his mind, Harry had not lost sight of the great object which had sent him from home to seek employment among strangers. He had undertaken to meet the note which his father had given Squire Green in payment for the cow. By the first of December he had saved up thirty-three dollars toward this object. By the middle of January the note would come due.

Of course he had not saved so much without the strictest economy, and by denying himself pleasures which were entirely proper. For instance, he was waited upon by Luke Harrison on the first day of December, and asked to join in a grand sleighing excursion to a town ten miles distant, where it was proposed to take dinner, and, after a social time, return late in the evening.

**Luke wants Harry to join them on a
sleighing expedition like this one.**

"I would like to go," said Harry, who was strongly, tempted, for he was by no means averse to pleasure; "but I am afraid I cannot. How much will it cost?"

"Three dollars apiece. That pays for the dinner too."

Harry shook his head. It was for rum a week's wages. If he were not trying to save money for his father, he might have ventured to incur this expense, but he felt that under present circumstances it would not be best.

"I can't go," said Harry.

"Oh, come along," urged Luke. "Don't make such a mope of yourself. You'll be sure to enjoy it."

"I know I should; but I can't afford it."

"I never knew a feller that thought so much of money as you," sneered Luke.

"I suppose it looks so," said Harry; "but it isn't true."

"Everybody says you are a miser."

"I have good reasons for not going."

"If you would come, it would make the expense lighter for the rest of us and you would have a jolly time."

This conversation took place as they were walking home from the store in the evening. Harry pulled out his handkerchief suddenly from his pocket and with it came his pocketbook, containing all his savings. He didn't hear if fall; but Luke did, and the latter, moreover, suspected what it was. He did not call Harry's attention to it, but, falling back, said: "I've got to go back to the store. I forgot something. Good night!"

"Good night!" said Harry, unsuspiciously.

Luke stooped swiftly while our hero's back was turned, and picked up the pocketbook. He slipped it into his own pocket, and, instead of going back to the store, went to his own room, locked the door, and then eagerly pulled out the pocketbook and counted the contents.

"Thirty-three dollars! What a miser that fellow is! It serves him right to lose his money."

CHAPTER XIX

AN UNWELCOME VISITOR

Luke Harrison had picked up Harry's pocketbook, and, though knowing it to be his, concealed the discovery upon the impulse of the moment.

"What I find is mine," he said to himself. "Of course it is. Harry Walton deserves to lose his money."

It will be seen that he had already decided to keep the money. It looked so tempting to him, as his eyes rested on the thick roll of bills—for, though insignificant in amount, the bills were ones and twos, and twenty in number—that he could not make up his mind to return it.

Luke was fond of new clothes. He wanted to re-establish his credit with Merrill, for he was in want of a new coat and knew that it would be useless to order one unless he had some money to pay on account. He decided to use a part of Harry's money for this purpose. It would be better, however, he thought, to wait a day or two, as the news of the loss would undoubtedly spread abroad, and his order might excite suspicion, particularly as he had been in Harry's company at the time the money disappeared. He therefore put the pocketbook into his trunk, and carefully locked it. Then he went to bed.

Meanwhile, Harry reached Mr. Leavitt's unconscious of the serious misfortune which had befallen him. He went into the sitting room and talked a while with Mr. Leavitt, and at ten o'clock took his lamp and went up to bed. While he was undressing he felt in his pocket for his money, intending to lock it up in his trunk as usual. His dismay may be conceived when he could not find it.

Poor Harry sank into a chair with that sudden sinking of the heart which unlooked-for misfortune brings and tried to think where he could have left the pocketbook.

That evening he found himself under the necessity of buying a necktie at the store, and so had taken it from his trunk. Could he have left it on the counter? No; he distinctly remembered replacing it in his pocket. He felt the need of consulting with somebody, and with his lamp in his hand went downstairs again.

"You haven't concluded to sit up all night, have you?" asked Mr. Leavitt, surprised at his reappearance.

—

"Are you sick, Harry?" asked Mrs. Leavitt. "You're looking dreadfully pale."

"I've lost my pocketbook," said Harry..

"How much was there in it?" asked his employer.

"Thirty-three dollars," answered Harry.

"Whew! That's a good deal of money to lose. I shouldn't want to lose so much myself. When did you have it last?"

Harry told his story, Mr. Leavitt listening attentively

"And you came right home?"

"Yes."

"Alone."

"No; Luke Harrison came with me."

"Are you two thick together?"

"Not at all. He doesn't like me, and I don't fancy him."

"What was he talking about?"

"He wanted me to join a sleighing party."

"What did you say?"

"I said I couldn't afford it. Then he charged me with being a miser, as he often does."

"Did he come all the way home with you?"

"No; he left me at Deacon Brewster's. He said he must go back to the store."

"There is something queer about this," said Mr. Leavitt, shrewdly. "Do you want my advice?"

"Yes; I wish you would advise me, for I don't know what to do."

"Then go to the store at once. Ask, but without attracting any attention, if Luke came back there after leaving you. Then ask Mr. Meade, the storekeeper, whether he noticed you put back your pocketbook."

"But I know I did."

"Then it will be well to say nothing about it, at least publicly. If you find that Luke's excuse was false, and that he did not go back, go at once to his boarding place, and ask him whether he saw you drop the pocketbook. You might have dropped it and he picked it up."

"Suppose he says no?"

"Then we must watch whether he seems flush of money for the next few days."

This seemed to Harry good advice. He retraced his steps to the store, carefully looking for the lost pocketbook. But of course, it was not to be seen and he entered the store troubled and out of spirits.

"I thought you went home, Harry," said Frank Heath.

"You see I am here again," said our hero.

"Time to shut up shop," said Mr. Meade, the storekeeper. "You boys will have to adjourn till tomorrow."

"Where's Luke Harrison?" asked Frank Heath.

"Didn't he go out with you?"

"Yes; but he left me some time ago. He came back here, didn't he?"

"No; he hasn't been here since."

"He spoke of coming," said Harry. "He wanted me to join that sleighing party."

"Good night, boys," said the storekeeper, significantly.

They took the hint and went out. Their way lay in different directions, and they parted company.

"Now I must call on Luke," said Harry to himself.

"I hope he found the pocketbook. He wouldn't be wicked enough to keep it."

But he was not quite so sure of this as he would like to have been. He felt almost sick as he thought of the possibility that he might never recover the money which he had saved so gladly, though with such painful economy. It represented the entire cash earnings of eleven weeks.

Luke Harrison boarded with a Mr. Glenham, a carpenter, and it was at his door that Harry knocked.

"Is Luke Harrison at home?" he inquired of Mrs. Glenham, who opened the door.

"At home and abed, I reckon," she replied.

"I know it's late, Mrs. Glenham, but it is about a matter of importance that I wish to see Luke."

"I reckon it's about the sleighing party."

"No, it is quite another thing. I won't stay but minute."

"Well, I suppose you can go up."

Harry went upstairs and knocked. Ordinarily, Luke would have been asleep, for generally he sank to sleep five minutes after his head touched the pillow; but tonight the excitement of his dishonest intention kept him awake, and he started uneasily when he heard the knock.

84

"Who's there?" he called out from the bed.

"It's I—Harry Walton."

"He's come about that pocketbook," thought Luke.

"I'm in bed," he answered.

"I want to see you a minute, on a matter of importance."

"Come tomorrow morning."

"I must see you now."

"Oh, well, come in, if you must," said Luke.

CHAPTER XX

"You seem to be in an awful hurry to see me," said Luke, grumbling. "I was just getting to sleep."

"I've lost my pocketbook. Have you seen it?"

"Have I seen it? That's a strange question. How should I have seen it?"

"I lost it on the way from the store to the house."

"Do you mean to charge me with taking it?"

"I haven't said anything of the sort," said Harry; "but you were with me, and I thought you might have seen it drop out of my pocket."

"Did you drop it out of your pocket?"

"I can't think of any other way I could lose it."

"Of course I haven't seen it. Was that all you woke me up about?"

"Is that all? You talk as if it was a little thing losing thirty-three dollars."

"Thirty-three dollars!" repeated Luke, pretending to be surprised. "You don't mean to say you've lost all that?"

"Yes, I do."

"Well," said Luke, yawning, "I wish I could help you; but I can't. Good night."

"Good night," said Harry, turning away disappointed.

"What success, Harry?" inquired Mr. Leavitt, who had deferred going to bed in order to hear his report.

"None at all," answered Harry.

"Is there anything by which you can identify any of the bills?"

"Yes," answered Harry, with sudden recollection, "I dropped a penful of ink on one of the bills—a two-dollar note—just in the center. I had been writing a letter, and the bill lay on the table near by."

"Good!" said Mr. Leavitt. "Now, supposing Luke has taken this money, how is he likely to spend it?"

"At the tailor's, most likely. He is always talking about new clothes; but lately he hasn't had any because Merrill shut down on him on account of an unpaid bill."

"Then you had better see Merrill and ask him to take particular notice of any bills that Luke pays him."

"Innocence must often be suspected, or guilt would never be detected. It is the only way to get on the track of the missing bills."

Harry saw that this was reasonable and decided to call on Merrill the next day.

"Do you think Luke took it?" asked the tailor.

"I don't know. I don't like to suspect him."

"I haven't much opinion of Luke. He owes me a considerable bill."

"He prefers your clothes to Hayden's, and if he has the money, he will probably come here and spend some of it."

"Suppose he does, what do you want me to do?"

"To examine the bills he pays you, and if you find an ink spot on the center of one let me know."

"I understand. I think I can manage it."

"My money was mostly in ones and twos."

"That may help you. I will bear it in mind."

Two days afterwards, Luke Harrison met Harry.

"Have you found your money, Walton?" he asked.

"No, and I am afraid I never shall," said our hero.

"What do you think has become of it?"

"That's just what I would like to find out," said Harry.

"The only thing you can do is to grin and bear it."

"And be more careful next time."

"Of course."

"He's given it up," said Luke to himself. "I think I can venture to use some of it now. I'll go round to Merrill's and see what he's got in the way of pants."

Accordingly he strolled into Merrill's that evening.

"Got any new cloths in, Merrill?" asked Luke.

"I've got some new cloths for pants."

"That's just what I want."

"You're owing me a bill."

"How much is it?"

"Some over thirty dollars."

"I can't pay it all, but I'll tell you what I'll do. I'll pay you fifteen dollars on account, and you can make me a new pair of pants. Will that answer?"

"All right. Of course I'd rather you'd pay the whole bill. Still I want to be accommodating."

"Let me look at your cloths."

The tailor displayed a variety of cloths, one of which suited Luke's fancy.

"Here's fifteen dollars," he said. "Just credit me with that on the bill, will you?"

"All right," said Merrill.

He proceeded to count the money, which consisted of consisted of ones and twos, and instantly came to the conclusion that it was from Harry's missing pocketbook, particularly as he came upon the identical note with the blot in the center.

**Luke tries to pay the tailor with a two dollar bill
that belonged to Harry.**

Unaware of the manner in which he had betrayed himself, Luke felt quite complacent over his re-established credit, and that without any expense to himself.

"Have you got any new cloth for coats?" he asked.

"I shall have some new cloths in next week."

"All right. When will you have the pants done?"

"You may call round in two or three days."

"Just make 'em in style, Merrill, and I'll send all my friends here."

"Very well. I hope you'll soon be able to pay me the balance of my bill."

"Oh, yes, to be sure. You won't have to wait long."

He swaggered out of the shop, lighting a cigar.

"My young friend," soliloquized the tailor, watching his exit, "you have walked into my trap neatly. Colman,"—turning to a young man present at the time—"did you see Luke Harrison pay me this money?"

"Yes; to be sure."

"Do you see this blot on one of the bills—a two?"

"Yes; What of it?"

"Nothing. I only called your attention to it."

"I don't see what there is strange about that. Anybody might get ink on a bill, mightn't he?"

"Of course."

Colman was puzzled. He could not understand why he should have been called upon to notice such a trifle; but the tailor had his reasons. He wanted to be able to prove by Colman's testimony that the blotted bill was actually put into his hands by Luke Harrison.

CHAPTER XXI

IN THE TAILOR'S POWER

"Is that the bill you spoke of, Walton?" asked the tailor, on Harry's next visit to the shop.

"Yes," said Harry, eagerly. "Where did you get it?"

"You can guess."

"From Luke Harrison?"

"Yes; he paid me, last evening, fifteen dollars on account. This note was among those he paid me."

"It is mine. I can swear to it."

"The rest of the money was yours, no doubt."

"What shall I do, Mr. Merrill?"

"The money is yours, and I will restore it to you after seeing Luke. I will send for him to be here at seven o'clock this evening."

As Luke was at work in his shop that day, the tailor's boy came in with a note.

Luke opened it and read as follows:

"Will you call at my shop at seven this evening about the pants you ordered?

"Henry Merrill."

"Tell your father I'll come," said Luke.

At seven o'clock he entered the tailor's shop once more.

"Well, Merrill, what do you want to see me about?" he asked. "Have you cut the pants?"

"No."

"You haven't? I wanted you to go to work on them at once."

"I know; but it was necessary to see you first."

"Why—didn't you take the measure right?"

"Luke," said Mr. Merrill, looking him steadily in the eye, "where did you get that money you paid me?"

"Where did I get the money?" repeated Luke, flushing up. "What makes you ask me that question? Isn't it good money? 'Tisn't counterfeit, is it?"

"I asked you where you got it from?"

"From the man I work for, to be sure," said Luke.

"Will you swear to that?"

"I don't see the use. Can't you take my word?"

"I may as well tell you that Harry Walton recognizes one of the bills as a part of the money he lost."

"He does, does he?" said Luke, boldly. "That's all nonsense. Bills all look alike."

"This one has a drop of ink just in the center. He remembered having dropped a blot upon it."

"What have I to do with that?"

"It is hardly necessary to explain. The evening he lost the money you were with him. Two days after, you pay me one of the bills which he lost," said the tailor.

"Do you mean to say I stole 'em?" demanded Luke.

"It looks like it, unless you can explain how you came by the blotted bill."

"I don't believe I paid you the bill. Very likely it was some one else."

I thought you would say that, so I called Colman's attention to it. However, if your employer admits paying you the bills, of course you are all right."

Luke remembered very well that he was paid in fives, and that such an appeal would do him no good.

"Does Walton know this?" he asked, sinking into a chair, and wiping the perspiration from his brow.

"Yes; he suspected you."

"I'd like to choke him!" said Luke, fiercely. "The miserly scoundrel!"

"It seems to me he is justified in trying to recover his money. What have you done with the rest of it?"

"Tell me what will be done to me," said Luke, sullenly.

"I didn't steal it. I only picked it up when he dropped it. He deserves to lose it, for being so careless."

"Why didn't you tell him you had found it?"

"I meant to give it to him after a while. I only wanted to keep it long enough to frighten him."

"That was dangerous, particularly as you used it."

"I meant to give him back other money."

"I don't think that excuse will avail you in court."

"Court of justice!" repeated Luke, turning pale.

"He won't have me taken up—will he?"

"He will unless you arrange to restore all the money."

"I've paid you part of it."

—

"That I shall hand over to him. Have you the rest?"

"I've spent a few dollars. I've got eight dollars left."

"You had better give it to me."

Reluctantly, Luke drew out his pocketbook and passed the eight dollars to Mr. Merrill.

"Now when will you pay the rest?"

"In a few weeks," said Luke.

"That won't do. How much do you earn a week?"

"Fifteen dollars."

"How much do you pay for board?"

"Four dollars."

"Then you will be able to pay eleven dollars at the end of this week."

"I can't get along without money," said Luke.

"You will have to till you pay back the money, unless you prefer appearing before a court of justice."

Luke was just going out when the tailor called him back.

"I believe you owe me thirty dollars. When are you going to pay it?"

"I can't pay it yet a while," said Luke.

"I think you had better," said the tailor quietly.

"I'll pay you as soon as I can."

"You make eleven dollars a week over and above your board and spend it on drink, billiards and fast horses. You are fully able to pay for your clothes promptly and I advise you to do it."

"I'll pay you as soon as I can."

"If you neglect to do it, I may as well tell you that I shall let it be known that you stole Walton's pocketbook."

An expression of alarm overspread Luke's face, and he hastily made the required promise. But he added, "I didn't steal it. I only found it."

"The whole story would be told, and people might think as they pleased. But it is much better for you to avoid all this by paying your bills."

Luke Harrison left the tailor's shop in a very unhappy and disgusted frame of mind.

"If I had the sense to wait till it blew over," he said to himself, "I should have escaped all this: I didn't think Merrill would act so mean. Now I'm in for paying his infernal bill besides. It's too bad."

Just then he came upon Frank Heath, who hailed him.

"Luke, come and play a game of billiards."

"If you'll promise not to beat me. I haven't got a cent of money."

"You haven't? What have you done with those bills you had this afternoon?"

"I've paid 'em over to Merrill," said Luke, hesitating.

"He was in a deuced stew about his bill."

"When are your pants going to be ready?"

"I don't know," said Luke, with a pang of sorrow.

"Merrill's making them, isn't he?"

"He says he won't till I pay the whole bill."

"Seems to me your credit ain't very good, Luke."

"It's good enough, be he's hard up for money. I guess he's going to fail. If you'll lend me a couple of dollars, I'll go around and have a game."

Frank Heath laughed.

"You'll have to go to some one else, Luke," he said.

Luke passed a disagreeable evening. Cut off by his want of money from his ordinary amusements, and depressed by the thought that things would be no better till he had paid his bills, he lounged about, feeling that he was a victim of ill luck. It did not occur to him that that ill luck was of his own bringing.

93

CHAPTER XXII

THE COMING OF THE MAGICIAN

The week passed and Luke carefully avoided our hero going so far as to cross the street so as not to meet him. On Saturday evening, according to his arrangement, Luke was to have paid the surplus of his wages, after meeting his board bill, to Mr. Merrill, for Harry.

But he did not go near him. On Monday, the tailor meeting him, inquired why he had not kept his agreement.

"The fact is," said Luke, "I have been unlucky."

"How unlucky?"

"I had my wages loose in my pocket, and managed to lose them somehow."

"That is very singular," said the tailor, suspiciously.

"Why is it singular?" asked Luke. "Didn't Harry Walton lose his money?"

"You seem to have lost yours at a very convenient time."

"It's hard on me," said Luke. "Owing so much, I want to pay as quick as I can, so as to have my wages to myself. Don't you see that?"

"Where do you think you lost the money?"

"I'm sure I don't know," said Luke.

"Well," said Merrill, dryly, "I hope you will take better care of your wages next Saturday evening."

"I mean to. I can't afford to lose anymore."

"I don't believe, a word of what he says about losing his money," said the tailor, privately, to Harry. "I think it's only a trick to get rid of paying you."

"Don't you think he'll pay me?" asked Harry.

"He won't if he can help it," was the answer. "He's a slippery customer. I believe his money is in his pocket at this moment."

Mr. Merrill was not quite right; but it was only as to the whereabouts of the money. It was in Luke's trunk. He intended to run away, leaving all his creditors in the lurch. This was the "new way to pay old debts," which occurred to Luke as much the easiest.

The next Saturday evening, Mr. Merrill waited in vain for a call from his debtor.

"What excuse will he have now?" he thought.

On Monday morning he learned that Luke had left town without acquainting anyone with his destination. It transpired, also, that he was owing at his boarding house for two weeks' board. He was thus enabled to depart with nearly thirty dollars, for parts unknown.

"He's a hard case," said Mr. Merrill to Harry. "I am afraid he means to owe us for a long time to come."

"Where do you think he is gone?" asked Harry.

"I have no idea. He has evidently been saving up money to help him out of town. Sometime we may get upon his track, and compel him to pay up."

"That won't do me much good," said Harry, despondently. And then he told the tailor why he wanted the money. "Now," he concluded, "I shan't be able to have the money ready in time."

"You'll have most of it ready, won't you?"

"I think I will."

"I would lend you the money myself," said the tailor, "but I've got a heavy payment to meet and some of my customers are slow pay, though I have not many as bad as Luke Harrison."

"Thank you, Mr. Merrill," said Harry. "I am as much obliged to you as if you could lend the money."

But it is said that misfortunes never come singly. The very next day Mr. Leavitt received a message from the wholesale dealer to whom he sold his shoes that the market was glutted and sales slow.

"I shall not want any more goods for a month or two," the letter concluded. "I will let you know, when I more."

Mr. Leavitt read this letter aloud in the shop.

"So it seems we are to have a vacation," he said. "That's the worst of the shoe trade. It isn't steady. When it's good everybody rushes into it, and the market soon gets overstocked. Then there's no work for weeks."

This was a catastrophe for which Harry was no prepared. He heard the announcement with a grave face, for to him it was a serious calamity. Twenty-three dollars were all that he had saved from the money lost and this would be increased by a dollar or two only, when he had settled up with Mr. Leavitt. If he stayed here did not obtain work, he must pay his board, and that would soon swallow up his money. Could he get work in any other shop? That was an important question.

"Do you think I can get into any other shop in town?" he inquired anxiously of Mr. Leavitt.

—

"You can try, Harry; but I guess you'll find others no better off than I."

This was not very encouraging, but Harry determined not to give up without an effort. He devoted the next day to going around among the shoe shops; but everywhere he met with unfavorable answers. Some had ready suspended. Others were about to do so.

"It seems as if all my money must go," thought Harry, looking despondently at his little hoard. "First the ten dollars Luke Harrison stole. Then work stopped. I don't know but it would be better for me to go home."

But the more Harry thought of this, the less he liked it. It would be an inglorious ending to his campaign. Probably now he would not be able to carry out his plan of paying for the cow; but if his father should lose it, he might be able, if he found work, to buy him another Squire Green's cow was not the only cow in the world and all would not be lost if he could not buy her.

"I won't give up yet," said Harry, pluckily. "I must expect to meet with some bad luck. I suppose everybody does. Something'll turn up for me if I try to make it."

This was good philosophy. Waiting passively for something to turn up is bad policy and likely to lead to disappointment; but waiting actively, ready to seize any chance that may offer, is quite different. The world is full of chances, and from such chances so seized has been based many a prosperous career.

During his first idle day, Harry's attention was drawn to a handbill which had been posted up in the store, the post office, the tavern, and other public places in the village. It was to this effect:

"PROFESSOR HENDERSON,

"The celebrated Magician,

"Will exhibit his wonderful feats of Magic and Sleight of Hand in the Town Hall this evening, commencing at 8 o'clock. In the course of the entertainment he will amuse the audience by his wonderful exhibition of ventriloquism, in which he is unsurpassed.

"Tickets 25 cents. Children under twelve, 15 cents."

In a country village, where amusements are few, such entertainments occupy a far more important place than in a city, where amusements abound.

"Are you going to the exhibition, Walton?" asked Frank Heath.

"I don't know," said Harry.

"Better come. It'll be worth seeing."

In spite of his economy, our hero wanted to go.

"The professor's stopping at the tavern. Come over, and we may see him," said Frank.

CHAPTER XXIII

THE VENTRILOQUIST

The boys went into the public room of the tavern. In the center was a stove, around which were gathered a miscellaneous crowd, who had assembled, as usual, to hear and talk over the news of the day. At the farther end of the room was a bar, where liquor and cigars were sold. The walls of the room, which was rather low-studded, were ornamented by sundry notices and posters of different colors, with here and there an engraving of no great artistic excellence—one representing a horse race, another a steamer of the Cunard Line, and still another, the Presidents of the United States grouped together, with Washington as the central figure.

Professor Henderson is a traveling ventriloquist. Traveling ventriloquists would advertise their shows with posters like this one.

"Have a cigar, Walton?" asked Frank Heath.

"No, thank you, Frank."

"You haven't got so far along, hey?"

"I don't think it would do me any good," said Harry.

"Maybe not; but jolly comfortable on a cold night. The worst of it is, it's mighty expensive."

Frank walked up to the bar and bought a ten-cent cigar. He returned and sat down on a settee.

"The magician isn't here," said Harry.

"Hush, he is here!" said Frank, in a low voice, as the door opened, and a tall, portly man entered the room.

Professor Henderson—for it was he—walked up the bar, and followed Frank Heath's example in the purchase of a cigar. Then he glanced leisurely round the apartment. Apparently, his attention was fixed by our hero, for he walked up to him, and said: "Young man, I would like to speak to you."

"All right, sir," said Harry, in surprise.

"If you are not otherwise occupied, will you accompany me to my room?"

"Certainly, sir," returned Harry, in fresh wonder.

"Perhaps he's going to take in Walton as partner," Frank Heath suggested to Tom Frisbie.

"I wonder what he want anyway?" said Frisbie. "Why didn't he take you?"

"Because I'm too sharp," said Frank. "I should see through his tricks."

Meanwhile, Harry had entered the professor's chamber.

"Sit down," said the magician. "I'll tell you what I want of you. I want you to take tickets at the door of hall tonight. Can you do it?"

"Yes, sir," said Harry, promptly.

"It seems easy enough," said the professor; "but not everyone can do it rapidly without making mistakes. Are you quick at figures?"

"I am usually considered so," said our hero.

"I won't ask whether you are honest, for you would so, of course."

"I hope—" commenced Harry.

—

99

"I know what you are going to say; but there is no need of saying it," interrupted the magician. "I judge from your face, which is an honest one. I have traveled about a good deal, and I am a good judge of faces."

"You shall not be disappointed, sir."

"I know that, in advance. Now, tell me if you are at work, or do you attend school?"

"I have been at work in a shoe shop in this village, sir."

"Not now?"

"No, sir; business is dull, and work has given out."

"What are you going to do next?"

"Anything by which I can earn an honest living."

"That's the way to talk. I'll take you into my employ, if you have no objection to travel."

Objection to travel! Who ever heard of a boy of fifteen who had an objection to travel?

"But will your parents consent? That is the next question. I don't want to entice any boys away from home against their parents' consent."

"My parents do not live here. They live farther north, in the town of Granton."

"Granton? I never was there. Is it a large place?"

"No, sir, it is a very small place. My father consented to have me leave home and he will have no objection to my earning my living in any honest way."

"Well, my young friend, I can assure you that my way is an honest one, though I frankly confess I do my best to deceive the people who come to my entertainments."

"What is it you want me to do, sir?"

"Partly what you are going to do tonight—take tickets at the door; but that is not all. I have to carry about considerable apparatus and I need help about arranging it. Sometimes, also, I need help in my experiments. I had a young man with me; but he is taken down with a fever and obliged to go home. It is not likely, as his health is delicate, that he will care to resume his position. I must have somebody in his place. I have no doubt you will answer my purpose."

"How much pay do you give, sir?"

"A practical question," said the professor, smiling.

"To begin with, of course I pay traveling expenses, and I can offer you five dollars a week besides. Will that be satisfactory?"

"Yes, sir," said Harry, his heart giving a great throb of exultation as he realized that his new business would give him two dollars week more than his work in the shop, besides being a good deal more agreeable, since it would give him a chance to see a little of the world.

"Can you start with me tomorrow morning?"

"Yes, sir."

"Then it is settled. But it is time you were at the hall. I will give you a supply of small bills and, change, as you may have to change some bills."

He drew from his side pocket a wallet, which he placed in the hands of our hero.

"This wallet contains twenty dollars," he said: "Of course you will bring me back that amount, in addition to what you take at the door this evening."

"Very well, sir."

"You can wait for me at the close of the evening, and hand me all together. Now go over to the hall, as the doors are to be open at half past seven o'clock."

When Frank Heath and his companion went over to the Town Hall they found Harry making change.

"Hello, Walton!" said Frank. "Are you the treasurer of this concern?"

"It seems so," said Harry.

"You'll let in your friends for nothing, won't you?"

"Not much. I charge them double price."

"Well here's our money. I say, Tom, I wonder the old fellow didn't take me instead of Walton."

"That's easily told. You don't look honest enough."

"Oh, if it comes to that, he passed over you, too, Tom."

"He wouldn't insult a gentleman of my dignity. Come on; there's room on the front seat."

Harry was kept busy till ten minutes after eight. By that time about all who intended to be present were in the hall and the magician was gratified by seeing that it was crowded. He was already well-known in the village, having been in the habit of visiting it every four years and his reputation for dexterity, and especially for ventriloquism, had called out this large audience.

The professor's tricks excited great wonder in the younger spectators. I will only dwell slightly on his ventriloquism. When he came to this part of the entertainment, he said: "Will any young gentleman assist me?"

Frank Heath immediately left his seat and took up his position beside the professor.

"Now, sir," said the professor, "I want to ask you a question or two. Will you answer me truly?"

A gruff voice appeared to proceed from Frank's mouth, saying: "Yes, sir."

"Are you married, sir?"

Again the same gruff voice answered: "Yes, sir; I wish I wasn't;" to the great delight of the small boys.

"Indeed, sir! I hope your wife doesn't make it uncomfortable for you."

"She licks me," Frank appeared to answer.

"I am sorry. What does she lick you with?"

"With a broomstick."

Frank looked foolish and there was a general laugh.

"I hope she doesn't treat you so badly very often, sir."

"Yes, she does, every day," was the answer. "If she known I was up here telling you, she'd beat me awful."

"In that case, sir, I won't be cruel enough to keep you here any longer. Take my advice, sir, and get a divorce."

"So I will, by hokey!"

And Frank, amid hearty laughter, resumed his seat, not having uttered a word, the professor being responsible for the whole conversation.

CHAPTER XXIV

HARRY'S LETTER

During Harry's absence, the little household at Granton had got along about as usual. They lived from hand to mouth. It required sharp financiering to provide food and clothes for the little family.

There was one neighbor who watched their progress sharply and this was Squire Green. It will be remembered that he had bound Mr. Walton to forfeit ten dollars, if, at the end of six months, he was not prepared to pay the forty dollars and interest which he had agreed to pay for the cow. It is a proof of the man's intense meanness that, though rich while his neighbor was poor, he was strongly in hopes that the latter would incur the forfeit and be compelled to pay it.

One morning Squire Green accosted Mr. Walton, the squire being at work in his own front yard.

"Good morning, neighbor Walton," he said.

"Good morning, squire."

"How is that cow a-doin'?"

"Pretty well."

"She's a good cow."

"Not so good as the one I lost."

"You're jokin' now, neighbor. It was my best cow. I wouldn't have sold her except to obleege."

"She doesn't give as much milk as my old one."

"Sho! I guess you don't feed her as well as I did."

"She fares just as well as the other one did. Of course, I don't know how you fed her."

"She allers had her fill when she was with me. Le' me see, how long is it since I sold her to ye?"

Though the squire apparently asked for information, he knew the time to a day and was not likely to forget.

"It's between four and five months, I believe."

"Jus'so. You was to be ready to pay up at the end of six months."

"That was the agreement."

"You'd better be a-savin' up for it."

"There isn't much chance of my saving. It's all I can do to make both ends meet."

"You don't say so," said the squire, secretly pleased.

"My farm is small and poor, and doesn't yield much."

"But you work out, don't you?"

"When I get a chance. You don't want any help, do you, squire? I might work off part of the debt that way."

"Mebbe next spring I'd like some help."

"That will be too late to meet my note, unless you'll renew."

"I'll see about it," said the squire, evasively. "What do you hear from that boy of yours? Is he doin' well?"

"He's at work in a shoe shop."

"Does it pay well?"

"He doesn't get much just at first."

"Then he won't be able to pay for the cow," thought the squire. "That's what I wanted to know."

"He'd better have gone to work for me," he said

"No, I think he will do better away from home. He will get a good trade that he can fall back upon hereafter, even if he follows some other business."

"Wal, I never learned no trade but I've got along middlin' well," said the squire, in a complacent tone. "Farmin's good enough for me."

"I would say the same if I had your farm, squire. You wouldn't exchange, would you?"

"That's a good joke, neighbor Walton. When I make up my mind to do it. I'll let you know."

"What a mean old curmudgeon he is!" thought Hiram Walton, as he kept on his way to the village store. "He evidently intends to keep me to my agreement and will exact the ten dollars in case I can't pay for the cow at the appointed time. It will be nothing but a robbery."

This was not the day for a letter from Harry but it occurred to Mr. Walton to call at the post office. Contrary to his anticipations, a letter was handed him.

"I won't open it till I get home," he said to himself.

"I've got a letter from Harry," he said, as he entered the house.

"A letter from Harry? It isn't his day for writing," said Mrs. Walton. "What does he say?"

"I haven't opened the letter yet. Here, Tom, open and read it aloud."

Tom opened the letter and read as follows:

"Dear Father:—I must tell you, to begin with, that I have been compelled to stop work in the shoe shop. The market is overstocked and trade has become very dull.

"Of course, I felt quite bad when Mr. Leavitt told me this, for I feared it would prevent my helping you pay for the cow, as I want so much to do. I went round to several other shops, hoping to get in, but I found it impossible. Still, I have succeeded in getting something to do that will pay me better than work in the shop. If you were to guess all day, I don't believe you would guess what business it is. So, to relieve your suspense, I will tell you that I have engaged as assistant to Professor Henderson, the famous magician and ventriloquist and am to start tomorrow on a tour with him."

"Assistant to a magician!" exclaimed Mrs. Walton

"What does the boy know about magic?"

"It's a bully business," said Tom, enthusiastically. "I only wish I was in Harry's shoes. I'd like to travel round with a magician first-rate."

"You're too thick-headed, Tom," said Marry.

"Shut up!" said Tom. "I guess I'm as smart as you, any day."

"Be quiet, both of you!" said Mr. Walton. "Now, Tom, go on with your brother's letter."

Tom proceeded: "I am to take money at the door. We are going about in the southern part of the state and shall visit some towns in Massachusetts, the professor says. You know I've never been round any and I shall like traveling and seeing new places. Professor Henderson is very kind and I think I shall like him. He pays my traveling expenses and five dollars a week, which is nearly twice as much money as I got from Mr. Leavitt. I can't help thinking I am lucky in getting so good a chance only a day after I lost my place in the shoe shop. I hope, yet, to be able to pay for the cow when the money comes due.

"Love to all at home.

"Harry."

"Harry's lucky," said Mary. "He can get along."

"He is fortunate to find employment at once," said his father; "though something which he can follow steadily is better. But the pay is good and I am glad he has it."

"How long it seems since Harry was at home," said his mother. "I wish I could see him."

"Yes, it would be pleasant," said Mr. Walton; "but the boy has his own way to make, so we will be thankful that he is succeeding so well."

This is a 19th-century shoe shop like the one where Harry first finds employment.

CHAPTER XXV

A STRANGE COMPANION

At ten o'clock the next day, Harry presented himself at the hotel. He carried in his hand a carpetbag lent him by Mr. Leavitt, which contained his small stock of underclothing. His outside suits he left at Mr. Leavitt's, not wishing to be encumbered with them while traveling.

"I see you are on time," said the professor.

"Yes, sir; I always mean to be."

"That's well; now if you'll jump into my buggy with me, we will ride round to the Town Hall and take in my apparatus. I have to keep a carriage," said the magician, as they rode along. "It saves me a great deal of trouble by making me independent of cars and stages."

The apparatus was transferred to a trunk in the back part of the buggy and securely locked.

"Now we are all ready," said Professor Henderson,

"Would you like to drive?"

"Yes, sir," answered Harry, with alacrity.

"I am going to give an entertainment in Holston this evening," said his new employer. "Were you ever there?"

"No, sir."

"It is a smart little place and although the population is not large, I always draw a full house."

"How far is it, sir?"

"About six miles."

**The professor gives Harry a ride in a carriage
much like this one pictured.**

Harry was sorry it was not farther, as he enjoyed driving. His companion leaned back at his ease and talked on various subjects. He paused a moment and Harry was startled by hearing a stifled child's voice just behind him: "Oh, let me out! Don't keep me locked up here!"

The reins nearly fell from his hands. He turned and heard the voice apparently proceeding from the trunk.

"What's the matter?" asked Professor Henderson.

"I thought I heard a child's voice."

"So you did," said the voice again.

The truth flashed upon Harry. His companion was exerting some of his powers as a ventriloquist.

"Oh, it is you, sir," he said, smiling.

His companion smiled.

"You are right," he said.

"I don't see how you can do it," said Harry.

"Practice, my boy."

"But practice wouldn't make everybody a ventriloquist, would it?"

"Most persons might become ventriloquists, though in an unequal degree. I often amuse myself by making use of it for playing practical jokes upon people.

"Do you see that old lady ahead?"

"Yes, sir."

"I'll offer her a ride. If she accepts, you'll see sport. I shall make you talk, but you must be careful to say nothing yourself."

A few rods farther on, they overtook an old woman.

"Good morning, ma'am," said the professor. "Won't you get in and ride? It's easier riding than walking."

The old women scanned his countenance and answered: "Thank you, sir, I'm obleeged to ye. I don't mind if I do."

She was assisted into the carriage and sat at one end of the seat, Harry being in the middle.

"I was going to see my darter, Nancy," said the old women. "Mrs. Nehemiah Babcock her name is. Mebbe you know her husband."

"I don't think I do," said the professor.

"He's got a brother in Boston in the dry goods business. Mebbe you've been at his store."

"Mebbe I have."

"I ginerally call to see my darter—her name is Nancy—once a week; but it's rather hard for me to walk, now I'm getting' on in years."

"You're most eighty, ain't you?" appeared to proceed from Harry's mouth. Our hero's face twitched and he had hard work to keep from laughing.

"Indeed, I'm not!" said the old lady, indignantly.

"I'm only sixty-seven and folks say I don't look more'n sixty," and the old lady looked angrily at Harry.

"You must excuse him, ma'am," said the professor, soothingly. "He is no judge of a lady's age."

"I should think not, indeed."

"Indeed, madam, you are very young looking."

The old lady was pacified by this compliment but looked askance at Harry.

"Is he your son?"

"No, ma'am."

The old lady sniffed, as if to say, "So much the better for you."

"Are you travelin' far?" asked the old lady.

"What do you want to know for?" Harry appeared to ask.

"You're a sassy boy!" exclaimed the old woman.

"Harry," said Professor Henderson, gravely, "how often have I told you not to be so unmannerly?"

"He orter be whipped," said the old lady. "Ef I had a boy that was so sassy, I'd larn him manners!"

"I'm glad I ain't your boy," Harry appeared to reply.

"I declare I won't ride another step if you let him insult me so," said the old woman, glaring at our hero.

Professor Henderson caught her eye and significantly touched his forehead, giving her to understand that Harry was only "half-witted."

"You don't say so," she exclaimed, taking the hint at once. "How long's he been so?"

"Ever since he was born."

"Ain't you afraid to have him drive?"

"Oh, not at all. He understands horses as well as I do."

"What's his name?"

Before the professor's answer could be heard, Harry appeared to rattle off the extraordinary name: "George Washington Harry Jefferson Ebenezer Popkins."

"My gracious! Has he got all them names?"

"Why not? What have you got to say about it, old women?" said the same voice.

"Oh, I ain't got no objection," said the old woman.

"You may have fifty-'leven names ef you want to."

"I don't interfere with his names," said the professor.

"If he chooses to call himself—"

"George Washington Harry Jefferson Ebenezer Popkins," repeated the voice, with great volubility.

"If he chooses to call himself by all those names, I'm sure I don't care. How far do you go, ma'am?"

"About quarter of a mile farther."

The professor saw that he must proceed to his final joke.

"Let me out! Don't keep me locked up here!" said the child's voice, from behind, in a pleading tone.

"What's that?" asked the startled old lady.

"What's what?" asked the professor, innocently.

"That child that wants to get out."

"You must have dreamed it, my good lady."

"No, there 'tis agin'," said the old lady, excited.

"It's in the trunk behind you," said the assumed voice, appearing to proceed from our hero.

"So 'tis," said the old lady, turning halfway round.

"Oh, I shall die! Let me out! Let me out!"

"He's locked up his little girl in the trunk," Harry seemed to say.

"You wicked man, let her out this minute," said the old lady, very much excited. "Don't you know no better than to lock up a child where she can't get no air?"

"There is no child in the trunk, I assure you," said Professor Henderson, politely.

"Don't you believe him," said Harry's voice.

"Do let me out, father!" implored the child's voice

"If you don't open the trunk, I'll have you took up for murder," said the old lady.

"I will open it to show you are mistaken."

The professor got over the seat, and, opening the trunk, displayed its contents to the astonished old lady.

"I told you that there was no child there," he said; "but you would not believe me."

"Le' me out," gasped the old woman. "I'd rather walk. I never heerd of such strange goin's on afore."

"If you insist upon it, madam, but I'm sorry to lose your company. Take this with you and read it."

He handed her one of his bills, which she put in her pocket, saying she couldn't see to read it.

When they were far enough off to make it safe, Harry gave vent to his mirth, which he had restrained till this at difficulty and laughed long and loud.

CHAPTER XXVI

PAGES FROM THE PAST

"What will the old lady think of you?" said Harry.

"She will have a very bad opinion till she puts on her specs and read the bill. That will explain all. I shouldn't be surprised to see her at my entertainment."

"I wonder if she'll recognize me," said Harry.

"No doubt; as soon as she learns with whom she rode, she'll be very curious to come and see me perform."

"How old were you when you began to be a ventriloquist?"

"I was eighteen. I accidentally made the discovery, and devoted considerable time to perfecting myself in it before acquainting anyone with it. That idea came later. You see when I was twenty-one, with a little property which I inherited from my uncle, I went into business for myself; but I was young and inexperienced in management, and the consequence was, that in about two years I failed. I found it difficult to get employment as a clerk, business being very dull at the time. While uncertain what to do, one of my friends, to whom I had communicated my power, induced me to give me a public entertainment, combining with it a few tricks of magic, which I had been able to pick up from books. I succeeded so well my vocation in life became Professor Henderson."

"It must be great fun to be a ventriloquist."

"So I regarded it at first. It may not be a very high vocation, but I make the people laugh and so I regard myself as a public benefactor. Indeed, I once did an essential service to a young man by means of my ventriloquism."

"I should like very much to hear the story."

"I will tell you. One day, a young man, a stranger, came to me and introduced himself under the name of Paul Dabney. He said that I might, if I would, do him a great service. His father had died the year previous, leaving a farm and other property to the value of fifteen thousand dollars. Of course, being as only son, he expected that this would be left to himself, or, at least, the greater part of it. Conceive his surprise, therefore, when the will came to be read, to find that the entire property was left to his Uncle Jonas, his father brother, who, for three years past, had been a member of the family.

Jonas had never prospered in life, and his brother, out of pity, had offered him an asylum on his farm. He had formerly been a bookkeeper and was an accomplished penman.

"The will was so extraordinary—since Paul and his father had always been on perfectly good terms—that the young man was thunderstruck. His uncle expressed hypocritical surprise at the nature of the will.

"'I don't believe my father made that will,' exclaimed Paul, angrily.

"'What do you mean by that?' demanded the uncle.

"His anger made Paul think that he had hit upon the truth, particularly as his uncle was an adroit penman.

"He carefully examined the will; but the writing so closely resembled his father's that he could see no difference. The witnesses were his Uncle Jonas and a hired man, who, shortly after witnessing the signature, had been discharged and had disappeared from the neighborhood. All this excited Paul's suspicions.

"His uncle offered him a home on the farm; but positively refused to give him any portion of the property.

"'I sympathize with you,' I said at the conclusion of Paul's story; 'but how can I help you?'

"'I will tell you, sir,' he replied. 'You must know that my Uncle Jonas is very superstitious. I mean, through your help, to play upon his fears and thus induce him to give up the property to me.'

"With this he unfolded his plan, and I agreed to help him. His uncle lived ten miles distant. I procured a laborer's disguise and the morning after—Paul having previously gone back—I entered the yard of the farmhouse. The old man was standing outside, smoking a pipe.

"'Can you give me work?' I asked.

"'What kind of work?' inquired Jonas.

"'Farm work,' I answered.

"'How much do you want?'

"'Eight dollars a month.'

"'I'll give you six,' he said.

"'That's too little.'

"'It's the most I'll give you.'

"'Then I'll take,' I replied, and was at once engaged.

"Delighted to get me so cheap, the sordid old man asked me no troublesome questions. I knew enough of farm work to get along pretty well and not betray myself.

"That night I concealed myself in the old man's apartment without arousing his suspicions, Paul helping me. After he had been in bed about twenty minutes, I thought it time to begin. Accordingly I uttered a hollow groan.

"'Eh! What's that?' cried the old man, rising in bed.

"'I am the spirit of your dead brother,' I answered, throwing my voice near the bed.

"'What do you want?' he asked, his teeth chattering.

"'You have cheated Paul out of his property.'

"'Forgive me!' he cried, terror-stricken.

"'Then give him back the property.'

"'The whole?' he groaned.

"'Yes, the whole.'

"'Are—are you really my brother?'

"'I will give you this proof. Unless you do as I order you, in three days you will be with me.'

"'What, dead?' he said, shuddering.

"'Yes,' I answered in sepulchral a tone as possible.

"'Are—are you sure of it?'

"'If you doubt it, disobey me.'

"'I'll do it, but—don't come again.'

"'Be sure you do it then.'

"I ceased to speak, being tired, and escaped as soon as I could. But the battle was not yet over. The next day gave Jonas courage. Afternoon came and he had done nothing. He was with me in the field when I threw a hollow voice, which seemed to be close to his ear. I said, 'Obey, or in three days you die.'

"He turned pale as a sheet and asked me if I heard anything. I expressed surprise and this confirmed him in his belief of the ghostly visitation. He went to the house, sent for a lawyer and transferred the entire property to his nephew. The latter made him a present of a thousand dollars and so the affair ended happily. Paul paid me handsomely for my share in the trick and the next day I made an excuse for leaving the farm."

"Did the old man ever discover your agency in the affair, Professor Henderson?"

114

"Never. He is dead now and my friend Paul is happily married, and has a fine family. His oldest boy is named after me. But here we are in Holston."

CHAPTER XXVII

A MYSTIFYING PERFORMANCE

The people of Holston turned out in large numbers. Among the first to appear was the old lady whom the professor had taken up on his way over.

"You're the boy that was so sassy to me this mornin'," she said, peering at Harry through her spectacles.

"I didn't say a word to you," said Harry.

"I'm afraid you're tellin' fibs. I heerd you."

"It was the professor. He put the words in my mouth."

"Well, come to think on't the voice was different from yours. Then there wa'n't nobody in the trunk?"

"No, ma'am," said Harry, smiling.

"It's wonderful, I declare for't. This is my darter, Mrs. Nehemiah Babcock," continued the old lady. "Nancy, this is the ventriloquer's boy. I thought he was sassy to me this mornin'; but he says he didn't speak a word. How much is to pay?" said the old lady.

"I won't charge you anything," said Harry. "Professor Henderson told me, if you came to let you in free, and any of your family."

"Really, now, that's very perlite of the professor," said the old lady. "He's a gentleman if ever there was one. Do you hear, Nancy, we can go in without payin' a cent. That's all on account of your marm's being acquainted with the professor. I'm glad I come."

The old lady and her party entered the hall, and being early, secured good seats. Tom, her grandson, was glad to be so near, as he was ambitious to assist the professor in case volunteers were called for.

"Will any young gentleman come forward and assist me in the next trick?" asked the professor, after a while.

Tom started from his seat. His grandmother tried to seize him by the coat but he was too quick for her.

"Oh, let him go," said his mother. "He won't come to any harm."

"Is this your first appearance as a magician?" asked the professor.

"Yes, sir," answered Tom, with a grin.

"Very good. I will get you to help me, but you mustn't tell anybody how the tricks are done."

"No, sir, I won't."

"As I am going trust you with a little money, I want to ask you whether you are strictly honest."

"Yes, sir."

"I am glad to hear it. Do you see this piece of gold?"

"Yes, sir."

"What is its value?"

"Ten dollars," answered Tom, inspecting it.

"Very good. I want you hold it for me. I give you warning that I mean to make it pass out of your hand."

"I don't think you can do it, sir."

"Well, perhaps not. You look like a pretty sharp customer. It won't be easy to fool you."

"You bet."

"Nancy," whispered the old lady to her daughter. "I hope you don't allow Tom to talk so."

"Look, mother, see want he's going to do."

"What I propose to do," said the professor, "is to make that coin pass into the box on the table. I may not be able to do it, as the young gentleman is on his guard. However, I will try. Presto, change!"

"It didn't go," said Tom. "I've got it here."

"Have you? Suppose you open your hand."

Tom opened his hand.

"Well, what have you got? Is it the gold piece?"

"No, sir," said Tom, astonished; "it's a cent."

"Then, sir, all I can say is, you have treated me badly. In order to prevent my getting the gold piece into the box, you changed it into a cent."

"No, I didn't," said Tom.

"Then perhaps I have succeeded, after all. The fact is, I took out the gold piece and put a penny in its place, so that you might not know the difference. Now here is the key of that box. Will you unlock it?"

Tom unlocked it, only to find another box inside. In fact, it was a perfect nest of boxes. In the very last of all was found the gold coin.

"It's very strange you didn't feel it go out of your hand," said the professor.

"I am afraid you are not quick enough to make a magician. Can you fire a pistol?"

"Yes, sir," said Tom.

"Will any lady lend me a ring?" asked the professor.

One was soon found

"I will load the pistol," said the professor, "and put the ring in with the rest of the charge. It appears to be rather too large. I shall have to hammer it down."

He brought down a hammer heavily upon the ring and soon bent it sufficiently to get it into the pistol.

"Now, sir," he said, "take the pistol, and stand off there. All right, sir. When I give the word, I want you to fire. One, two, three!"

Tom fired, his grandmother uttering a half suppressed shriek at the report. When the smoke cleared away, the professor was holding the ring between his thumb and finger, quite uninjured.

Professor Henderson's attention had been drawn to his companion of the morning. He observed that she had taken off her bonnet. He went up to her, and said, politely, "Madam, will you kindly lend me your bonnet?"

"Massy sakes, what do you want of it?"

"I won't injure it, I assure you."

"You may take it, ef you want to," said the old lady; "but be keerful and don't bend it."

"I will be very careful; but, madam," he said, in seeming surprise, "what have you got in it?"

"Nothing, sir."

"You are mistaken. See there, and there, and there"; and he rapidly drew out three onions, four turnips and a couple of potatoes. "Really, you must have thought you were going to market."

"They ain't mine," gasped the old lady.

"Then it's very strange how they got into your bonnet. And—let me see—here's an egg, too."

"I never see sich doin's."

"Granny, I guess a hen made her nest in your bonnet," whispered Tom.

The old lady shook her head in helpless amazement.

Professor Henderson gives the boy a ten dollar gold coin, and turns it into a penny.

CHAPTER XXVII

AN UNEXPECTED PAYMENT

A week later, Harry reached a brisk manufacturing place which I will call Centreville. He assisted the professor during the afternoon to get ready the hall for his evening performance and, at half past five, took his seat at the dinner table in the village hotel.

Just as Harry began to eat, he lifted his eyes, and started in surprise as he recognized, in his opposite neighbor, Luke Harrison, whose abrupt departure without paying his debts the reader will remember. Under the circumstances, it will not be wondered at that our hero's look was not exactly cordial. As for Luke, he was disagreeably startled at Harry's sudden appearance. Not knowing his connection with Professor Henderson, he fancied that our hero was in quest of him and not being skilled in the law, felt a little apprehension as to what course he might take. It was best, he concluded to conciliate him.

"How are you, Walton?" he said.

"I am well," said Harry, coldly.

"How do you happen to be in this neighborhood?"

"On business," said Harry, briefly.

Luke jumped to the conclusion that the business related to him and, conscious of wrong-doing, felt disturbed.

"I'm glad to see you," he said. "It seems pleasant to see an old acquaintance"—he intended to say "friend."

"You left us rather suddenly," said Harry.

"Why, yes," said Luke, hesitating. "I had reasons. I'll tell you about it after dinner."

As Harry rose from the table, Luke joined him.

"Come upstairs to my room, Walton," he said, "and have a cigar."

"I'll go upstairs with you; but I don't smoke."

"You'd better learn. It's a great comfort."

"Do you board here?"

"Yes. I found I shouldn't have to pay any more than at a boarding house and the grub's better. Here's my room. Walk in."

He led the way into a small apartment on the top floor.

"This is my den," he said. "There isn't but one chair; but I'll sit on the bed. When did you reach town?"

120

"About noon."

"Are you going to stop long?" asked Luke.

"I shall stay here till I get through with my errand," answered Harry, shrewdly; for he saw what Luke thought, and it occurred to him that he might turn it to advantage.

Luke looked a little uneasy.

"By the way, Walton," he said, "I believe I owe you a little money."

"Yes. I believe so."

"I'm sorry I can't pay you the whole of it. It costs considerable to live, you know; but I'll pay part."

"Here are five dollars," he said. "I'll pay you the rest as soon as I can—in a week or two."

Harry took the bank note with secret self-congratulation, for he had given up the debt as bad, and never expected to realize a cent of it.

"I am glad to get it," he said. "I have a use for all my money. Are you working in this town?"

"Yes. The shoe business is carried on here considerably. Are you still working for Mr. Leavitt?"

"No; I've left him."

"What are you doing, then?"

"I'm traveling with Professor Henderson."

"What, the magician?"

"Yes."

"And is that what brought you to Centreville?"

"Yes."

Luke whistled.

"I thought—" he began.

"What did you think?"

"I thought," answered Luke, evasively, "that you might be looking for work in some of the shoe shops here."

"Is there any chance, do you think?"

"No, I don't think there is," said Luke; for he was by no means anxious to have Harry in the same town.

"Then I shall probably stay with the professor."

"What do you do?"

"Take tickets at the door and help him beforehand with his apparatus."

"You'll let me in free, tonight, won't you?"

"That isn't for me to decide."

"I should think the professor would let your friends go in free."

"I'll make you an offer, Luke," said he.

"What is it?"

"Just pay me the rest of; that money tonight and I'll let you in free at my own expense."

"I can't do it. I haven't got the money. If 'you'll give it back, I'll call it a dollar more and pay you the whole at the end of next week."

"I'm afraid your calling it a dollar more wouldn't do much good," said Harry, shrewdly.

"Do you doubt my word?" blustered Luke, who had regained courage now that he had ascertained the real object of Harry's visit and that it had no connection with him.

"I won't express any opinion on that subject," answered Harry; "but there's an old saying that a 'bird in the hand's worth two in the bush.'"

"I hate old sayings."

"Some of them contain a great deal of truth."

"What a fool I was to pay him that five dollars!" thought Luke, regretfully. "If I hadn't been such a simpleton, I should have found out what brought him here, before throwing away nearly all I had."

This was the view Luke took of paying his debts. He regarded it as money thrown away. Apparently, a good many young men are of a similar opinion. This was not, however, according to Harry's code, and was never likely to be. He believed in honesty and integrity. If he hadn't, I should feel far less confidence in his ultimate success.

"I think I must leave you," said Harry, rising. "The professor may need me."

"Do you like him? Have you got a good place?"

"Yes, I like him. He is a very pleasant man."

"How does it pay?"

"Pretty well."

"I wouldn't mind trying it myself. Do you handle all the money?"

"I take the money at the door."

"I suppose you might keep back a dollar or so, every night, and he'd never know the difference."

"I don't know. I never thought about that," said Harry, dryly.

"Oh, I remember, you're one of the pious boys."

"I'm too pious to take money that doesn't belong to me, if that's what you mean," said Harry.

This was a very innocent remark; but Luke, remembering how he had kept Harry's pocketbook, chose to interpret it as a fling to himself.

"Do you mean that for me?" he demanded, angrily.

"Mean what for you?"

"That about keeping other people's money."

"I wasn't talking about you at all. I was talking about myself."

"You'd better not insult me," said Luke, still suspicious.

"I'm not in the habit of insulting anybody."

"I don't believe in people that set themselves up to be so much better than everybody else."

"Do you mean that for me?" asked Harry, smiling.

"Yes, I do. What are you going to do about it?"

"Nothing, except to deny that I make any such claims. Shall you come round to the hall, tonight?"

"Perhaps so."

"Then I shall see you. I must be going now."

He went out, leaving Luke vainly deploring the loss of the five dollars which he had so foolishly squandered in paying his debt.

CHAPTER XXIX

IN THE PRINTING OFFICE

"Harry," said the professor, after breakfast the next morning, "I find we must get some more bills printed. You may go round to the office of the Centreville Gazette, and ask them how soon they can print me a hundred large bills and a thousand small ones."

"All right, sir. Suppose they can't have them done by the ready to start?"

"They can send them to me by express."

Harry had never been in a printing office; but he had a great curiosity to see one ever since he had read the "Life of Benjamin Franklin." If there was anyone in whose steps he thought he should like to follow, it was Franklin, and Franklin was a printer.

He had no difficulty in finding the office. It was in the second story of a building, just at the junction of two roads near the center of the town, the post office being just underneath. He ascended a staircase, and saw on the door, at the head of the stairs:

"CENTREVILLE GAZETTE"

He opened the door and entered. He saw a large room, containing a press at the end, while two young men, with paper caps on their heads, were standing in their shirt sleeves at upright cases setting type. On one side there was a very small office partitioned off. Within, a man was seen seated at a desk, with a pile of exchange papers on the floor, writing busily. This was Mr. Jotham Anderson publisher and editor of the Gazette.

"I want to get some printing done," said Harry, looking toward the journeymen.

"Go to Mr. Anderson," said one, pointing to the office.

Harry went in. The editor looked up as he entered.

"What can I do for you?" he asked.

"I want to get some printing done."

"For yourself?"

"No; for Professor Henderson."

"I've done jobs for him before. What does he want?"

Our hero explained.

"Very well, we will do it."

"Can you have it done before two o'clock?"

"Impossible. I am just bringing out my paper."

"When can you have the job finished?"

"Tomorrow noon."

"I suppose that will do. We perform tomorrow at Berlin and they can be sent over to the hotel there."

"You say 'we'?"

Answered Harry, amused, "I take tickets, and assist him generally."

"How do you like the business?"

"Very well; but I should like your business better."

"What makes you think so?"

"I have been reading the 'Life of Benjamin Franklin.' He was a printer."

"That's true; but I'm sorry to say Franklins are scarce in our printing offices. I never met one yet."

"I shouldn't expect to turn out a Franklins; but I think one couldn't help being improved by the business."

"True again, though, of course, it depends on the wish to improve. How long have you been working for Professor Henderson?"

"Not long. Only two or three weeks."

"What did you do before?"

"I was pegger in a shoe shop."

"Didn't you like it?"

"Well enough, for I needed to earn money and it paid me; but I don't think I should like to be a shoemaker all my life. It doesn't give any chance to learn."

"Then you like learning?"

"Yes. 'Live and learn'—that is my motto."

"It is a good one. Do you mean to be a printer?"

"If I get a chance."

"You may come into my office on the first of April, if you like. One of my men will leave me by the first of May. If you are a smart boy, and really wish to learn the business, you can break in so as to be useful in four weeks."

"I should like it," said Harry; "but," he added, with hesitation, "I am poor, and could not afford to work for nothing while I was learning."

125

"I'll tell you what I'll do, then," said the editor. "I'll give you your board for the first month, on condition that you'll work for six months afterwards for two dollars a week and board. That's a fair offer. I wouldn't make it if I didn't feel assured that you were smart, and would in time be valuable to me."

"I'll come if my father does not object."

"Quite tight. I should not like to have you act contrary to his wishes. I suppose, for the present, you will remain with Professor Henderson."

"Yes, sir."

"Very well. Let me hear from you when you have communicated with your father."

Harry left the office plunged in thought. It came upon him with surprise, that he had engaged himself to learn a new business, and that the one which he had longed to follow ever since he had become acquainted with Franklin's early life. He realized that he was probably making immediate sacrifice. He could, undoubtedly, make more money in the shoe shop than in the printing office, for the present at least. By the first of April the shoe business obtain employment. But then he was sure he should like printing better, and if he was ever going to change, why, the sooner he made the change the better.

When he returned to the hotel, he told the professor what he had done.

"I am glad you are not going at once," said his employer, "for I should be sorry to lose you. I generally give up traveling for the season about the first of April, so that I shall be ready to release you. I commend your choice of a trade. Many of our best editors have been practical printers in their youth."

"I should like to be an editor, but I don't know enough."

"Not at present; but you can qualify yourself to become one— that is, if you devote you spare time to reading and studying."

"I mean to do that."

"Then you will fair chance of becoming what you desire. To a certain extent, a boy, or young man, holds the future in his own hands."

At the end of the story, Harry leaves Professor Henderson to work in a printing office like this one.

Harry wrote to father, at once, in regard to the plan which he had in view. The answer did not reach him for nearly a week; but we will so far anticipate matters as to insert that part which related to it.

"If you desire to be a printer, Harry, I shall not object. It is a good trade, and you can make yourself, through it, useful to the community. I do not suppose it will ever make you rich. Still, I should think it might, in time, give you a comfortable living—better, I hope, than I have been able to earn as a farmer. If you determine to win success, you probably will. If you should leave your present place before the first of April, we shall be very glad to have you come home, if only for a day or two. We all miss you very much— your mother, particularly. Tom doesn't say much about it; but I know he will be as glad to see you as the rest of us."

Harry read this letter with great pleasure, partly because it brought him permission to do as he desired, and partly because it was gratifying to him to feel that he was missed at home. He determined, if it was a possible thing, to leave the professor a week before his new engagement, and spend that time in Granton.

CHAPTER XXX

THE YOUNG TREASURER

On the morning after receiving the letter from his father, Harry came down to breakfast, but looked in vain for the professor. Supposing he would be down directly, he sat down to the breakfast table. When he had nearly finished eating, a boy employed about the hotel came to his side.

"That gentleman you're with is sick. He wants you to come to his room as soon as you are through breakfast."

Harry did not wait to finish, but got up from the table at once, and went up to his employer's room.

"Are you sick, sir?" he inquired, anxiously.

The professor's face was flushed, and he was tossing about in bed.

"Yes," he answered. "I am afraid I am threatened with a fever."

"I hope not, sir."

"I am subject to fevers; but I hope I might not have another for some time to come. I must have caught cold yesterday, and the result is, that I am sick this morning."

"What can I do for you, sir?"

"I should like to have you go for the doctor. Inquire of the landlord who is the best in the village."

"I will go at once."

On inquiry, our hero was informed that Dr. Parker was the most trusted physician in the neighborhood, and he proceeded to his house at once. The doctor was, fortunately, still at home, and answered the summons immediately. He felt the sick man's pulse, asked him a variety of questions, and finally announced his opinion.

"You are about to have a fever," he said, "if, indeed, the fever has not already set in."

"A serious fever, doctor?" asked the sick man, anxiously.

"I cannot yet determine."

"Do you think I shall be long sick?"

"That, also, is uncertain. I suppose you will be likely to be detained here a fortnight, at least."

"I wish I could go home."

"It would not be safe for you to travel, under present circumstances."

"If I were at home, I could be under my wife's care."

"Can't she come here?"

"She has three young children. It would be difficult for her to leave them."

"Who is the boy that called at my house?"

"Harry Walton. He is my assistant—takes money at the door, and helps me other ways."

"Is he trustworthy?"

"I have always found him so."

"Why can't he attend upon you?"

"I mean to retain him with me—that is, if he will stay. It will be dull work for a boy of his age."

"You can obtain a nurse, besides, if needful."

"You had better engage one for me, as I cannot confine him here all the time."

"I will do so. I know of one, skillful and experienced, who is just now at leisure. I will send her round here this morning."

"What is her name?"

"Not a very romantic one—Betsy Chase."

"I suppose that doesn't prevent her being a good nurse," said the professor, smiling.

"Not at all."

Here Harry entered the room.

"Harry," said the professor, "the doctor tells me I am going to be sick."

"I am very sorry, sir," said our hero, with an air of concern.

"I shall probably be detained here at least a fortnight. Are you willing to remain with me?"

"Certainly, sir. I should not think of leaving you, sick and alone, if you desired me to stay. I hope I can make myself useful to you."

"You can. I shall need you to do errands for me and to sit with me a part of the time."

"I shall be very willing to do so, sir."

"You will probably find it dull."

"Not so dull as you will find it, sir. The time must seem very long to you, lying on that bed."

"I suppose it will; but that can't be helped."

"A nurse will be here this afternoon," said the doctor.

"Until she comes, you will be in attendance here."

"Yes, sir."

_____

129

"I will direct you what to do, and how often to administer the medicines. Can remember?"

"Yes, sir, I shall not forget."

Dr. Parker here gave Harry minute instructions, which need not be repeated, since they were altogether of a professional nature.

After the doctor was gone, Professor Henderson said:

"As soon as the nurse comes, I shall want you to ride over to the next town, Carmansville, and countermand the notices for an exhibition tonight. I shall not be able to give entertainments for some time to come. Indeed, I am not sure but I must wait till next season."

"How shall I go over?" asked Harry.

"You may get a horse and buggy at the stable, and drive over there. If I remember rightly, it is between little seven and eight miles. The road is a little winding, but I think you won't lose your way."

"Oh, I'll find it," said Harry, confidently.

It was not till three o'clock that the nurse made her appearance, and it was past three before Harry started on his way.

"You need not hurry home," said the professor. "In fact, you had better take dinner at the hotel in Carmansville, as you probably could not very well get back here till eight o'clock."

"Very well, sir," said Harry. "But shan't you need me?"

"No; Miss Chase will attend to me."

"Mrs. Chase, if you please," said the nurse. "I've been a widder for twenty years."

"I beg your pardon, Mrs. Chase," said the sick man smiling.

"When my husband was alive, I never expected to go out nursin'; but I've had come to it."

"The doctor says you are a very skillful and experienced nurse."

"I'd ought to be. I've nussed people in almost all sorts of diseases, from measles to smallpox. You needn't be frightened, sir; I haven't had any smallpox case lately. Isn't it most time to take your medicine?"

Harry left the room, and was soon on his way to Carmansville. Once he got off the road, which was rather a perplexing one, but he soon found it again. However, it was half past five before he reached the village, and nearly an hour later before he had done the errand which brought him over. Finally, he came back to the tavern, and being by this time hungry, went in at once to the tavern, and being

---

130

by this time hungry, went in at once to dinner. He did full justice to the meal which was set before him. The day was cold, and his ride had stimulated his appetite.

When he sat down to the table he was alone; but a minute afterward a small, dark-complexioned man, with heavy black whiskers, came in, and sat down beside him. He had a heavy look, and a forbidding expression; but our hero was too busy to take particular notice of him till the latter commenced a conversation.

We first meet Professor Henderson in a tavern like this one.

"It's a pretty cold day," he remarked.

"Very cold," said Harry. "I am dreading my ride back to Pentland."

"Are you going to Pentland tonight?" asked the stranger, with interest.

"Yes, sir."

"Do you live over there?"

"No; I am there for a short time only," Harry replied.

"Business?"

"Yes."

"You seem rather young to be in business," said the stranger.

"Oh," said Harry, smiling, "I am in the employ of Professor Henderson, the ventriloquist. I suppose it is hardly proper to say that I am in business."

"Professor Henderson! Why, he is going to give an entertainment here tonight, isn't he?"

"He was; but I have come over to countermand the notice."

"What is that for?"

131

"He is taken sick at Pentland, and won't be able to come."

"Oh, that's it. Well, I'm sorry, for I should like to have gone to hear him. So you are his assistant, are you?"

"Yes, sir."

"Can you perform tricks, too?"

"I don't assist him in that way. I take money at the door, and help him with his apparatus."

"Have you been with him long?"

"Only a few weeks."

"So you are his treasurer, are you?" asked the stranger smiling.

"Ye—es," said Harry, slowly, for it brought to his mind that he had one hundred and fifty dollars of the professor's money in his pocket, besides the pocketbook containing his own. He intended to have left it with his employer, but in the hurry of leaving he had forgotten to do so. Now he was about to take a long ride in the evening with this large sum of money about him.

"However," he said, reassuring himself, "there is nothing to be afraid of. Country people are not robbers. Burglars stay in the cities. I have nothing to fear."

Still he prudently resolved, if compelled to be out late again, to leave his money at home.

He rose from table, followed by the stranger.

"Well," said the latter, "I must be going. How soon do you start?"

"In a few minutes."

"Well, good night."

"Good night."

"He seems inclined to be social," thought Harry, "but I don't fancy him much."

CHAPTER XXXI

Harry was soon on his way home. It was already getting dark, and he felt a little anxious lest he should lose his way. He was rather sorry that he had not started earlier, though he had lost no time.

He had gone about two miles, when he came to a place where two roads met. There was no guideboard, and he could not remember by which road he had come. Luckily, as he thought, he described a man a little ahead. He stopped the horse, and hailed him.

"Can you tell me which road to take to Pentland?" he asked.

The man addressed turned his head, and, to his surprise, our hero recognized his table companion at the inn.

"Oh, it's you, my young friend!" he said.

"Yes, sir. Can you tell me the right road to Pentland? I have never been this way before today, and I have forgotten how I came."

"I am thinking of going to Pentland myself," said the other.

"My sister lives there. If you don't mind giving me a lift, I will jump in with you, and guide you."

Now, though Harry did not fancy the man's appearance, he had no reason to doubt him, nor any ground for refusing his request.

"Jump in, sir," he said. "There is plenty of room."

The stranger was speedily seated at his side.

"Take the left-hand road," he said.

Harry turned to his left.

"It's rather a blind road," observed the stranger.

"I think I could remember in the daytime," said Harry; "but it is so dark now, that I am in doubt."

"So I suppose."

The road on which they had entered was very lonely. Scarcely a house was passed, and the neighborhood seemed quite uninhabited.

"I don't remember this road," said Harry, anxiously.

"Are you sure we are right?"

"Yes, yes, we are right. Don't trouble yourself."

"It's a lonely road."

"So it is. I don't suppose there's anybody lives within half a mile."

"The road didn't seem so lonely when I came over it this afternoon."

"Oh, that's the effect of sunshine. Nothing seems lonely in the daytime. Turn down that lane."

133

"What for?" asked Harry, in surprise. "That can't be the road to Pentland."

"Never mind that. Turn, I tell you."

His companion spoke fiercely, and Harry's mind began to conceive alarming suspicions as to his character. But he was brave, and not easily daunted.

"The horse and carriage are mine, or, at least, are under my direction," he said, firmly, "and you have no control over them. I shall not turn."

"Won't you?" retorted the stranger, with an oath, and drew from his pocket a pistol. "Won't you?"

"What do you mean? Who are you?" demanded Harry.

"You will find out before I get through with you. Now turn into the lane."

"I will not," said Harry, pale, but determined.

"Then I will save you the trouble," and his companion snatched the reins from him, and turned the horse himself. Resistance was, of course, useless, and our hero was compelled to submit.

"There, that suits me better. Now to business."

"To business. Produce your pocketbook."

"Would you rob me?" asked Harry, who was in a measure prepared for the demand.

"Oh, of course not," said the other. "Gentlemen never do such things. I want to borrow your money, that is all."

"I don't want to lend."

"I dare say not," sneered the other; "but I shan't be able to respect your wishes. The sooner you give me the money the better."

Harry had two pocketbooks. The one contained his own money—about forty dollars—the other the money of his employer. The first was in the side pocket of his coat, the second in the pocket of his pants. The latter, as was stated in the preceding chapter, contained one hundred and fifty dollars. Harry heartily repented not having left it behind, but it was to late for repentance. He could only hope that the robber would be satisfied with one pocketbook, and not suspect the existence of the other. There seemed but little hope of saving his own money. However, he determined to do it, if possible.
"Hurry up," said the stranger, impatiently. "You needn't pretend you have no money. I know better than that. I saw you pay the landlord."

"Then he saw the professor's pocketbook," thought Harry, uneasily. "Mine is of different appearance. I hope he won't detect the difference."

"I hope you will leave me some of the money," said Harry, producing the pocketbook.

"It is all I have."

"How much is there?"

"About forty dollars."

"Humph! That isn't much."

"It is all I have in the world."

"Pooh! You are young and can soon earn some more. I must have the whole of it."

"Can't you leave me five dollars?"

"No, I can't. Forty dollars are little enough to serve my turn."

So saying, he coolly deposited the pocketbook in the pocket of his pants.

"So far so good. It's well, youngster, you didn't make any more fuss, or I might have had to use my little persuader;" and he displayed the pistol.

"Will you let me go now, sir?"

"I have not got through my business yet. That's a nice overcoat of yours."

Harry looked at him, in doubt as to his meaning, but he was soon enlightened.

"I am a small person," proceeded the man with black whiskers, "scarcely any larger than you. I think it'll be a good fit."

"Must I lose my overcoat, too?" thought Harry, in trouble.

"You've got an overcoat of your own, sir," he said.

"You don't need mine."

"Oh, I wouldn't rob you of yours on any account. A fair exchange is no robbery. I am going to give you mine in exchange for yours."

The stranger's coat was rough and well-worn, and, at its best, had been inferior to Harry's coat. Our hero felt disturbed at the prospect of losing it, for he could not tell when he could afford to get another.

"I should think you might be satisfied with the pocketbook," he said. "I hope you will leave me my coat."

"Off with the coat, youngster!" was the sole reply.

"First, get out of the buggy. We can make the exchange better outside."

As opposition would be unavailing, Harry obeyed. The robber took from him the handsome overcoat, the possession of which had afforded him so much satisfaction, and handed him his own. In great disgust and dissatisfaction our hero invested himself in it.

"Fits you as if it was made for you," said the stranger, with a short laugh. "Yours is a trifle slow for me, but I can make it go. No, don't be in such a hurry."

He seized Harry by the arm as he was about to jump into the carriage.

"I must go," said Harry. "You have already detained me some time."

"I intend to detain you some time longer."

"Have you got any more business with me?"

"Yes, I have. You've hit it exactly. You'll soon know what it is."

He produced a ball of cord from a pocket of his inside coat, and with a knife severed a portion. "Do you know what this is for?" he asked, jeeringly.

"No."

"Say, 'No, sir.' It's more respectful. Well, I'll gratify your laudable curiosity. It's to tie your hands and feet."

"I won't submit to it," said Harry, angrily.

"Won't you?" asked the other, coolly. "This is a very pretty pistol, isn't it? I hope I shan't have to use it."

"What do you want to tie my hands for?" asked Harry.

"For obvious reasons, my young friend."

"I can't drive if my hands are tied."

"Correct, my son. I don't intend you to drive tonight. Give me your hands."

**Professor Henderson would travel from town to town
on a horse and buggy like this one.**

Harry considered whether it would be advisable to resist. The stranger was not much larger than himself. He was a man, however, and naturally stronger. Besides, he had a pistol. He seceded that it was necessary to submit. After all, he had saved his employer's money, even if he had lost his own, and this was something. He allowed himself to be bound.

"Now," said the stranger, setting him up against the stone wall, which bordered the lane, "I will bid you good night. I might take your horse, but, on the whole, I don't want him. I will fasten him to this tree, where he will be all ready for you in the morning. That's considerate in me. Good night. I hope you are comfortable."

He disappeared in the darkness, and Harry was left alone.

CHAPTER XXXII

THE GOOD SAMARITAN

Harry's reflections, as he sat on the ground were not the most cheerful. He was sitting in a constrained posture, his hands and feet being tied, and, moreover, the cold air chilled him. The cold was not intense, but as he was unable to move his limbs he, of course, felt it the more.

"I suppose it will get colder," thought Harry, uncomfortably. "I wonder if there is any danger of freezing."

The horse evidently began to feel impatient, for he turned round and looked at our hero. "Why don't you keep on?"

"I wish somebody would come this way," thought Harry, and he looked up and down the lane as well as he could, but could see no one.

"If I could only get at my knife," said Harry, to himself, "I could cut theses cords. Let me try."

He tried to get his hands into his pockets, but it was of no avail. The pocket was too deep, and though he worked his body round, he finally gave it up. It seemed likely that he must stay here all night. The next day probably some one would come by, as they were so near a public road, upon whom he could call to release him.

"The night will seem about a week long," poor Harry considered. "I shan't dare to go to sleep, for fear I may freeze to death."

The horse whinnied again, and again looked inquiringly at his young driver, but the latter was not master of the situation, and was obliged to disregard the mute appeal.

"I wonder the robber didn't carry off the horse," thought Harry. "I suppose he had his reasons. It isn't likely he left him out of his regard for me."

Two hours passed, and Harry still found himself a prisoner. His constrained position became still more uncomfortable. He longed for the power of jumping up and stretching his legs, now numb and chilled, but the cord was strong, and defied his efforts. No person had passed, not had he heard any sound as he lay there, except the occasional whinny of the horse which was tied as well as himself, and did not appear to enjoy his confinement any better.

It was at this moment that Harry's heart leaped with sudden hope, as he heard in the distance the sound of a whistle. It might be a boy, or it might be a man; but, as he listened intently, he perceived that it was coming nearer.

"I hope I can make him hear," thought Harry, earnestly.

It was a boy of about his own age, who was advancing along the road from which he had turned into the lane. The boy was not alone, as it appeared, for a large dog ran before him. The dog first noticed the horse and buggy, and next our hero, lying on the ground, and, concluding that something was wrong, began to bark violently, circling uncomfortably near Harry, against whom he seemed to cherish hostile designs.

"What's the matter, Caesar?" shouted his young master.

"Good dog!" said Harry, soothingly, in momentary fear that the brute would bite him.

But Caesar was not to be cajoled by flattery. "Bow, wow, wow!" he answered, opening his large mouth, and displaying a formidable set of teeth.

"Good dog! I'd like to choke him!" added Harry, in an undertone to himself.

There was another volley of barks, which seemed likely to be followed by an attack. Just at this moment, however, luckily for our hero, the dog's master came up.

"Why, Caesar," he called, "what is the matter with you?"

"Please take your dog away," said Harry. "I am afraid he will bite me."

"Who are you?" inquired the boy, in surprise.

"Come and untie these cords, and I will tell you."

"What! Are you tied?"

"Yes, hand and foot."

"Who did it?" asked the boy, in increasing surprise.

"I don't know his name, but he robbed me of my pocketbook before doing it."

"What, a robber around here!" exclaimed the boy, incredulous.

"Yes; I met him first over in Carmansville. Thank you; now my feet, if you please. It seems good to be free again;" and Harry swung his arms, and jumped up and down to bring back the sense of warmth to his chilled limbs.

"Is this horse yours?" asked the boy.

"Yes; I took up the man and he promised to show me the road to Pentland."

"This isn't the road to Pentland."

"I suppose not. He took me wrong on purpose."

"How much money did he take from you?"

"Forty dollars."

"That's a good deal," said the country boy. "Was it yours?"

"Yes."

"I never had so much money in my life."

"It has taken me almost six months to earn it. But I had more money with me, only he didn't know it."

"How much?"

"A hundred and fifty dollars."

"Was it yours?" asked the boy, surprised.

"No; it belonged to my employer."

"Who is he?"

"Professor Henderson, the ventriloquist."

"Where is he stopping?"

"Over at Pentland. He is sick at the hotel there."

"It's lucky for you I was out tonight. I ain't often out so late but I went to see a friend of mine, and stayed later than I meant to."

"Do you live near here?"

"I live about a quarter of a mile up this lane."

"Do you know what time it is?"

"I don't know, but I think it is past ten."

"I wonder whether I can get anybody to go with me to Pentland. I can't find my way in the dark."

"I will go with you tomorrow morning."

"But what shall I do tonight?"

"I'll tell you. Come home with me. The folks will take you in, and the horse can be put up in the barn."

Harry hesitated

"I suppose they will feel anxious about me over at Pentland. They won't know what has become of me."

"You can start early in the morning—as early as you like."

"Perhaps it will be better," said Harry, after a pause.

"It won't trouble your family too much, will it?"

"Not a bit," answered the boy, heartily. "Very likely they won't know till morning," he added, laughing. "They go to bed early, and I told them they needn't wait up for me."

"I am very much obliged to you," said Harry. "I will accept your kind invitation. As I've got a horse, we may as well ride. I'll untie him, and you jump into the buggy."

"All right," said the boy, well pleased.

"You may drive, for you know the way better than I."

"Where did this horse come from?"

"From the stable in Pentland."

"Perhaps they will think you have run away with it."

"I hope not."

"What is your name?"

"Harry Walton. What is yours?"

"Jefferson Selden. The boys usually call me Jeff."

"Is that your dog?"

"Yes. He's a fine fellow."

"I didn't think so when he was threatening to bite me," said Harry laughing.

"I used to be afraid of dogs," said Jeff; "but I got cured of it after a while. When I go out at night, I generally take Caesar with me. If you had had him, you would have been a match for the robber."

"He had a pistol."

"Caesar would have had him down before he could use it."

"I wish he had been with me, then."

They had, by this time, come in sight of Jeff's house. It was a square farmhouse, with a barn in the rear.

"We'll go right out to the barn," said Jeff, "and put up the horse. Then we'll come back to the house and go to bed."

There was a little difficulty in unharnessing the horse, on account of the absence of light; but at last, by a combined effort, it was done, and the buggy was drawn into the barn and the doors shut.

"There, all will be safe till tomorrow morning," said Jeff. "Now we'll go into the house."

He entered by the back shed door, and Harry followed him. They went into the broad, low kitchen, with its ample fireplace, in which a few embers were glowing. By these Jeff lighted a candle, and asked Harry if he would have anything to eat.

"No, thank you," said Harry. "I ate a hearty dinner at Carmansville."

"Then we'll go upstairs to bed. I sleep in a small room over the shed. You won't mind sleeping with me?"

"I should like your company," said Harry, who was attracted to his good-natured companion.

"Then come up. I guess we'll find the bed wide enough."

He led the way up a narrow staircase, into a room low studded, and very plainly but comfortably furnished.

"The folks will be surprised to see you here in the morning," said Jeff.

"I may be gone before they are up."

"I guess not. Father'll be up by five o'clock, and I think that'll be as early as you'll want to be stirring."

CHAPTER XXXIII

THE REWARD OF FIDELITY

"Where am I?" asked Harry, the next morning, as he sat up in bed and stared around him.

"Don't you remember?" asked Jeff, smiling.

Jeff was standing by the bedside, already dressed.

"Yes; I remember now," said Harry, slowly. "What time is it?"

"Seven o'clock."

"Seven o'clock! I meant to be dressed at six."

"That is the time I got up," said Jeff.

"Why didn't you wake me up?"

"You looked so comfortable that I thought it was a pity to wake you. You must have felt tired."

"I think it was the cold that made me sleepy. I got chilled through when I lay on the ground there, tied hand and foot. But I must get up in hurry now."

He jumped out of bed, and hurried on his clothes.

"Now," said Jeff, "come down into the kitchen, and mother'll give you some breakfast."

"I am giving you a great deal of trouble, I am afraid," said Harry.

"No, you're not. It's no trouble at all. The rest of the family has eaten breakfast, but I waited for you. I've been up an hour, and feel as hungry as a wolf. So come down, and we'll see who'll eat the most."

"I can do my part," said Harry. "I've got a good appetite, though I've been up a good deal less than an hour."

"Take your overcoat alone," said Jeff; "or will you come up and get after breakfast?"

"I'll take it down with me. It isn't my coat, you know. Mine was a much better one. I wish I had it back."

Jeff, meanwhile, had taken up the coat.

"There's something in the pocket," he said. "What is it?"

"I didn't put anything in."

Harry thrust his hand into the side pocket for the first time, and drew out a shabby leather wallet.

"Perhaps there's money in it," Jeff suggested.

The same thought had occurred to Harry. He hastily opened it, and his eyes opened wide with astonishment as he drew out a thick roll of bills.

"By hokey!" said Jeff, "you're in luck. The robber took your pocketbook, and left his own. Maybe there's as much as you lost. Count it."

This Harry eagerly proceeded to do.

"Three—eight—eleven—thirteen—twenty," he repeated, aloud. He continued his count, which resulted in showing that the wallet contained ninety-seven dollars.

"Ninety-seven dollars!" exclaimed Jeff. "How much did you lose?"

"Forty dollars."

"Then you've made just fifty-seven dollars. Bully for you!"

"But I've exchanged a good overcoat for a poor one."

"There can't be more than seventeen dollars difference."

"Not so much."

"Then you're forty dollars better off, at any rate."

"But I don't know as I can claim this money," said Harry, doubtfully. "It isn't mine."

"He won't be likely to call for it. When he does, and returns you the money and the coat, it will be time to think about it."

"I will ask Professor Henderson about that. At any rate I've got my money back, that's one good thing."

This timely discovery made Harry decidedly cheerful, and, if anything, sharpened his appetite for breakfast.

**At the demand of the highwayman, Harry trades
his overcoat with the robber, only to find the
robber's wallet still in the pocket.**

Now Mr. Selden had gone out to oversee some farm work; but Mrs. Selden received our hero very kindly, and made him feel that he was heartily welcome. She had many questions to ask about the bold robber who had waylaid him, and expressed the hope that he had left the neighborhood.

"Perhaps he'll come back for his wallet, Harry," said Jeff. "You'd better look out for him."

"I shall take care how I carry much money about with me, after this," said Harry. "That was what got me into a scrape yesterday."

"He wouldn't make out much if he tried to rob me," said Jeff. "I haven't got money enough about me to pay the board of a full-grown fly for twenty-four hours."

"You don't look as if your poverty troubled you much," said his mother.

"I don't have any board bills to pay," said Jeff, "so I can get along."

"I should think you would feel nervous about riding to Pentland alone," said Mrs. Selden, "for fear of meeting the man who robbed you yesterday."

"I do dread it a little," said Harry, "having so much money about me. Besides this ninety-seven dollars, I've got a hundred and fifty dollars belonging to my employer."

"Suppose I go with you to protect you," said Jeff.

"I wish you would."

"I don't think Jefferson would make a very efficient protector," said his mother.

"You don't know how brave I am, mother," said Jeff, in the tone of an injured hero.

"No, I don't," said his mother, smiling. "I believe there was a time when you were not very heroic in the company of dogs."

"That's long ago, mother. I've got over it now."

"If you would like to ride over with your friend, you may do so. But how will you get back?"

"Major Pinkham will be up there this afternoon. I can wait, and ride home with him."

"Very well; I have no objection."

The two boys rode off together. Harry was glad to have a companion who knew the road well, for he did not care to be lost again till he had delivered up the money which he had in charge. There was no opportunity to test Jeff's courage, for the highwayman did not make his appearance. Indeed, it was not till the next morning that he discovered the serious blunder he had made in leaving his own wallet behind, and, though he was angry and disgusted, prudential considerations prevented his going back. He was forced to the unpleasant conviction that he had overreached himself, and that his intended victim had come out best in the "exchange" which "was no robbery." I may as well add here that, though he deserved to be caught, he was not, and Harry has never, to this day, set eyes either upon him or upon the coat.

When Harry arrived at Pentland, he found that no little anxiety had been felt about him.

"Has Harry come yet?" asked the sick man, at ten o'clock the evening previous.

"No, he hasn't," answered the nurse.

"It's strange what keeps him."

"Did he have any money of yours with him?"

"Yes, I believe he had."

"Oh!" exclaimed Mrs. Chase, significantly.

"What do you mean by that?"

"I didn't say anything, did I?"

"I am afraid he may have been attacked and robbed on the road."

Mrs. Chase coughed.

"Don't you think so?"

"I'll tell you what I think, professor," said the nurse, proceeding to speak plainly, "I don't think you'll ever see anything of that boy ag'in."

"Why not?"

"It ain't safe to trust boys with money," she answered, sententiously.

"Oh, I'm not afraid of his honesty."

"You don't say! Maybe you haven't seen as much of boys as I have."

"I was once a boy myself," said the professor, smiling.

"Oh, you—that's different."

"Why is it different? I wasn't any better than boys generally."

"I don't know anything about that; but you mark my words—as like as not he's run away with your money. How much did he have?"

"I can't say exactly. Over a hundred dollars, I believe."

"Then he won't come back," said Mrs. Chase, decidedly.

Here the conference closed, as it was necessary for Mr. Henderson to take medicine.

"Has the boy returned?" asked the professor, the next morning.

"You don't expect him—do you?"

"Certainly I expect him."

"Well, he ain't come, and I guess he won't come."

"I am sure that boy is honest," said Professor Henderson to himself. "If he isn't, I'll never trust a boy again."

Mrs. Chase was going downstairs with her patient's breakfast dishes, when she was nearly run into by our hero, who had just returned, and was eager to report to his employer.

147

"   Do be keerful," she expostulated, when, to her surprise, she recognized Harry.

So he had come back, after all, and falsified her prediction. Such is human nature, that for an instant she was disappointed.

"Here's pretty work," she said, "stayin' out all night, and worryin' the professor out of his wits."

"I couldn't help it, Mrs. Chase."

"Why couldn't you help it, I'd like to know?"

"I'll tell you afterwards. I must go up now, and see the professor."

Mrs. Chase was so curious that she returned, with the dishes, to hear Harry's statement.

"Good morning," said Harry, entering the chamber.

"I'm sorry to have been so long away, but I couldn't help it. I hope you haven't worried much about my absence."

"I knew you would come back, but Mrs. Chase had her doubts," said Professor Henderson, pleasantly. "Now tell me what it was that detained you?"

"A highwayman," said Harry.

"A highwayman!" exclaimed both in concert.

"Yes, I'll tell you all about it. But first, I'll say that he stole only my money, and didn't suspect that I had a hundred and fifty dollars of yours with me. That's all safe. Here it is. I think you had better take care of that yourself, sir, hereafter."

The professor glanced significantly at Mr. Chase, as much as to say, "You see how unjust your suspicions were. I am right, after all."

"Tell us all about it, Harry."

Our hero obeyed instructions; but it is not necessary to repeat a familiar tale.

"Massy sakes!" exclaimed Betsy Chase. "Who ever heerd the like?"

"I congratulate you, Harry, on coming off with such flying colors. I will, at my own expense, provide you with a new overcoat, as a reward for bringing home my money safe. You shall not lose anything by your fidelity."

148

CHAPTER XXXIV

IN DIFFICULTY

We must now transfer the scene to the Walton homestead.

It looks very much the same as on the day when the reader was first introduced to it. There is not a single article of new furniture, nor is any of the family any better dressed. Poverty reigns with undisputed sway. Mr. Walton is reading a borrowed newspaper by the light of a candle—for it is evening—while Mrs. Walton is engaged in her never-ending task of mending old clothes, in the vain endeavor to make them look as well as new. It is so seldom that anyone of the family has new clothes, that the occasion is one long remembered and dated from.

"It seems strange we don't hear from Harry," said Mrs. Walton, looking up from her work.

"When was the last letter received?" asked Mr. Walton, laying down the paper.

"Over a week ago. He wrote that the professor was sick, and he was stopping at the hotel to take care of him."

"I remember. What was the name of the place?"

"Pentland."

"Perhaps his employer is recovered, and he is going about with him."

"Perhaps so; but I should think he would write. I am afraid he is sick himself. He may have caught the same fever."

"It is possible; but I think Harry would let us know in some way. At any rate, it isn't best to worry ourselves about uncertainties."

"I wonder if Harry's grown?" said Tom.

"Of course he's grown," said Mary.

"I wonder if he's grown as much as I have," said Tom, complacently.

"I don't believe you've grown a bit."

"Yes, I have; if you don't believe it, see how short my pants are."

Tom did, indeed, seem to be growing out of his pants, which were undeniably too short for him.

"You ought to have some new pants," said his mother, sighing; "but I don't see where the money is to come from."

"Nor I," said Mr. Walton, soberly. "Somehow I don't seem to get ahead at all. Tomorrow my note for the cow comes due, and I haven't but two dollars to meet it."

"How large it the note?"

"With six months' interest, it amounts to forty-one dollars and twenty cents."

"The cow isn't worth that. She doesn't give as much milk as the one we lost."

"That's true. It was a hard bargain, but I could do no better."

"You say you won't be able to meet the payment. What will be the consequence?"

"I suppose Squire Green will take back the cow."

"Perhaps you can get another somewhere else, on better terms."

"I am afraid my credit won't be very good. I agreed to forfeit ten dollars to Squire Green, if I couldn't pay at the end of six months."

"Will he insist on that condition?"

"I am afraid he will. He is a hard man."

"Then," said Mrs. Walton, indignantly, "he won't deserve to prosper."

"Worldly prosperity doesn't always go by merit. Plenty of mean men prosper."

Before Mrs. Walton had time to reply, a knock was heard at the door.

"Go to the door, Tom," said his father.

Tom obeyed, and shortly reappeared, followed by a small man with a thin figure and wrinkled face, whose deep-set, crafty eyes peered about him curiously as he entered the room.

"Good evening, Squire Green," said Mr. Walton, politely, guessing his errand.

"Good evenin', Mrs. Walton. The air's kinder frosty. I ain't so young as I was once, and it chills my blood."

"Come up to the fire, Squire Green," said Mrs. Walton, who wanted the old man to be comfortable, though she neither liked nor respected him.

The old man sat down and spread his hands before the fire.

"Anything new stirring, Squire?" asked Hiram Walton.

"Nothin' that I know on. I was lookin' over my papers tonight, neighbor, and I come across that note you give for the cow. Forty dollars with interest, which makes the whole come to forty-one dollars and twenty cents. Tomorrow's the day for payin'. I suppose you'll be ready?" and the old man peered at Hiram Walton with his little keen eyes.

"Now for it," thought Hiram. "I'm sorry to say, Squire Green," he answered, "that I can't pay the note. Times have been hard, and my family expenses have taken all I could earn."

The squire was not much disappointed, for now he was entitled to exact the forfeit of ten dollars.

"The contrack provides that if you can't meet the note you shall pay ten dollars," he said. "I 'spose you can do that."

"Squire Green, I haven't got but two dollars laid by."

"Two dollars!" repeated the squire, frowning. "That ain't honest. You knew the note was comin' due, and you'd oughter have provided ten dollars, at least."

"I've done as much as I could. I've wanted to meet the note, but I couldn't make money, and I earned all I could."

"You hain't been equinomical," said the squire, testily. "Folks can't expect to lay up money ef they spend it fast as it comes in"; and he thumped on the floor with his cane.

"I should like to have you tell us how we can economize any more than we have," said Mrs. Walton, with spirit. "Just look around you, and see if you think we have been extravagant in buying clothes. I am sure I have to darn and mend till I am actually ashamed."

"There's other ways of wastin' money," said the squire. "If you think we live extravagantly, come in any day to lunch, and we will convince you to the contrary," said Mrs. Walton, warmly.

"Tain't none of my business, as long as you pay me what you owe me," said the squire. "All I want is my money, and I'd orter have it."

"It doesn't seem right that my husband should forfeit ten dollars and lose the cow."

"That was the contrack, Mrs. Walton. Your husband 'greed to it, and—"

"That doesn't make it just."

"Tain't no more'n a fair price for the use of the cow six months. Ef you'll pay the ten dollars tomorrow, I'll let you have the cow six months longer on the same contrack."

"I don't see any possibility of my paying you the money, Squire Green. I haven't got it."

"Why don't you borrer somewhere?"

"I might as well owe you as another man, Besides, I don't know anybody that would lend me the money."

"You haven't tried, have you?"

"No."

"Then you'd better. I thought I might as well come round and remind you of the note as you might forget it."

"Not much danger," said Hiram Walton. "I've had it on my mind ever since I gave it."

"Well, I'll come round tomorrow night, and I hope you'll be ready. Good night."

No very cordial good night followed Squire Green as he hobbled out of the cottage—for he was lame—not—I am sure the reader will agree with me—did he deserve any. He was a mean, miserly, grasping man, who had no regard for the feelings or comfort of anyone else; whose master passion was a selfish love of accumulating money. His money did him little good, however, for he was as mean with himself as with others, and grudged himself even the necessaries of life, because, if purchased, it must be at the expense of his hoards. The time would come when he and his money must part, but he did not think of that.

CHAPTER XXXV

SETTLED

There was a general silence after Squire Green's departure. Hiram Walton looked gloomy, and the rest of the family also.

"What an awful mean man the squire is!" Tom broke out, indignantly.

"You're right, for once," said Mary.

In general, such remarks were rebuked by the father or mother; but the truth of Tom's observation was so clear, that for once he was not reproved.

"Squire Green's money does him very little good," said Hiram Walton. "He spends very little of it on himself, and it certainly doesn't obtain him respect in the village. Rich as he is, and poor as I am, I would rather stand in my shoes than his."

"I should think so," said his wife. "Money isn't everything."

"No; but it is a good deal I have suffered too much from the want of it, to despise it."

"Well, Hiram," said Mrs. Walton, who felt that it would not do to look too persistently upon the dark side, "you know that the song says, 'There's a good time coming.'"

"I've waited for it a long time, wife," said the farmer, soberly.

"Wait a little longer," said Mrs. Walton, quoting the refrain of the song.

He smiled faintly.

"Very well, I'll wait a little longer; but if I have to wait too long, I shall get discouraged."

"Children, it's time to go to bed," said Mrs. Walton.

"Mayn't I sit up a little longer?" pleaded Mary.

"'Wait a little longer,' mother," said Tom, laughing, as he quoted his mother's words against her.

"Ten minutes, only, then."

Before the ten minutes were over, there was great and unexpected joy in the little house. Suddenly the outer door opened, and, without the slightest warning to anyone, Harry walked in. He was immediately surrounded by the delighted family, and in less time than I am taking to describe it he had shaken hands with his father, kissed his mother and sister, and given Tom a bearlike hug, which nearly suffocated him.

"Where did you come from, Harry?" asked Mary.

"Dropped down from the sky," said Harry, laughing.

"Has the professor been giving exhibitions up there?" asked Tom.

"I've discharge the professor," said Harry, gayly. "I'm my own man now."

"And you've come home to stay, I hope," said his mother.

"Not long, mother," said Harry. "I can only stay a few days."

"What a bully overcoat you've got on!" said Tom.

"The professor gave it to me."

"Hasn't he got one for me, too?"

Harry took off his overcoat, and Tom was struck with fresh admiration as he surveyed his brother's inside suit.

"I guess you spent all you money on clothes," he said.

"I hope not," said Mr. Walton, whom experience had made prudent.

"Not quite all," said Harry, cheerfully. "How much money do you think I have brought home?"

"Ten dollars," said Tom.

"More."

"Fifteen."

"More."

"Twenty," said Mary.

"More."

"Twenty-five."

"I won't keep you guessing all night. What do you say to fifty dollars?"

"Oh, what a lot of money!" said Mary.

"You have done well, my son," said Mr. Walton. "You must have been very economical."

"I tried to be, father. But I didn't say fifty dollars was all I had."

"You haven't got more?" said his mother, incredulously.

"I've got a hundred dollars, mother," said Harry.

"Here are fifty dollars for you, father. It'll pay your note to Squire Green, and a little over. Here are thirty dollars, mother, of which you must use for ten for yourself, ten for Mary and ten for Tom. I want you all to have some new clothes, to remember me by."

"But Harry, you will have nothing left for yourself."

"Yes, I shall. I have kept twenty dollars, which will be enough till I can earn some more."

"I don't see how you could save so much money, Harry," said his father.

"It was partly luck, father, and partly hard work. I'll tell you all about it."

He sat down before the fire and they listened to his narrative.

"Well, Harry," said Mr. Walton, "I am very glad to find that you are more fortunate than your father. I have had a hard struggle; but I will not complain if my children can prosper."

The cloud that Squire Green had brought with him had vanished, and all was sunshine and happiness.

It was agreed that no hint should be given to Squire Green that his note was to be paid. He did not even hear of Harry's arrival, and was quite unconscious of any change in the circumstances of the family, when he entered the cottage the next evening.

"Well, neighbor," he said, "I've brought along that ere note. I hope you've raised the money to pay it."

"Where do you think I could raise money, Squire?" asked Hiram Walton.

"I thought mebbe some of the neighbors would lent it to you."

"Money isn't very plenty with any of them, Squire, except with you."

"I calc'late better than they. Hev you got the ten dollars that you agreed to pay ef you couldn't meet the note?"

"Yes," said Hiram, "I raised the ten dollars."

"All right," said the squire, briskly, "I thought you could. As long as you pay that, you can keep the cow six months more, one a new contrack."

"Don't you think, Squire, it's rather hard on a poor man, to make him forfeit ten dollars because he can't meet his note?"

"A contrack's a contrack," said the squire. "It's the only way to do business."

"I think you are taking advantage of me, Squire."

"No, I ain't. You needn't hev come to me ef you didn't want to. I didn't ask you to buy the cow. I'll trouble you for that ten dollars, neighbor, as I'm in a hurry."

"On the whole, Squire, I think I'll settle up the note. That'll be cheaper than paying the forfeit."

"What! Pay forty-one dollars and twenty cents!" exclaimed the squire, incredulously.

———

"Yes; it's more than the cow's worth, but as I agreed to pay it I suppose I must."

"I thought you didn't hev the money," said the squire, his lower jaw falling; for he would have preferred the ten dollars' forfeit, and a renewal of the usurious contract.

"I didn't have it when you were in last night; but I've raised it since."

"You said you couldn't borrow it."

"I didn't borrow it."

"Then where did it come from?"

"My son Harry has got home, Squire. He has supplied me with the money."

"You don't say! Where is he? Been a-doin' well, has he?"

"Harry!"

Harry entered the room, and nodded rather coldly to the squire, who was disposed to patronize him, now that he was well dressed, and appeared to be doing well.

"I'm glad to see ye, Harry. So you've made money, have ye?"

"A little."

"Hev you come home to stay?"

"No sir; I shall only stay a few days."

"What hev ye been doin'"

"I am going to be a printer."

"You don't say! Is it a good business?"

"I think it will be," said Harry. "I can tell better by and by."

"Well, I'm glad you're doin' so well. Neighbor Walton, when you want another cow I'll do as well by you as anybody. I'll give you credit for another on the same terms."

"If I conclude to buy any, Squire, I may come round."

"Well, good night, all. Harry, you must come round and see me before you go back."

Harry thanked him, but did not propose to accept the invitation. He felt that the squire was no true friend, either to himself or to his family, and he should feel no pleasure in his society. It was not in his nature to be hypocritical, and he expressed no pleasure at the squire's affability and politeness.

I have thus detailed a few of Harry's early experiences; but I am quite aware that I have hardly fulfilled the promise of the title. He has neither lived long nor learned much as yet, nor has he risen very high in the world. In fact, he is still at the bottom of the ladder. I propose, therefore, to devote another volume to his later fortunes, and hope, in the end, to satisfy the reader. The most that can be said thus far is, that he has made a fair beginning, and I must refer the reader who is interested to know what success he met with as a printer, to the next volume, which will be entitled: "Risen From The Ranks."

THE END

~ ~ ~

TEACHERS GUIDE QUESTIONS FOR BOUND TO RISE

1.   Describe the main character Harry Walton. Who inspires him? How does he come to be inspired by him?
2.   Who is Squire Green? Describe his personality and his relationship with the Walton family.
3.   Two mottos are given during this story: Squire Green's motto and the Walton family motto. What are they?
4.   What pushes Harry out of Walton family home?
5.   What is Harry's first occupation after he leaves home?
6.   Compare Harry's behavior to that of his acquaintance Luke. What message is the author sending with Luke's character?
7.   What causes Harry to lose his job? How long is Harry out of work, and what is his next occupation?
8.   What makes Harry decide to start working at the printing office?
9.   When the highwaymen robbed Harry, he could have betrayed his employer. How could he have done this? What happens instead, and what lesson is learned here?
10. Has Harry lived up to his inspiration? How?
11. How did Harry live up to his family motto during this story?

TEACHERS GUIDE ANSWERS FOR BOUND TO RISE

1.   Harry Walton is the son of a poor farmer. He's a very good student, and even won a competition. The prize for winning the academic competition was a book about the life of Benjamin Franklin. Harry is inspired by the life of Benjamin Franklin after reading this book, and wants to live like him.

2.   Squire Green is the rich man of their town. He's very cheap, saves all of his money, and also likes to exploit unfortunate people whenever he can. The Walton family, much like the rest of the townsfolk, don't like him, but they are forced to do business with him when their cow dies.

3.   The Walton family motto is "live and learn." Squire Green's motto, while not said directly by Squire Green, is "live and earn."

4.   Inspired by Benjamin Franklin's rise to prominence from poor beginnings, Harry decides to leave the home to help earn money to pay for the cow, and also to make his own way in the world.

5.   Harry's first occupation after leaving home is at a shoe shop working as a pegger. He makes $3 per week.

6.   Harry saves all of his money so he will have enough to pay Squire Green for the cow. Luke is very foolish with his money, and runs up debt at the local tailor's shop. Luke thinks that he is unlucky because he never has money, but the author is trying to teach how smart it is to save your money.

7.   Harry loses his job at the shoe shop because they've made too many, and their store has to sell them before they can make more. He's out of work for two days before he becomes the assistant to Professor Henderson the ventriloquist.

8.   Harry decides to start working at the printing office because Benjamin Franklin was a printer. It pays less than he made at the shoe shop and with the magician, but he feels that the work has much more of a future.

9. Harry could have given the highwayman the wallet with Professor Henderson's money, and still had the money to pay for the family cow. He gives up his own money, and in trading jackets with the robber finds that the robber left his own wallet in the jacket, which had much more than was stolen from Harry. In rewarding Harry's honesty, the author is stressing the importance of being honest.

10. Harry is doing well so far in living up to his inspiration. He's out on his own, and slowly moving up in the world. He's on his way to becoming a printer, and he's not relying on anyone to lift him out of poverty.

11. He lives up to the family motto in several ways. First, he's an excellent student, and values education as being very important. Even after he leaves the home, he takes up night school at his own expense, and reads whenever he can. Finally he takes a lower paying job at the end of the story because it will allow him to learn more.

Stories of Success

"I was taught very early that I would have to depend entirely upon myself; that my future lay in my own hands"
Darius Ogden Mills

Stories of Success:

Bound To Rise
(Illustrated)

CHAPTER I

HARRY WALTON

"I am sorry to part with you, Harry," said Professor Henderson. "You have been a very satisfactory and efficient assistant, and I shall miss you."

"Thank you, sir," said Harry. "I have tried to be faithful to your interests."

"You have been so," said the Professor emphatically. "I have had perfect confidence in you, and this has relieved me of a great deal of anxiety. It would have been very easy for one in your position to cheat me out of a considerable sum of money."

"It was no credit to me to resist such a temptation as that," said Harry.

"I am glad to hear you say so, but it shows your inexperience nevertheless. Money is the great tempter nowadays. Consider how many defalcations and breaches of trust we read of daily in confidential positions, and we are forced to conclude that honesty is a rarer virtue than we like to think it. I have every reason to believe that my assistant last winter purloined, at the least, a hundred dollars, but I was unable to prove it, and submitted to the loss. It may be the same next winter. Can't I induce you to change your resolution, and remain in my employ? I will advance your pay."

"Thank you, Professor Henderson," said Harry gratefully. "I appreciate your offer, even if I do not accept it. But I have made up mind to learn the printing business."

"You are to enter the office of the Centreville Gazette, I believe."

"Yes, sir."

"How much pay will you get?"

"I shall receive my board the first month, and for the next six months have agreed to take two dollars a week and board."

"That won't pay your expenses."

"It must," said Harry, firmly.

"You have laid up some money while with me, haven't you?"

"Yes, sir; I have fifty dollars in my wallet, besides having given eighty dollars at home."

"That is doing well, but you won't be able to lay up anything for the next year."

"Perhaps not in money, but I shall be gaining the knowledge of a good trade."

"And you like that better than remaining with me, and learning my business?"

"Yes, sir."

"Well, perhaps you are right. I don't fancy being a magician myself; but I am too old to change. I like moving round, and I make a good living for my family. Besides I contribute to the innocent amusement of the public, and earn my money fairly."

"I agree with you, sir," said Harry. "I think yours is a useful employment, but it would not suit everybody. Ever since I read the life of Benjamin Franklin, I have wanted to learn to be a printer."

Young Benjamin Franklin working as a "Printer's Devil."

"It is an excellent business, no doubt, and if you have made up your mind I will not dissuade you. When you have a paper of your own, you can give your old friend, Professor Henderson, an occasional puff."

"I shall be glad to do that," said Harry, smiling, "but I shall have to wait some time first."

"How old are you now?"

"Sixteen."

"Then you may qualify yourself for an editor in five or six years. I advise you to try it at any rate. The editor in America is a man of influence."

"I do look forward to it," said Harry, seriously. "I should not be satisfied to remain a journeyman all my life, nor even the half of it."

"I sympathize with your ambition, Harry," said the Professor, earnestly, "and I wish you the best success. Let me hear from you occasionally."

"I should be very glad to write you, sir."

"I see the stage is at the door, and I must bid you good-bye. When you have a vacation, if you get a chance to come our way, Mrs. Henderson and myself will be glad to receive a visit from you. Good-bye!" And with a hearty shake of the hand, Professor Henderson bade farewell to his late assistant.

Those who have read "Bound to Rise," and are thus familiar with Harry Walton's early history, will need no explanation of the preceding conversation. But for the benefit of new readers, I will recapitulate briefly the leading events in the history of the boy of sixteen who is to be our hero.

Harry Walton was the oldest son of a poor New Hampshire farmer, who found great difficulty in wresting from his few sterile acres a living for his family. Nearly a year before, he had lost his only cow by a prevalent disease, and being without money, was compelled to buy another of Squire Green, a rich but mean neighbor, on a six months' note, on very unfavorable terms. As it required great economy to make both ends meet, there seemed no possible chance of his being able to meet the note at maturity. Besides, Mr. Walton was to forfeit ten dollars if he did not have the principal and interest ready for Squire Green. The hard-hearted creditor was mean enough to take advantage of his poor neighbor's necessities, and there was not the slightest chance of his receding from his unreasonable demand. Under these circumstances Harry, the oldest boy, asked his father's permission to go out into the world and earn his own living. He hoped not only to do this, but to save something toward paying his father's note. His ambition had been kindled by reading the life of Benjamin Franklin, which had been awarded to him as a school prize. He did not expect to emulate Franklin, but he thought that by imitating him he might attain an honorable position in the community.

Harry's request was not at first favorably received. To send a boy out into the world to earn his own living is a hazardous experiment, and fathers are less sanguine than their sons. Their experience suggests difficulties and obstacles of which the inexperienced youth knows and possesses nothing. But in the present case Mr. Walton reflected that the little farming town in which he lived offered small inducements for a boy to remain there, unless he was content to be a farmer, and this required capital. His farm was too small for himself, and of course he could not give Harry a part when he came of age. On the whole, therefore, Harry's plan of becoming a mechanic seemed not so bad a one after all. So permission was accorded, and our hero, with his little bundle of clothes, left the paternal roof, and went out in quest of employment.

After some adventures Harry obtained employment in a shoe-shop as pegger. A few weeks sufficed to make him a good workman, and he was then able to earn three dollars a week and board. Out of this sum he hoped to save enough to pay the note held by Squire Green against his father, but there were two unforeseen obstacles. He had the misfortune to lose his wallet, which was picked up by an unprincipled young man, by name Luke Harrison, also a shoemaker, who was always in pecuniary difficulties, though he earned much higher wages than Harry. Luke was unable to resist the temptation, and appropriated the money to his own use. This Harry ascertained after a while, but thus far had succeeded in obtaining the restitution of but a small portion of his hard-earned savings. The second obstacle was a sudden depression in the shoe trade which threw him out of work. More than most occupations the shoe business is liable to these sudden fluctuations and suspensions, and the most industrious and ambitious workman is often compelled to spend in his enforced weeks of idleness all that he had been able to save when employed, and thus at the end of the year finds himself, through no fault of his own, no better off than at the beginning. Finding himself out of work, our hero visited other shoe establishments in the hope of employment. But his search was in vain. Chance in this emergency made him acquainted with Professor Henderson, a well-known magician and conjurer, whose custom it was to travel, through the fall and winter, from town to town, giving public exhibitions of his skill. He was in want of an assistant, to sell tickets and help him generally, and he offered the position to our hero, at a salary of five dollars a week. It is needless to say that the position was gladly accepted. It was not the business that Harry preferred, but he reasoned justly that it was honorable, and was far better than remaining idle. He found Professor Henderson as he called himself, a considerate and agreeable employer, and as may be inferred from the conversation with which this chapter begins, his services were very satisfactory. At the close of the six months, he had the satisfaction of paying the note which his father had given, and so of disappointing the selfish schemes of the grasping creditor.

This was not all. He met with an adventure while travelling for the Professor, in which a highwayman who undertook to rob him, came off second best, and he was thus enabled to add fifty dollars to his savings. His financial condition at the opening of the present story has already been set forth.

Though I have necessarily omitted many interesting details, to be found in "Bound to Rise," I have given the reader all the information required to enable him to understand the narrative of Harry's subsequent fortunes.

CHAPTER II

THE PRINTING OFFICE

Jotham Anderson, editor and publisher of the Centreville Gazette, was sitting at his desk penning an editorial paragraph, when the office door opened, and Harry Walton entered.

"Good-morning, Mr. Anderson," said our hero, removing his hat.

"Good-morning, my friend. I believe you have the advantage of me," replied the editor.

Our hero was taken aback. It didn't occur to him that the engagement was a far less important event to the publisher than to himself. He began to be afraid that the job had not been kept open for him.

"My name is Harry Walton," he explained. "I was travelling with Prof. Henderson last winter, and called here to get some bills printed."

"Oh yes, I remember you now. I agreed to take you into the office," said the editor, to Harry's great relief.

"Yes, air."

"You haven't changed your mind, then? You still want to be a printer?"

"Yes, sir."

"You have left the Professor, I suppose."

"I left him yesterday."

"What did he pay you?"

"Five dollars a week. He offered me six, if I would stay with him."

"Of course you know that I can't pay you any such wages at present."

"Yes, sir. You agreed to give me my board the first month, and two dollars a week for six months afterward."

"That is all you will be worth to me at first. It is a good deal less than you would earn with Professor Henderson."

"I know that, sir; but I am willing to come for that."

"Good. I see you are in earnest about printing, and that is a good sign. I wanted you to understand just what you had to expect, so that you need not be disappointed."

"I sha'n't be disappointed, sir," said Harry confidently. "I have made up my mind to be a printer, and if you didn't receive me into your office, I would try to get in somewhere else."

"Then no more need be said. When do you want to begin?"

"I am ready any time."

"Where is your trunk?"

"At the tavern."

"You can have it brought over to my house whenever you please. The hotel-keeper will send it over for you. He is our expressman. Come into the house now, and I will introduce you to my wife."

The editor's home was just across the street from his printing office. Followed by Harry he crossed the street, opened the front door, and led the way into the sitting-room, where a pleasant-looking lady of middle age was seated.

"My dear," he said, "I bring you a new boarder."

She looked at Harry inquiringly.

"This young man," her husband explained, "is going into the office to learn printing. I have taken a contract to make a second Benjamin Franklin of him."

"Then you'll do more for him than you have been able to do for yourself," said Mrs. Anderson, smiling.

"You are inclined to be severe, Mrs. Anderson, but I fear you are correct. However, I can be like a guide-post, which points the way which it does not travel. Can you show Harry Walton—for that is his name—where you propose to put him?"

"I am afraid I must give you a room in the attic," said Mrs. Anderson. "Our house is small, and all the chambers on the second floor are occupied."

"I am not at all particular," said Harry. "I have not been accustomed to elegant accommodations."

"If you will follow me upstairs, I will show you your room."

Pausing on the third landing, Mrs. Anderson found the door of a small but comfortable bed-room. There was no carpet on the floor, but it was painted yellow, and scrupulously clean. A bed, two chairs, a bureau and wash-stand completed the list of furniture.

"I shall like this room very well," said our hero.

"There is a closet," said the lady, pointing to a door in the corner. "It is large enough to contain your trunk, if you choose to put it in there. I hope you don't smoke."

171

"Oh, no, indeed," said Harry, laughing. "I haven't got so far along as that."

"Mr. Anderson's last apprentice—he is a journeyman now—was a smoker. He not only scented up the room, but as he was very careless about lights, I was continually alarmed lest he should set the house on fire. Finally, I got so nervous that I asked him to board somewhere else."

"Is he working for Mr. Anderson now?"

"Yes; you probably saw him in the office."

"I saw two young men at the case."

"The one I speak of is the youngest. His name is John Clapp."

"There is no danger of my smoking. I don't think it would do me any good. Besides, it is expensive, and I can't afford it."

"I see we think alike," said Mrs. Anderson, smiling. "I am sure we will get along well together."

"I shall try not to give you any trouble," said our hero, and his tone, which was evidently sincere, impressed Mrs. Anderson still more favorably.

"You won't find me very hard to suit, I hope. I suppose you will be here for dinner?"

"If it will be quite convenient. My trunk is at the tavern, and I could stay there till morning, if you wished."

"Oh, no, come at once. Take possession of the room now, if you like, and leave an order to have your trunk brought here."

"Thank you. What is your hour for dinner?"

"Half-past five."

"Thank you. I will go over and speak to Mr. Anderson a minute."

The editor looked up as Harry reappeared.

"Well, have you settled arrangements with Mrs. Anderson?" he asked.

"Yes, sir, I believe so."

"I hope you like your room."

"It is very comfortable. It won't take me long to feel at home there."

"Did she ask you whether you smoked?"

"Yes, sir."

"I thought she would. That's where Clapp and she fell out."

Harry's attention was drawn to a thin, sallow young man of about twenty, who stood at a case on the opposite side of the room.

"Mrs. Anderson was afraid I would set the house on fire," said the young man thus referred to.

"Yes, she felt nervous about it. However, it is not surprising. An uncle of hers lost his house in that way. I suppose you don't smoke, Walton?"

"No, sir."

"Clapp smokes for his health. You see how stout and robust he is," said the editor, a little satirically.

"It doesn't do me any harm," said Clapp, a little testily.

"Oh, well, I don't interfere with you, though I think you would be better off if you should give up the habit. Ferguson don't smoke."

This was the other compositor, a man of thirty, whose case was not far distant from Clapp's.

"I can't afford it," said Ferguson; "nor could Clapp, if he had a wife and two young children to support."

"Smoking doesn't cost much," said the younger journeyman.

"So you think; but did you ever reckon it up?"

"No."

"Don't you keep any accounts?"

"No; I spend when I need to, and I can always tell how much I have left. What's the use of keeping accounts?"

"You can tell how you stand."

"I can tell that without taking so much trouble."

"You see we must all agree to disagree," said Mr. Anderson. "I am afraid Clapp isn't going to be a second Benjamin Franklin."

"Who is?" asked Clapp.

"Our young friend here," said the editor.

"Oh, is he?" queried the other with a sneer. "It'll be a great honor I'm sure, to have him in the office."

"Come, no chaffing, Clapp," said Mr. Anderson.

Harry hastened to disclaim the charge, for Clapp's sneer affected him disagreeably.

"I admire Franklin," he said, "but there isn't much danger of my turning out a second edition of him."

"Professional already, I see, Walton," said the editor.

"When shall I go to work, Mr. Anderson?"

"Whenever you are ready."

"I am ready now."

"You are prompt."

"You won't be in such a hurry to go to work a week hence," said Clapp.

"I think I shall," said Harry. "I am anxious to learn as fast as possible."

"Oh, I forgot. You want to become a second Franklin."

"I sha'n't like him," thought our hero. "He seems to try to make himself disagreeable."

"Mr. Ferguson will give you some instruction, and set you to work," said his employer.

Harry was glad that it was from the older journeyman that he was to receive his first lesson, and not from the younger.

CHAPTER III

HARRY STUMBLES UPON

AN ACQUAINTANCE

After dinner Harry went round to the tavern to see about his trunk. A group of young men were in the bar-room, some of whom looked up as he entered. Among these was Luke Harrison, who was surprised and by no means pleased to see his creditor. Harry recognized him at the same instant, and said, "How are you, Luke?"

"Is that you, Walton?" said Luke. "What brings you to Centreville? Professor Henderson isn't here, is he?"

"No; I have left him."

"Oh, you're out of a job, are you?" asked Luke, in a tone of satisfaction, for we are apt to dislike those whom we have injured, and for this reason he felt by no means friendly.

"No, I'm not," said Harry, quietly. "I've found work in Centreville."

"Gone back to pegging, have you? Whose shop are you in?"

"I am in a different business."

"You don't say! What is it?" asked Luke, with some curiosity.

"I'm in the office of the Centreville Gazette. I'm going to learn the printing business."

"You are? Why, I've got a friend in the office—John Clapp. He never told me about your being there."

"He didn't know I was coming. I only went to work this afternoon."

"So you are the printer's devil?" said Luke, with a slight sneer.

"I believe so," answered our hero, quietly.

"Do you get good pay?"

"Not much at first. However, I can get along with what money I have, and what is due me."

Luke Harrison understood the last allusion, and turned away abruptly. He had no wish to pay up the money which he owed Harry, and for this reason was sorry to see him in the village. He feared, if the conversation were continued, Harry would be asking for the money, and this would be disagreeable.

At this moment John Clapp entered the bar-room. He nodded slightly to Harry, but walked up to Luke, and greeted him cordially. There were many points of resemblance between them, and this drew them into habits of intimacy.

"Will you have something to drink, Harrison?" said Clapp.

"I don't mind if I do," answered Luke, with alacrity.

They walked up to the bar, and they were soon pledging each other in a fiery fluid which was not very likely to benefit either of them. Meanwhile Harry gave directions about his trunk, and left the room.

"So you've got a new 'devil' in your office," said Luke, after draining his glass.

"Yes. He came this afternoon. How did you hear?"

"He told me."

"Do you know him?" asked Clapp, in some surprise.

"Yes. I know him as well as I want to."

"What sort of a fellow is he?"

"Oh, he's a sneak—one of your pious chaps, that 'wants to be an angel, and with the angels stand.'"

"Then he's made a mistake in turning 'devil,'" said Clapp.

"Good for you!" said Luke, laughing. "You're unusually brilliant tonight, Clapp."

"So he's a saint, is he?"

"He set up for one; but I don't like his style myself. He's as mean as dirt. Why I knew him several months, and he never offered to treat in all that time. He's as much afraid of spending a cent as if it were a dollar."

"He won't have many dollars to spend just at present. He's working for his board."

"Oh, he's got money saved up," said Luke. "Fellows like him hang on to a cent when they get it. I once asked him to lend me a few dollars, just for a day or two, but he wouldn't do it. I hate such mean fellows."

"So do I. Will you have a cigar?"

"I'll treat this time," said Luke, who thought it polite to take his turn in treating once to his companion's four or five times.

"Thank you. From what you say, I am sorry Anderson has taken the fellow into the office."

"You needn't have much to say to him."

"I shan't trouble myself much about him. I didn't like his looks when I first set eyes on him. I suppose old Mother Anderson will like him. She couldn't abide my smoking, and he won't trouble her that way."

"So, he's too mean to buy the cigars."

"He said he couldn't afford it."

"That's what it comes to. By the way, Clapp, when shall we take another ride?"

"I can get away next Monday afternoon, at three."

"All right. I'll manage to get off at the same time. We'll go to Whiston and take dinner at the hotel. It does a fellow good to get off now and then. It won't cost more than five dollars apiece altogether."

"We'll get the carriage charged. The fact is, I'm a little low on funds."

"So am I, but it won't matter. Griffin will wait for his pay."

While Harry's character was being so unfavorably discussed, he was taking a walk by himself, observing with interest the main features of his new home. He had been here before with Professor Henderson, but had been too much occupied at that time to get a very clear idea of Centreville, nor had it then the interest for him which it had acquired since. He went upon a hill overlooking the village, and obtained an excellent view from its summit. It was a pleasant, well-built village of perhaps three thousand inhabitants, with outlying farms and farm-houses. Along the principal streets the dwellings and stores were closely built, so as to make it seem quite city-like. It was the shire town of the county, and being the largest place in the neighborhood, country people for miles around traded at its stores. Farmers' wives came to Centreville to make purchases, just as ladies living within a radius of thirty miles visit New York and Boston, for a similar purpose. Altogether, therefore, Centreville was quite a lively place, and a town of considerable local importance. The fact that it had a weekly paper of its own, contributed to bring it into notice. Nor was that all. Situated on a little hillock was a building with a belfry, which might have been taken for a church but for a play-ground nearby, which indicated that it had a different character. It was in fact the Prescott Academy, so called from the name of its founder, who had endowed it with a fund of ten thousand dollars, besides erecting the building at his own expense on land bought for the purpose. This academy also had a

---

local reputation, and its benefits were not confined to the children of Centreville. There were about twenty pupils from other towns who boarded with the Principal or elsewhere in the town, and made up the whole number of students in attendance—about eighty on an average.

Standing on the eminence referred to, Harry's attention was drawn to the Academy, and he could not help forming the wish that he, too, might share in its advantages.

"There is so much to learn, and I know so little," he thought.

But he did not brood over the poverty which prevented him from gratifying his desire. He knew it would do no good, and he also reflected that knowledge may be acquired in a printing office as well as within the walls of an academy or college.

"As soon as I get well settled," he said to himself, "I mean to get some books and study a little every day. That is the way Franklin did. I never can be an editor, that's certain, without knowing more than I do now. Before I am qualified to teach others, I must know something myself."

Looking at the village which lay below him, Harry was disposed to congratulate himself on his new residence.

"It looks like a pleasant place," he said to himself, "and when I get a little acquainted, I shall enjoy myself very well, I am sure. Of course I shall feel rather lonely just at first."

He was so engrossed by his thoughts that he did not take heed to his steps, and was only reminded of his abstraction by his foot suddenly coming in contact with a boy who was lying under a tree, and pitching headfirst over him.

"Holloa!" exclaimed the latter, "what are you about? You didn't take me for a foot-ball, did you?"

"I beg your pardon," said Harry, jumping up in some confusion. "I was so busy thinking that I didn't see you. I hope I didn't hurt you."

"Nothing serious. Didn't you hurt yourself?"
"I bumped my head a little, but it only struck the earth. If it had been a stone, it might have been different. I had no idea there was anyone up here except myself."

"It was very kind of you to bow so low to a perfect stranger," said the other, his eyes twinkling humorously. "I suppose it would only be polite for me to follow your example."

"I'll excuse you," said Harry laughing.

"Thank you. That takes a great burden off my mind. I don't like to be outdone in politeness, but really I shouldn't like to tumble over you. My head may be softer than yours. There's one thing clear. We ought to know each other. As you've taken the trouble to come up here, and stumble over me, I really feel as if we ought to strike up a friendship. What do you say?"

"With all my heart," said our hero.

CHAPTER IV

OSCAR VINCENT

"Allow me to introduce myself," said the stranger boy. "My name is Oscar Vincent, from Boston, at present a student at the Prescott Academy, at your service."

As he spoke, he doffed his hat and bowed, showing a profusion of chestnut hair, a broad, open brow, and an attractive face, lighted up by a pleasant smile.

Harry felt drawn to him by a feeling which was not long in ripening into friendship.

Imitating the other's frankness, he also took off his hat and replied—

"Let me introduce myself, in turn, as Harry Walton, junior apprentice in the office of the Centreville Gazette, sometimes profanely called 'printer's devil.'"

"Good!" said Oscar, laughing. "How do you like the business?"

"I think I shall like it, but I have only just started in it. I went into the office for the first time today."

"I have an uncle who started as you are doing," said Oscar. "He is now chief editor of a daily paper in Boston."

"Is he?" said Harry, with interest. "Did he find it hard to rise?"

"He is a hard worker. I have heard him say that he used to sit up late of nights during his apprenticeship, studying and improving himself."

"That is what I mean to do," said Harry.

"I don't think he was as lazy as his nephew," said Oscar. "I am afraid if I had been in his place I should have remained in it."

"Are you lazy?" asked Harry, smiling at the other's frankness.

"A little so; that is, I don't improve my opportunities as I might. Father wants to make a lawyer of me so he has put me here, and I am preparing for Harvard."

"I envy you," said Harry. "There is nothing I should like so much as entering college."

"I daresay I shall like it tolerably well," said Oscar; "but I don't hanker after it, as the boy said after swallowing a dose of castor oil. I'll tell you what I should like better—"

"What?" asked Harry, as the other paused.

"I should like to enter the Naval Academy, and qualify myself for the naval service. I always liked the sea."

"Doesn't your father approve of your doing this?"

"He wouldn't mind my entering the Navy as an officer, but he is not willing to have me enter the merchant service."

"Then why doesn't he send you to the Naval Academy?"

"Because I can't enter without receiving the appointment from a member of Congress. Our member can only appoint one, and there is no vacancy. So, as I can't go where I want to, I am preparing for Harvard."

"Are you studying Latin and Greek?"

"Yes."

"Have you studied them long?"

"About two years. I was looking over my Greek lesson when you playfully tumbled over me."

"Will you let me look at your book? I never saw a Greek book."

"I sometimes wish I never had," said Oscar; "but that's when I am lazy."

Harry opened the book—a Greek reader—in the middle of an extract from Xenophon, and looked with some awe at the unintelligible letters.

ΞΕΝΟΦΩΝΤΟΣ

ΑΘΗΝΑΙΩΝ ΠΟΛΙΤΕΙΑ.

ΚΕΦ. α'.

ΠΕΡΙ ἢ ἢ Ἀθηναίων πολιτείας, ὅτι ἢ εἵλοντο τῦτον ἢ τρόπον ἢ πολιτείας, ὐκ ἐπαινῶ διὰ τόδε· ὅτι ταῦθ' ἑλόμενοι, εἵλοντο τὺς πονηρὺς ἄμεινον πράττειν ἢ τὺς χρηστύς. Διὰ ἢ ὀν τῦτο ὐκ ἐπαινῶ. Ἐπεὶ ἢ ταῦτα ὅτως ἔδοξεν αὐτοῖς, ὡς εὖ διασώζονῖ ἢ πολιτείαν, κ̀ τἆλλα διαπράτῖοῖ), ἃ δοκῦσιν ἁμαρτάνειν τοῖς ἄλλοις Ἕλλησι, τῦτ' ἀποδείξω.

XENOPHONTIS

ATHENIENSIUM RESPUBLICA.

CAP. I.

JAM de Athenienfium republicâ, quòd eam reipublicæ formam fecuti fint, proptereà non laudo : quia dum illam voluerunt, voluerunt improbos *homines* meliori efle conditione, quàm probos. Hanc itaque ob caufam non laudo. Quia verò ita eis vifum eft, equidem oftendam, rempublicam eos fuam incolumem confervare, atque etiam alia perficere, in quibus aberrare Græcis cæteris exiftimentur.

Xenophon, the book that Oscar Vincent was studying for his Greek class when Harry first meets him.

"Can you read it? Can you understand what it means?" he asked, looking up from the book.

"So-so."

"You must know a great deal."

Oscar laughed.

"I wonder what Dr. Burton would say if he heard you," he said.

"Who is he?"

"Principal of our Academy. He gave me a blowing up for my ignorance today, because I missed an irregular Greek verb. I'm not exactly a dunce, but I don't think I shall ever be a Greek professor."

"If you speak of yourself that way, what will you think of me? I don't know a word of Latin, of Greek, or any language except my own."

"Because you have had no chance to learn. There's one language I know more about than Latin or Greek."

"English?"

"I mean French; I spent a year at a French boarding-school, three years ago."

"What! Have you been in France?"

"Yes; an uncle of mine—in fact, the editor—was going over, and urged father to send me. I learned considerable French, but not much else. I can speak and understand it pretty well."

"How I wish I had had your advantages," said Harry. "How did you like your French schoolmates?"

"They wouldn't come near me at first. Because I was an American they thought I carried a revolver and a dirk-knife, and was dangerous. That is their idea of American boys. When they found I was tame, and carried no deadly weapons, they ventured to speak with me, and after that we got along pretty well."

"How soon do you expect to go to college?"

"A year from next summer. I suppose I shall be ready by that time. You are going to stay in town, I suppose?"

"Yes, if I keep my job."

"Oh, you'll do that. Then we can see something of each other. You must come up to my room, and see me. Come almost any evening."

"I should like to. Do you live in Dr. Barton's family?"

"No, I hope not."

"Why not?"

"Oh, the Doctor has a way of looking after the fellows that room in the house, and of keeping them at work all the time. That wouldn't suit me. I board at Mrs. Greyson's, at the south-east corner of the church common. Have you got anything to do this evening?"

"Nothing in particular."

"Then come round and take a look at my den, or sanctum I ought to call it; as I am talking to a member of the editorial profession."

"Not quite yet," said Harry, smiling.

"Oh, well that'll come in due time. Will you come?"

"Sha'n't I be disturbing you?"

"Not a bit. My Greek lesson is about finished, and that's all I've got to do this evening. Come round, and we will sit over the fire, and chat like old friends."

"Thank you, Oscar," said Harry, irresistibly attracted by his bright and lively acquaintance, "I shall enjoy calling. I have made no acquaintances yet, and I feel lonely."

"I have got over that," said Oscar. "I am used to being away from home and don't mind it."

The two boys walked together to Oscar's boarding-place. It was a large house, of considerable pretension for a village, and Oscar's room was large and handsomely furnished. But what attracted Harry's attention was not the furniture, but a collection of over a hundred books, ranged on shelves at one end of the room. In his father's house it had always been so difficult to obtain the necessaries of life that books had necessarily been regarded as superfluities, and beyond a dozen volumes which Harry had read and re-read, he was compelled to depend on such as he could borrow. Here again his privileges were scanty, for most of the neighbors were as poorly supplied as his father.

"What a fine library you have, Oscar!" he exclaimed.

"I have a few books," said Oscar. "My father filled a couple of boxes, and sent me. He has a large library."

"This seems a large library to me," said Harry. "My father likes reading, but he is poor, and cannot afford to buy books."

He said that in a matter-of-fact tone, without the least attempt to conceal what many boys would have been tempted to hide. Oscar noted this, and liked his new friend the better for it.

"Yes," he said, "books cost money, and one hasn't always the money to spare."

"Have you read all these books?"

"Not more than half of them. I like reading better than studying, I am afraid. I am reading the Waverley novels now. Have you read any of them?"

"So; I never saw any of them before."

"If you see anything you would like to read, I will lend it to you with pleasure," said Oscar, noticing the interest with which Harry regarded the books.

"Will you?" said Harry, eagerly. "I can't tell you how much obliged I am. I will take good care of it."

"Oh, I am sure of that. Here, try Ivanhoe. I've just read it, and it's tip-top."

"Thank you; I will take it on your recommendation. What a nice room you have!"

"Yes, it's pretty comfortable. Father told me to fix it up to suit me. He said he wouldn't mind the expense if I would only study."

"I should think anybody might study in such a room as this, and with such a fine collection of books."

"I'm rather lazy sometimes," said Oscar, "but I shall turn over a new leaf one of these days, and astonish everybody. Tonight, as I have no studying to do, I'll tell you what we'll do. Did you ever pop corn?"

"Sometimes."

"I've got some corn here, and Ma'am Greyson has a popper. Stay here alone a minute, and I'll run down and get it."

Oscar ran down stairs, and speedily returned with a corn-popper.

"Now we'll have a jolly time," said he. "Draw up that arm-chair, and make yourself at home. If Xenophon, or Virgil, or any of those Greek and Latin chaps call, we'll tell 'em we are transacting important business and can't be disturbed. What do you say?"

"They won't be apt to call on me," said Harry. I haven't the pleasure of knowing them."

"It isn't always a pleasure, I can assure you, Harry. Pass over the corn-popper."

CHAPTER V

A YOUNG F. F. B.

As the two boys sat in front of the fire, popping and eating the corn, and chatting of one thing and another, their acquaintance improved rapidly. Harry learned that Oscar's father was a Boston merchant, in the Calcutta trade, with a counting-room on Long Wharf. Oscar was a year older than himself, and the oldest child. He had a sister of thirteen, named Florence, and a younger brother, Charlie, now ten. They lived on Beacon Street, opposite the Common. Though Harry had never lived in Boston, he knew that this was a fashionable street, and he had no difficulty in inferring that Mr. Vincent was a rich man. He felt what a wide gulf there was socially between himself and Oscar; one the son of a very poor country farmer, the other the son of a merchant prince. But nothing in Oscar's manner indicated the faintest feeling of superiority, and this pleased Harry. I may as well say, however, that our hero was not one to show any foolish subserviency to a richer boy; he thought mainly of Oscar's superiority in knowledge; and although the latter was far ahead of Harry on this score, he was not one to boast of it.

Harry, in return for Oscar's confidence, acquainted him with his own adventures since he had started out to earn his own living. Oscar was most interested in his apprenticeship to the ventriloquist.

"It must have been jolly fun," he said. "I shouldn't mind travelling round with him myself. Can you perform any tricks?"

"A few," said Harry.

"Show me some, that's a good fellow."

"If you won't show others. Professor Henderson wouldn't like to have his tricks generally known. I could show more if I had the articles he uses. But I can do some without."

"Go ahead, Professor. I'm all attention."

Not having served an apprenticeship to a magician, as Harry did, I will not undertake to describe the few simple tricks which he had picked up, and now exhibited for the entertainment of his companion. It is enough to say that they were quite satisfactory, and that Oscar professed his intention to puzzle his Boston friends with them, when his vacation arrived.

About half-past eight, a knock was heard at the door.

"Come in!" called out Oscar.

The door was opened, and a boy about his own age entered. His name was Fitzgerald Fletcher. He was also a Boston boy, and the son of a retail merchant, doing business on Washington Street. His father lived handsomely, and was supposed to be rich. At any rate Fitzgerald supposed him to be so, and was very proud of the fact. He generally let any new acquaintances understand very speedily that his father was a man of property, and that his family moved in the first circles of Boston Society. He cultivated the acquaintance of those boys who belonged to rich families, and did not fail to show the superiority which he felt to those of less abundant means. For example, he liked to be considered close with Oscar, as the social position of Mr. Vincent was higher than that of his own family. It gave him an excuse also for calling on Oscar in Boston. He had tried to ingratiate himself also with Oscar's sister Florence, but had only disgusted her with his airs, so that he could not flatter himself with his success in this direction. Oscar had very little liking for him, but as schoolfellows they often met, and Fitzgerald often called upon him. On such occasions he treated him politely enough, for it was not in his nature to be rude without cause.

Fitz was elaborately dressed, feeling that handsome clothes would help convey the impression of wealth, which he was anxious to establish. In particular he paid attention to his neckties, of which he boasted a greater variety than any of his schoolmates. It was not a lofty ambition, but, such as it was, he was able to gratify it.

"How are you, Fitz?" said Oscar, when he saw who was his visitor.

"Draw up a chair to the fire, and make yourself comfortable."

"Thank you, Oscar," said Fitzgerald, leisurely drawing off a pair of kid gloves; "I thought I would drop in and see you."

"All right! Will you have some popped corn?"

"No, thank you," answered Fitzgerald, shrugging his shoulders. "I don't fancy the article."

"Don't you? Then you don't know what's good."

"Fancy passing round popped corn at a party in Boston," said the other. "How people would stare!"

"Would they? I don't know about that. I think some would be more sensible and eat. But, I beg your pardon, I haven't introduced you to my friend, Harry Walton. Harry, this is a classmate of mine. Fitzgerald Fletcher, Esq., of Boston."

187

Kid gloves, which Fitzgerald Fletcher is usually described as wearing.

Fitzgerald did not appear to perceive that the title Esquire was sportively added to his name. He took it seriously, and was pleased with it, as a recognition of his social superiority. He bowed ceremoniously to our hero, and said, formally, "I am pleased to make your acquaintance, Mr. Walton."

"Thank you, Mr. Fletcher," replied Harry, bowing in turn.

"I wonder who he is," thought Fitzgerald.

He had no idea of the true position of our young hero, or he would not have wasted so much politeness upon him. The fact was, that Harry was well dressed, having on the suit which had been given him by a friend from the city. It was therefore fashionably cut, and had been so well kept as still to be in very good condition. It occurred to Fitz—to give him the short name he received from his school-fellows—that it might be a Boston friend of Oscar's, just entering the Academy. This might account for his not having met him before. Perhaps he was from an aristocratic Boston family. His intimacy with Oscar rendered it probable, and it might be well to cultivate his acquaintance. On this hint he spoke.

"Are you about to enter the Academy, Mr. Walton?"

"No; I should like to do so, but cannot."

"You are one of Oscar's friends from the city, I suppose, then?"

"Oh no; I am living in Centreville."

"Who can he be?" thought Fitz. With considerable less cordiality in his manner, he continued, impelled by curiosity, "I don't think I have met you before."

"No: I have only just come to the village."

Oscar understood thoroughly the bewilderment of his visitor, and enjoyed it. He knew the weakness of Fitz, and he could imagine how his feelings would change when be ascertained the real position of Harry.

"My friend," he explained, "is connected with the Centreville Gazette."

"In what capacity?" asked Fitz, by surprise.

"He is profanely termed the 'printer's devil.' Isn't that so, Harry?"

"I believe you are right," said our hero, smiling. He had a suspicion that this relation would shock his new acquaintance.

"Indeed!" exclaimed Fitz, pursing up his lips, and, I was about to say, turning up his nose, but nature had saved him the little trouble of doing that.

"What in the world brings him here, then?" he thought; but there was no need of saying it, for both Oscar and Harry read it in his manner. "Strange that Oscar Vincent, from one of the first families of Boston, should demean himself by keeping company with a low printer boy!"

"Harry and I have had a jolly time popping corn this evening!" said Oscar, choosing to ignore his schoolmate's changed manner.

"Indeed! I can't see what fun there is in it."

"Oh, you've got no taste. Has he, Harry?"

"His taste differs from ours," said our hero, politely.

"I should think so," remarked Fitz, with significant emphasis. "Was that all you had to amuse yourself?"

In using the singular pronoun, he expressly ignored the presence of the young printer.

"No, that wasn't all. My friend Harry has been amusing me with some tricks which he learned while he was travelling round with Professor Henderson, the ventriloquist and magician."

189

"Really, he is quite accomplished," said Fitz, with a covert sneer. "Pretty company Oscar has taken up with!" he thought. "How long were you in the circus business?" he asked, turning to Harry.

"I never was in the circus business."

"Excuse me. I should say, travelling about with the ventriloquist."

"About three months. I was with him when he performed here last winter."

"Ah! Indeed. I didn't go. My father doesn't approve of my attending such common performances. I only attend first-class theatres, and the Italian opera."

"That's foolish," said Oscar. "You miss a good deal of fun, then. I went to Professor Henderson's entertainment, and I now remember seeing you there, Harry. You took money at the door, didn't you?"

"Yes."

"Now I understand what made your face seem so familiar to me, when I saw it this afternoon. By the way, I have never been into a printing office. If I come round to yours, will you show me round?"

"I should be very glad to, Oscar, but perhaps you had better wait till I have been there a little while, and learned the ropes. I know very little about it yet."

"Won't you come too, Fitz?" asked Oscar.

"You must really excuse me," drawled Fitz. "I have heard that a printing office is a very dirty place. I should be afraid of soiling my clothes."

"Especially that stunning cravat."

"Do you like it? I flatter myself it's something a little extra," said Fitz, who was always gratified by a compliment to his cravats.

"Then you won't go?"

"I haven't the slightest curiosity about such a place, I assure you."

"Then I shall have to go alone. Let me know when you are ready to receive me, Harry."

"I won't forget, Oscar."

"I wonder he allows such a low fellow to call him by his first name," thought Fitz. "Really, he has no proper pride."

"Well," he said, rising, "I must be going."

"What's your hurry, Fitz?"

"I've got to write a letter home this evening. Besides, I haven't finished my Greek. Good-evening, Oscar."

"Good-evening, Fitz."

"Good-evening, Mr. Fletcher," said Harry.

"Evening!" said Fitz, briefly; and without a look at the low "printer-boy," he closed the door and went downstairs.

CHAPTER VI

OSCAR BECOMES A PROFESSOR

"I am afraid your friend won't thank you for introducing me to him," said Harry, after Fitz had left the room.

"Fitz is a snob," said Oscar. "He makes himself ridiculous by putting on airs, and assuming to be more than he is. His father is in a good business, and may be rich—I don't know about that—but that isn't much to boast of."

"I don't think we shall be very close," said Harry, smiling.

"Evidently a printer's apprentice is something very low in his eyes."

"When you are an influential editor he will be willing to recognize you. Let that stimulate your ambition."

"It isn't easy for a half-educated boy to rise to such a position. I feel that I know very little."

"If I can help you any, Harry, I shall be very glad to do it. I'm not much of a scholar, but I can help you a little. For instance, if you wanted to learn French, I could hear your lessons, and correct your exercises."

"Will you?" said Harry, eagerly. "There is nothing I should like better."

"Then I'll tell you what I'll do. You shall buy a French grammar, and come to my room two evenings a week, and recite what you get time to study at home."

"Won't it give you a great deal of trouble, Oscar?"

"Not a bit of it; I shall rather like it. Until you can buy a grammar, I will lend you mine. I'll set you a lesson out of it now."

He took from the book-shelves a French grammar, and inviting Harry to sit down beside him, gave him some necessary explanations as to the pronunciation of words according to the first lesson.

"It seems easy," said Harry. "I can take more than that."

"It is the easiest of the modern languages, to us at least, on account of its having so many words similar to ours."

"What evening shall I come, Oscar?"

"Tuesday and Friday will suit me as well as any. And remember, Harry, I mean to be very strict in discipline. And, by the way, how will it do to call myself Professor?"

"I'll call you Professor if you want me to."

"We'll leave all high titles to Fitz, and I won't use the rod any oftener than it is absolutely necessary."

"All right, Professor Vincent," said Harry laughing, "I'll endeavor to behave with propriety."

"I wonder what they would say at home," said Oscar, "if they knew I had taken up the profession of teacher. Strange as it may seem to you, Harry, I have the reputation in the home-circle of being decidedly lazy. How do you account for it?"

"Great men are seldom appreciated."

"You hit the nail on the head that time—glad I am not the nail, by the way. Henceforth I will submit with resignation to injustice and misconstruction, since I am only meeting with the common fate of great men."

"What time is it, Oscar?"

"Nearly ten."

"Then I will bid you good-night," and Harry rose to go. "I can't tell how much I am obliged to you for your kind offer."

"Just postpone thanks till you find out whether I am a good teacher or not."

"I am sure of that."

"I am not so sure, but I will do what I can for you. Good-night. I'll expect you Friday evening. I shall see Fitz tomorrow. Shall I give him your love?"

"Never mind!" said Harry, smiling. "I'm afraid it wouldn't be appreciated."

"Perhaps not."

As Harry left his lively companion, he felt that he had been most fortunate in securing his friendship—not only that he found him very agreeable and attractive, but he was likely to be of great use to him in promoting his plans of self-education. He had too much good sense not to perceive that the only chance he had of rising to an influential position lay in qualifying himself for it, by enlarging his limited knowledge and improving his mind.

"I have made a good beginning," he thought. "After I have learned something of French, I will take up Latin, and I think Oscar will be willing to help me in that too."

The next morning he commenced work in the printing office. With a few hints from Ferguson, he soon comprehended what he had to do, and made very rapid progress.

"You're getting on fast, Harry," said Ferguson approvingly.

"I like it," said our hero. "I am glad I decided to be a printer."

"I wish I wasn't one," grumbled Clapp, the younger journeyman.

"Don't you like it?"

"Not much. It's hard work and poor pay. I just wish I was in my brother's shoes. He is a bookkeeper in Boston, with a salary of twelve hundred a year, while I am plodding along on fifteen dollars week."

"You may do better some day," said Ferguson.

"Don't see any chance of it."

"If I were in your place, I would save up part of my salary, and by and by have an office, and perhaps a paper of my own."

"Why don't you do it, then?" sneered Clapp.

"Because I have a family to support from my earnings—you have only yourself."

"It doesn't help me any; I can't save anything out of fifteen dollars a week."

"You mean you won't," said Ferguson quietly.

"No I don't. I mean I can't."

"How do you expect I get along, then? I have a wife and two children to support, and only get two dollars a week more than you."

"Perhaps you get into debt."

"No; I owe no man a dollar," said Ferguson emphatically. "That isn't all. I save two dollars a week; so that I actually support four on fifteen dollars a week—your salary. What do you say to that?"

"I don't want to be mean," said Clapp.

"Nor I. I mean to live comfortably, but of course I have to be economical."

"Oh, hang economy!" said Clapp impatiently. "The old man used to lecture me about economy till I got sick of hearing the word."

"It is a good thing, for all that," persisted Ferguson. "You'll think so some day, even if you don't now."

"I guess you mean to run opposition to young Franklin, over there," sneered Clapp, indicating Harry, who had listened to the discussion with not a little interest.

"I think he and I will agree together pretty well," said Ferguson, smiling. "Franklin's a good man to imitate."

"If there are going to be two Franklins in the office, it will be time for me to clear out," returned Clapp.

"You can do better."

"How is that?"

"Become Franklin No. 3."

"You don't catch me imitating any old fogy like that. As far as I know anything about him, he was a mean, stingy old curmudgeon!" exclaimed Clapp with irritation.

"That's rather strong language, Clapp," said Mr. Anderson, looking up from his desk with a smile. "It doesn't correspond with the general estimate of Franklin's character."

"I don't care," said Clapp doggedly, "I wouldn't be like Franklin if I could. I have too much self-respect."

Ferguson laughed, and Harry wanted to, but feared he should offend the younger journeyman, who evidently had worked himself into a bad humor.

"I don't think you're in any danger," said Ferguson, who did not mind his fellow-workman's little ebullitions of temper.

Clapp scowled, but did not deign to reply, partly, perhaps, because he knew that there was nothing to say.

From the outset Ferguson took a fancy to the young apprentice.

"He's got good, solid ideas," said he to Mr. Anderson, when Harry was absent. "He isn't so thoughtless as most boys of his age. He looks ahead."

"I think you are right in your judgment of him," said Mr. Anderson.

"He promises to be a faithful workman."

"He promises more than that," said Ferguson. "Mark my words, Mr. Anderson; that boy is going to make his mark some day."

"It is a little too soon to say that, isn't it?"

"No; I judge from what I see. He is industrious and ambitious, and is bound to succeed. The world will hear of him yet."

Mr. Anderson smiled. He liked what he had seen of his new apprentice, but he thought Ferguson altogether too sanguine.

"He's a good, faithful boy," he admitted, "but it takes more than that to rise to distinction. If all the smart boys turned out smart men, they'd be a drug in the market."

But Ferguson held to his own opinion, notwithstanding. Time will show which was right.

The next day Ferguson said, "Harry, come round to my house, and take tea tonight. I've spoken to my wife about you, and she wants to see you."

"Thank you, Mr. Ferguson," said Harry. "I shall be very glad to come."

"I'll wait till you are ready, and you can walk along with me."

"All right; I will be ready in five minutes."

They set out together for Ferguson's modest home, which was about half a mile distant. As they passed up the village street Harry's attention was drawn to two boys who were approaching them. One he recognized at once as Fitzgerald Fletcher. He had an even more stunning necktie than when Harry first met him, and sported a jaunty little cane, which he swung in his neatly gloved hand.

"I wonder if he'll notice me," thought Harry. "At any rate, I won't be wanting in politeness."

"Good-afternoon, Mr. Fletcher," he said, as they met.

Fitzgerald stared at him superciliously, and made the slightest possible nod.

"Who is that?" asked Ferguson.

"It is a boy who has great contempt for printers' devils and low apprentices," answered Harry. "I was introduced to him two evenings ago, but he evidently doesn't care about keeping up the acquaintance."

"Who is that, Fitz?" asked his companion in turn.

"It's a low fellow—a printer's devil," answered Fitz, shortly.

"How do you happen to know him?"

"Oscar Vincent introduced him to me. Oscar's a queer fellow. He belongs to one of the first families in Boston—one of my set, you know, and yet he actually invited that boy to his room."

"He's rather a good-looking boy—the printer."

"Think so?" drawled Fitz. "He's low—all apprentices are. I mean to keep him at a distance."

CHAPTER VII

A PLEASANT EVENING

A 19th-century New England cottage, which is the kind of house where Ferguson lived with his family.

"This is my house," said Ferguson, pausing at the gate.

Harry looked at it with interest.

It was a cottage, containing four rooms, and a kitchen in the ell part. There was a plot of about a quarter of an acre connected with it. Everything about it was neat, though very unpretentious.

"It isn't a palace," said Ferguson, "but," he added cheerfully, "it's a happy home, and from all I've read, that is more than can be said of some palaces. Step right in and make yourself at home."

They entered a tiny entry, and Mrs. Ferguson opened the door of the sitting room. She was a pleasant-looking woman, and her face wore a smile of welcome.

"Hannah," said Ferguson, "this is our new apprentice, Harry Walton."

"I am glad to see you," she said, offering her hand. "My husband has spoken of you. You are quite welcome, if you can put up with humble fare."

"That is what I have always been accustomed to," said Harry, beginning to feel quite at home.

"Where are the children, Hannah?"

Two children, a boy and a girl, of six and four years respectively, bounded into the room and answered for themselves. They looked shyly at Harry, but before many minutes their shyness had worn off, and the little girl was sitting on his knee, while the boy stood beside him. Harry was fond of children, and readily adapted himself to his young acquaintances.

Dinner was soon ready—a plain meal, but one that Harry enjoyed. He could not help comparing Ferguson's plain, but pleasant home, with Clapp's mode of life.

The latter spent on himself as much as sufficed his fellow-workman to support a wife and two children, yet it was easy to see which found the best enjoyment in life.

"How do you like your new business?" asked Mrs. Ferguson, as she handed Harry a cup of tea.

"I like all but the name," said our hero, smiling.

"I wonder how the name came to be applied to a printer's apprentice any more than to any other apprentice," said Mrs. Ferguson.

"I never heard," said her husband. "It seems to me to be a libel upon our trade. But there is one comfort. If you stick to the business, you'll outgrow the name."

"That is lucky; I shouldn't like to be called the wife of a ——. I won't pronounce the word lest the children should catch it."

"What is it, mother?" asked Willie, with his mouth full.

"It isn't necessary for you to know, my boy."

"Do you know Mr. Clapp?" asked Harry.

"I have seen him, but never spoke with him."

"I never asked him round to tea," said Ferguson.

"I don't think he would enjoy it any better than I. His tastes are very different from mine, and his views of life are equally different."

"I should think so," said Harry.

"Now I think you and I would agree very well. Clapp dislikes the business, and only sticks to it because he must get his living in some way. As for me, if I had a sum of money, say five thousand dollars, I would still remain a printer, but in that case I would probably buy out a paper, or start one, and be a publisher, as well as a printer."

"That's just what I should like," said Harry.

"Who knows but we may be able to go into partnership some day, and carry out our plan."

"I would like it," said Harry; "but I am afraid it will be a good while before we can raise the five thousand dollars."

"We don't need as much. Mr. Anderson started on a capital of a thousand dollars, and now he is in comfortable circumstances."

"Then there's hopes for us."

"At any rate I cherish hopes of doing better some day. I shouldn't like always to be a journeyman. I manage to save up a hundred dollars a year. How much have we in the savings bank, Hannah?"

"Between four and five hundred dollars, with interest."

"It has taken me four years to save it up. In five more, if nothing happens, I should be worth a thousand dollars. Journeymen printers don't get rich very fast."

"I hope to have saved up something myself, in five years," said Harry.

"Then our plan may come to pass, after all. You shall be editor, and I publisher."

"I should think you would prefer to be an editor," said his wife.

"I am diffident of my powers in the line of composition," said Ferguson. "I shouldn't be afraid to undertake local items, but when it comes to an elaborate editorial, I should rather leave it in other hands."

"I always liked writing," said Harry. "Of course I have only had a school-boy's practice, but I mean to practice more in my leisure hours."

"Suppose you write a poem for the Gazette, Walton."

Harry smiled.

"I am not ambitious enough for that," he replied. "I will try plain prose."

"Do so," said Ferguson, earnestly. "Our plan may come to something after all, if we wait patiently. It will do no harm to prepare yourself as well as you can. After a while you might write something for the Gazette. I think Mr. Anderson would put it in."

"Shall I sign it P. D.?" asked Harry.

"P. D. stands for Doctor of Philosophy."

"I don't aspire to such a learned title. P. D. also stands for Printer's Devil."

"I see. Well, joking aside, I advise you to improve yourself in writing."

"I will. That is the way Franklin did."

"I remember. He wrote an article, and slipped it under the door of the printing office, not caring to have it known that he was the author."

"Shall I give you a piece of pie, Mr. Walton?" said Mrs. Ferguson.

"Thank you."

"Me too," said Willie, extending his plate.

"Willie is always fond of pie," said his father, "In a printing office pi is not such a favorite."

When dinner was over, Mr. Ferguson showed Harry a small collection of books, about twenty-five in number, neatly arranged on shelves.

"It isn't much of a library," he said, "but a few books are better than none. I should like to buy as many every year; but books are expensive, and the outlay would make too great an inroad upon my small surplus."

"I always thought I should like a library," said Harry, "but my father is very poor, and has fewer books than you. As for me, I have but one book besides the school-books I studied, and that I gained as a school prize—The Life of Franklin."

"If one has few books he is apt to prize them more," said Ferguson, "and is apt to profit by them more."

"Have you read the History of China?" asked Harry, who had been looking over his friend's books.

"No; I have never seen it."

"Why, there it is," said our hero, "In two volumes."

"Take it down," said Ferguson, laughing.

Harry did so, and to his surprise it opened in his hands, and revealed a checker-board.

"You see appearances are deceitful. Can you play checkers?"

"I never tried."

"You will easily learn. Shall I teach you the game?"

"I wish you would."

They sat down; and Harry soon became interested in the game, which requires a certain degree of thought and foresight.

"You will make a good player after a while," said his companion.

"You must come in often and play with me."

"Thank you, I should like to do so. It may not be often, for I am taking lessons in French, and I want to get on as fast as possible."

"I did not know there was any one in the village who gave lessons in French."

"Oh, he's not a professional teacher. Oscar Vincent, one of the Academy boys, is teaching me. I am to take two lessons a week, on Tuesday and Friday evenings."

"Indeed, that is a good arrangement. How did it come about?"

Harry related the particulars of his meeting with Oscar.

"He's a capital fellow," he concluded. "Very different from another boy I met in his room. I pointed him out to you in the street. Oscar seems to be rich, but he doesn't put on any airs, and he treated me very kindly."

"That is to his credit. It's the sham aristocrats that put on most airs. I believe you will make somebody, Walton. You have lost no time in getting to work."

"I have no time to lose. I wish I was in Oscar's place. He is preparing for Harvard, and has nothing to do but to learn."

"I heard a lecturer once who said that the printing office is the poor man's college, and he gave a great many instances of printers who had risen high in the world, particularly in our own country."

"Well, that is encouraging. I should like to have heard the lecture."

"I begin to think, Harry, that I should have done well to follow your example. When I was in your position, I might have studied too, but I didn't realize the importance as I do now. I read some useful books, to be sure, but that isn't like studying."

"It isn't too late now."

Ferguson shook his head.

"Now I have a wife and children," he said. "I am away from them during the day, and the evening I like to pass socially with them."

"Perhaps you would like to be divorced," said his wife, smiling. "Then you would get time for study."

"I doubt if that would make me as happy, Hannah. I am not ready to part with you just yet. But our young friend here is not quite old enough to be married, and there is nothing to prevent his pursuing his studies. So, Harry, go on, and prepare yourself for your editorial duties."

Harry smiled thoughtfully. For the first time he had formed definite plans for his future. Why should not Ferguson's plans be realized?

"If I live long enough," he said to himself, "I will be an editor, and exert some influence in the world."

At ten o'clock he bade goodnight to Mr. and Mrs. Ferguson, feeling that he had passed a pleasant and what might prove a profitable evening.

CHAPTER VIII

FLETCHER'S VIEWS ON

SOCIAL POSITION

"You are getting on finely, Harry," said Oscar Vincent, a fortnight later. "You do credit to my teaching. As you have been over all the regular verbs now, I will give you a lesson in translating."

"I shall find that interesting," said Harry, with satisfaction.

"Here is a French Reader," said Oscar, taking one down from the shelves. "It has a dictionary at the end. I won't give you a lesson. You may take as much as you have time for, and at the same time three or four of the irregular verbs. You are going about three times as fast as I did when I commenced French."

"Perhaps I have a better teacher than you had," said Harry, smiling.

"I shouldn't wonder," said Oscar. "That explains it to my satisfaction. Well, now that the lesson is over, sit down and we'll have a chat. Oh, by the way, there's one thing I want to speak to you about. We've got a debating society at our school. It is called 'The Clionian Society.' Most of the students belong to it. How would you like to join?"

"I should like it very much. Do you think they would admit me?"

"I don't see why not. I'll propose you at the next meeting, Thursday evening. Then the nomination will lie over a week, and be acted upon at the next meeting."

"I wish you would. I never belonged to a debating society, but I should like to learn to speak."

"It's nothing when you're used to it. It's only the first time, you know, that troubles you. By Jove! I remember how my knees trembled when I first got up and said Mr. President. I felt as if all eyes were upon me, and I wanted to sink through the floor. Now I can get up and chatter with the best of them. I don't mean that I can make an eloquent speech or anything of that kind, but I can talk at a minute's notice on almost any subject."

"I wish I could."

"Oh, you can, after you've tried a few times. Well, then, it's settled. I'll propose you at the next meeting."

"How lucky I am to have fallen in with you, Oscar."

"I know what you mean. I'm your guide, philosopher, and friend, and all that sort of thing. I hope you'll have proper veneration for me. It's rather a new character for me. Would you believe it, Harry, at home I am regarded as a rattle-brained chap, instead of the dignified Professor that you know me to be. Isn't it a shame?"

"Great men are seldom appreciated at home, Oscar."

"I know that. I shall have to get a certificate from you, certifying to my being a steady and erudite young man."

"I'll give it with the greatest pleasure."

"Holloa, there's a knock. Come in!" shouted Oscar.

The door opened, and Fitzgerald Fletcher entered the room.

"How are you, Fitz?" said Oscar. "Sit down and make yourself comfortable. You know my friend, Harry Walton, I believe?"

"I believe I had the honor to meet him here one evening," said Fitzgerald stiffly, slightly emphasizing the word "honor."

"I hope you are well, Mr. Fletcher," said Harry, more amused than disturbed by the manner of the aristocratic visitor.

"Thank you, my health is good," said Fitzgerald with equal stiffness, and forthwith turned to Oscar, not deigning to devote any more attention to Harry.

Our hero had intended to remain a short time longer, but, under the circumstances, as Oscar's attention would be occupied by Fletcher, with whom he was not on close terms, he thought he might spend the evening more profitably at home in study.

"If you'll excuse me, Oscar," he said, rising, "I will leave you now, as I have something to do this evening."

"If you insist upon it, Harry, I will excuse you. Come round Friday evening."

"Thank you."

"Do you have to work at the printing office in the evening?" Fletcher deigned to inquire.

"No; I have some studying to do."

"Reading and spelling, I suppose," sneered Fletcher.

"I am studying French."

"Indeed!" returned Fletcher, rather surprised. "How can you study it without a teacher?"

"I have a teacher."

"Who is it?"

"Professor Vincent," said Harry, smiling.

"You didn't know that I had developed into a French Professor, did you, Fitz? Well, it's so, and whether it's the superior teaching or not, I can't say, but my scholar is getting on famously."

"It must be a great bore to teach," said Fletcher.

"Not at all. I like it."

"Every one to his taste," said Fitzgerald unpleasantly.

"Good-night, Oscar. Good-night, Mr. Fletcher," said Harry, and made his exit.

"You're a strange fellow, Oscar," said Fletcher, after Harry's departure.

"Very likely, but what particular strangeness do you refer to now?"

"No one but you would think of giving lessons to a printer's devil."

"I don't know about that."

"No one, I mean, that holds your position in society."

"I don't know that I hold any particular position in society."

"Your family live on Beacon Street, and move in the first circles. I am sure my mother would be disgusted if I should demean myself so far as to give lessons to any vulgar apprentice."

"I don't propose to give lessons to any vulgar apprentice."

"You know whom I mean. This Walton is only a printer's devil."

"I don't know that that is any objection to him. It isn't morally wrong to be a printer's devil, is it?"

"What a queer fellow you are, Oscar. Of course I don't mean that. I daresay he's well enough in his place, though he seems to be very forward and presuming, but you know that he's not your equal."

"He is not my equal in knowledge, but I shouldn't be surprised if he would be some time. You'd be astonished to see how fast he gets on."

"I daresay. But I mean in social position."

"It seems to me you can't think of anything but social position."

"Well, it's worth thinking about."

"No doubt, as far as it is deserved. But when it is founded on nothing but money, I wouldn't give much for it."

"Of course we all know that the higher classes are more refined—"

"Than printers' devils and vulgar apprentices, I suppose," put in Oscar, laughing, "Yes."

"Well, if refinement consists in wearing kid gloves and stunning neckties, I suppose the higher classes, as you call them, are more refined."

"Do you mean me?" demanded Fletcher, who was noted for the character of his neckties.

"Well, I can't say I don't. I suppose you regard yourself as a representative of the higher classes, don't you?"

"To be sure I do," said Fletcher, complacently.

"So I supposed. Then you see I had a right to refer to you. Now listen to my prediction. Twenty-five years from now, the boy whom you look down upon as a vulgar apprentice will occupy a high position, and you will be glad to number him among your acquaintances."

"Speak for yourself, Oscar," said Fletcher, scornfully.

"I speak for both of us."

"Then I say I hope I can command better associates than this friend of yours."

"You may, but I doubt it."

"You seem to be carried away by him," said Fitzgerald, pettishly. "I don't see anything very wonderful about him, except dirty hands."

"Then you have seen more than I have."

"Of course a fellow who meddles with printer's ink must have dirty hands. Faugh!" said Fletcher, turning up his nose.

At the same time he regarded complacently his own fingers, which he carefully kept aloof from anything that would soil or mar their aristocratic whiteness.

"The fact is, Fitz," said Oscar, argumentatively, "our upper ten, as we call them, spring from just such beginnings as my friend Harry Walton. My own father commenced life in a printing office. But, as you say, he occupies a high position at present."

"Really!" said Fletcher, a little taken aback, for he knew that Vincent's father ranked higher than his own.

"I daresay your own ancestors were not always patricians."

Fletcher winced. He knew well enough that his father commenced life as a boy in a country grocery, but in the mutations of fortune had risen to be the proprietor of a large dry-goods store on Washington Street. None of the family cared to look back to the beginning of his career. They overlooked the fact that it was creditable to him to have risen from the ranks, though the rise was only in wealth, for Mr. Fletcher was a purse-proud parvenu, who owed all the consideration he enjoyed to his commercial position. Fitz liked to have it understood that he was of patrician lineage, and carefully ignored the little grocery, and certain country relations who occasionally paid a visit to their wealthy relatives, in spite of the rather frigid welcome they received.

"Oh, I suppose there are exceptions," Fletcher admitted reluctantly. "Your father was smart."

"So is Harry Walton. I know what he is aiming at, and I predict that he will be an influential editor some day."

"Have you got your Greek lesson?" asked Fletcher, abruptly; who did not relish the course the conversation had taken.

"Yes."

"Then I want you to translate a passage for me. I couldn't make it out."

"All right."

Half an hour later Fletcher left Vincent's room.

"What a snob he is!" thought Oscar.

And Oscar was right.

CHAPTER IX

THE CLIONIAN SOCIETY

On Thursday evening the main school of the Academy building was lighted up, and groups of boys, varying in age from thirteen to nineteen, were standing in different parts of the room. These were members of the Clionian Society, whose weekly meeting was about to take place.

A debating society, much like the Clionian Society at the academy.

At eight o'clock precisely the President took his place at the teacher's desk, with the Secretary at his side, and rapped for order. The presiding officer was Alfred DeWitt, a member of the Senior Class, and now nearly ready for college. The Secretary was a member of the same class, by name George Sanborn.

"The Secretary will read the minutes of the last meeting," said the President, when order had been obtained.

George Sanborn rose and read his report, which was accepted.

"Are any committees prepared to report?" asked the President.

The Finance Committee reported through its chairman, recommending that the fee for admission be established at one dollar, and that each member be assessed twenty-five cents monthly.

"Mr. President," said Fitzgerald Fletcher, rising to his feet, "I would like to say a word in reference to this report."

"Mr. Fletcher has the floor."

"Then, Mr. President, I wish to say that I disagree with the Report of the Committee. I think a dollar is altogether too small. It ought to be at least three dollars, and I myself should prefer five dollars. Again, sir, the Committee has recommended for the monthly assessment the ridiculously small sum of twenty-five cents. I think it ought to be a dollar."

"Mr. President, I should like to ask the gentleman his reason," said Henry Fairbanks, Chairman of the Finance Committee. "Why should we tax the members to such an extent, when the sums reported are sufficient to defray the ordinary expenses of the Society, and to leave a small surplus besides?"

"Mr. President," returned Fletcher, "I will answer the gentleman. We don't want to throw open the Society to every one that can raise a dollar. We want to have an exclusive society."

"Mr. President," said Oscar Vincent, rising, "I should like to ask the gentleman for how many he is speaking. He certainly is not speaking for me. I don't want the Society to be exclusive. There are not many who can afford to pay the exorbitant sums which he desires fixed for admission fee and for monthly assessments, and I for one am not willing to exclude any good fellow who desires to become one of us, but does not boast as heavy a purse as the gentleman who has just spoken."

These remarks of Oscar were greeted with applause, general enough to show that the opinions of nearly all were with him.

"Mr. President," said Henry Fairbanks, "though I am opposed to the gentleman's suggestion, (does he offer it as an amendment?) I have no possible objection to his individually paying the increased rates which he recommends, and I am sure the Treasurer will gladly receive them."

Laughter and applause greeted this hit, and Fletcher once more arose, somewhat vexed at the reception of his suggestion.

"I don't choose—" he commenced.

"The gentleman will address the chair," interrupted the President.

"Mr. President, I don't choose to pay more than the other members, though I can do it without inconvenience. But, as I said, I don't believe in being too democratic. I am not in favor of admitting anybody and everybody into the Society."

209

"Mr. President," said James Hooper, "I congratulate the gentleman on the flourishing state of his finances. For my own part, I am not ashamed to say that I cannot afford to pay a dollar a month assessment, and, were it required, I should be obliged to offer my resignation."

"So much the better," thought Fitzgerald, for, as Hooper was poor, and went coarsely clothed, he looked down upon him. Fortunately for himself he did not give utterance to his thought.

"Does Mr. Fletcher put his recommendation into the form of an amendment?" asked the President.

"I do."

"Be kind enough to state it, then."

Fletcher did so, but as no one seconded it, no action was of course taken.

"Nominations for membership are now in order," said the President.

"I should like to propose my friend Harry Walton."

"Who is Harry Walton?" asked a member.

"Mr. President, may I answer the gentleman?" asked Fitzgerald Fletcher, rising to his feet.

"As the nominee is not to be voted upon this evening, it is not in order."

"Mr. President," said Oscar, "I should be glad to have the gentleman report his information."

"Mr. Fletcher may speak if he desires it, but as the name will be referred to the Committee on Nominations, it is hardly necessary."

"Mr. President, I merely wish to inform the Society that Mr. Walton occupies the dignified position of printer's devil in the office of the Centreville Gazette."

"Mr. President," said Oscar, "may I ask the indulgence of the Society long enough to say that I am quite aware of the fact. I will add that Mr. Walton is a young man of excellent abilities, and I am confident will prove an accession to the Society."

"I cannot permit further remarks on a matter which will come in due course before the Committee on Nominations," said the President.

"The next business in order is the debate."

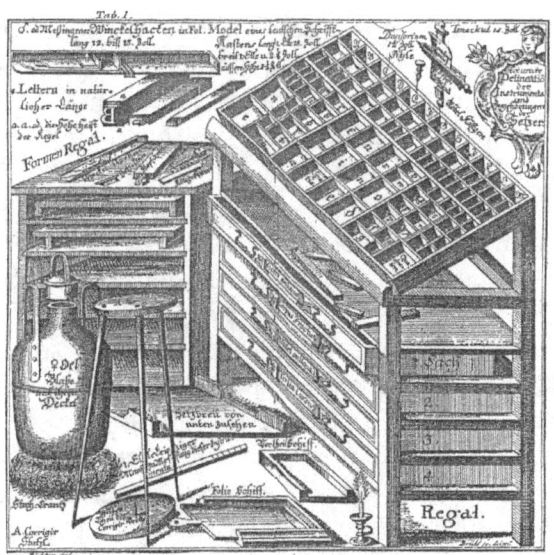

A typesetter's case. Harry works at one when he works as a printer's apprentice.

Of the debate, and the further proceedings, I shall not speak, as they are of no special interest. But after the meeting was over, groups of members discussed matters which had come up during the evening. Fletcher approached Oscar Vincent, and said, "I can't see, Oscar, why you are trying to get that printer's devil into our Society."

"Because he's a good fellow, and smart enough to do us credit."

"If there were any bootblacks in Centreville I suppose you'd be proposing them?" said Fletcher with a sneer.

"I might, if they were as smart as my friend Walton."

"You are not very particular about your friends," said Fletcher in the same tone.

"I don't ask them to open their wallets and show me how much money they have."

"I prefer to associate with gentlemen."

"So do I."

"Yet you associate with that printer's devil."

"I consider him a gentleman."

Fletcher laughed scornfully.

"You have strange ideas of a gentleman," he said.

"I hold the same," said James Hooper, who had come up in time to hear the last portion of the conversation. "I don't think a full wallet is the only or the chief qualification of a gentleman. If labor is to be a disqualification, then I must resign all claims to be considered a gentleman, as I worked on a farm for two years before coming to school, and in that way earned the money to pay my expenses here."

Fletcher turned up his nose, but did not reply.

Hooper was a good scholar and influential in the Society, but in Fletcher's eyes he was unworthy of consideration.

"Look here, Fletcher—what makes you so confoundedly exclusive is your ideas?" asked Henry Fairbanks.

"Because I respect myself," said Fletcher in rather a surly tone.

"Then you have one admirer," said Fairbanks.

"What do you mean by that?" asked Fletcher, suspiciously.

"Nothing out of the way. I believe in self-respect, but I don't see how it is going to be endangered by the admission of Oscar's friend to the Society."

"Am I expected to associate on equal terms with a printer's devil?"

"I can't answer for you. As for me, if he is a good fellow, I shall welcome him to our ranks. Some of our most eminent men have been apprenticed to the trade of printer. I believe, after all, it is the name that has prejudiced you."

"No it isn't. I have seen him."

"Harry Walton?"

"Yes."

"Where?"

"In Oscar's room."

"Well?"

"I don't like his appearance."

"What's the matter with his appearance?" asked Oscar.

"He looks low."

"That's where I must decidedly contradict you, Fitz, and I shall appeal confidently to the members of the Society when they come to know him, as they soon will, for I am sure no one else shares your ridiculous prejudices. Harry Walton, in my opinion, is a true gentleman, without reference to his wallet, and he is bound to rise hereafter, take my word for it."

"There's plenty of room for him to rise," said Fletcher with a sneer.

212

"That is true not only of him, but of all of us, I take it."

"Do you refer to me?"

"Oh no," said Oscar with sarcasm. "I am quite aware that you are at the pinnacle of eminence, even if you do flunk in Greek occasionally."

Fitzgerald had failed in the Greek recitation during the day, and that in school parlance is sometimes termed a "flunk." He bit his lip in mortification at this reference, and walked away, leaving Oscar master of the situation.

"You had the best of him there, Vincent," said George Sanborn. "He has gone off in disgust."

"I like to see Fletcher taken down," said Henry Fairbanks. "I never saw a fellow put on so many airs. He is altogether too aristocratic to associate with ordinary people."

"Yes," said Oscar, "he has a foolish pride, which I hope he will some time get rid of."

"He ought to have been born in England, and not in a republic."

"If he had been born in England, he would have been unhappy unless he had belonged to the nobility," said Alfred DeWitt.

"Look here, boys," said Tom Carver, "what do you say to mortifying Fitz's pride?"

"Have you got a plan in view, Tom? If so, out with it."

"Yes: you know the peddler that comes into town about once a month to buy up rags, and sell his tinwares."

"I have seen him. Well, what of him?"

"He is coming early next week. Some of us will see him privately, and post him up as to Fitz's relations and position, and hire him to come up to school, and inquire for Fitz, representing himself as his cousin. Of course Fitz will deny it indignantly, but he will persist and show that he knows all about the family."

"Good! Splendid!" exclaimed the boys laughing. "Won't Fitz be raving?"

"There's no doubt about that. Well, boys, I'll arrange it all, if you'll authorize me."

"Go ahead, Tom. You can draw upon us for the necessary funds."

Fletcher had retired to his room, angry at the opposition his proposal had received, and without any warning of the humiliation which awaited him.

213

CHAPTER X

THE TIN-PEDDLER

Those of my readers who live in large cities are probably not familiar with the travelling tin-peddler, who makes his appearance at frequent intervals in the country towns and villages of New England. His stock of tinware embraces a large variety of articles for culinary purposes, ranging from milk-pans to nutmeg-graters. These are contained in a wagon of large capacity, in shape like a box, on which he sits enthroned a merchant prince. Unlike most traders, he receives little money, most of his transactions being in the form of a barter, whereby he exchanges his merchandise for rags, white and colored, which have accumulated in the household, and are gladly traded off for bright tinware. Behind the cart usually depend two immense bags, one for white, the other for colored rags, which, in time, are sold to paper manufacturers. It may be that the very paper on which this description is printed, was manufactured from rags so collected.

Abner Bickford was the proprietor of such an establishment as I have described. No one, at first sight, would have hesitated to class him as a Yankee. He was long in the limbs, and long in the face, with a shrewd twinkle in the eye, a long nose, and the expression of a man who respected himself and feared nobody. He was unpolished, in his manners, and knew little of books, but he belonged to the same resolute and hardy type of men who in years past sprang to arms, and fought bravely for an idea. He was strong in his manhood, and would have stood unabashed before a king. Such was the man who was to mortify the pride of Fitzgerald Fletcher.

Tom Carver watched for his arrival in Centreville, and walking up to his cart, accosted him.

"Good-morning, Mr. Bickford."

"Good-mornin', young man. You've got the advantage of me. I never saw you before as I know of."

"I am Tom Carver, at your service."

"Glad to know you. Where do you live? Maybe your wife would like some tinware this mornin'?" said Abner, relaxing his gaunt features into a smile.

"She didn't say anything about it when I came out," said Tom, entering into the joke.

"Maybe you'd like a tin-dipper for your youngest boy?"

"Maybe I would, if you've got any to give away."

"I see you've cut your eye-teeth. Is there anything else I can do for you? I'm in for a trade."

"I don't know, unless I sell myself for rags."

"Anything for a trade. I'll give you two cents a pound."

"That's too cheap. I came to ask your help in a trick we boys want to play on one of our number."

"Sho! You don't say so. That ain't exactly in my line."

"I'll tell you all about it. There's a chap at our school—the Academy, you know—who's awfully stuck up. He's all the time bragging about belonging to a first family in Boston, and turning up his nose at poorer boys. We want to mortify him."

"Just so!" said Abner, nodding. "Drive ahead!"

"Well, we thought if you'd call at the school and ask after him, and pretend he was a cousin of yours, and all that, it would make him mad."

"Oh, I see," said Abner, nodding, "he wouldn't like to own a tin-peddler for his cousin."

"No," said Tom; "he wants us to think all his relations are rich. I wouldn't mind at all myself," he added, it suddenly occurring to him that Abner's feelings might be hurt.

"Good!" said Abner. "I see you ain't one of the stuck-up kind. I've got some relations in Boston myself, that are rich and stuck up. I never go near 'em. What's the name of this chap you're talkin' about?"

"Fletcher—Fitzgerald Fletcher."

"Fletcher!" repeated Abner. "Whew! Well, that's a joke!"

"What's a joke?" asked Tom, rather surprised.

"Why, he is my relation—a sort of second cousin. Why, my mother and his father are own cousins. So, don't you see we're second cousins?"

"That's splendid!" exclaimed Tom. "I can hardly believe it."

"It's so. My mother's name was Fletcher—Roxanna Fletcher—afore she married. Jim Fletcher—this boy's father—used to work in my grandfather's store, up to Hampton, but he got kinder discontented, and went off to Boston, where he's been lucky, and they do say he's mighty rich now. I never go nigh him, 'cause I know he looks down on his country cousins, and I don't believe in pokin' my nose in where I ain't wanted."

"Then you are really and truly Fitz's cousin?"

___

215

"If that's the boy's name. Seems to me it's a kinder queer one. I s'pose it's a fust-claas name. Sounds rather stuck up."

"Won't the boys roar when they hear about it! Are you willing to enter into our plan?"

"Well," said Abner, "I'll do it. I can't abide folks that's stuck up. I'd rather own a cousin like you."

"Thank you, Mr. Bickford."

"When do you want me to come round?"

"How long do you stay in town?"

"Well, I expect to stop overnight at the tavern; I can't get through in one day."

"Then come round to the Academy tomorrow morning, about half-past eight. School don't begin till nine, but the boys will be playing ball alongside. Then we'll give you an introduction to your cousin."

"That'll suit me well enough. I'll come."

Tom Carver returned in triumph, and communicated to the other boys the arrangement he had made with Mr. Bickford, and his unexpected discovery of the genuine relationship that existed between Fitz and the tin-peddler. His communication was listened to with great delight, and no little hilarity, and the boys discussed the probable effect of the projected meeting.

"Fitz will be perfectly raving," said Henry Fairbanks. "There's nothing that will take down his pride so much."

"He'll deny the relationship, probably," said Oscar.

"How can he?"

"He'll do it. See if he don't. It would be death to all his aristocratic claims to admit it."

"Suppose it were yourself, Oscar?"

"I'd say, 'How are you, cousin? How's the business?'" answered Oscar, promptly.

"I believe you would, Oscar. There's nothing of the snob about you."

"I hope not."

"Yet your family stands as high as Fletcher's."

"That's a point I leave to others to discuss," said Oscar. "My father is universally respected, I am sure, but he rose from the ranks. He was once a printer's devil, like my friend Harry Walton. Wouldn't it be ridiculous in me to turn up my nose at Walton, just because he stands now where my father did thirty years ago? It would be the same thing as sneering at father."

"Give us your hand, Oscar," said Henry Fairbanks. "You've got no nonsense about you—I like you."

"I'm not sure whether your compliment is deserved, Henry," said Oscar, "but if I have any nonsense it isn't of that kind."

"Do you believe Fitz has any suspicion that he has a cousin in the tin business?"

"No; I don't believe he has. He must know he has poor relations, living in the country, but he probably thinks as little as possible about them. As long as they don't intrude themselves upon his greatness, I suppose he is satisfied."

"And as long as no one suspects that he has any connection with such plebeians."

"Of course."

"What sort of a man is this tin-peddler, Tom?" asked Oscar.

"He's a pretty sharp fellow—not educated, or polished, you know, but he seems to have some sensible ideas. He said he had never seen the Fletchers; because he didn't want to poke his nose in where he wasn't wanted. He showed his good sense also by saying that he had rather have me for a cousin than Fitz."

"That isn't a very high compliment—I'd say the same myself."

"Thank you, Oscar. Your compliment exalts me. You won't mind my strutting a little."

And Tom humorously threw back his head, and strutted about with mock pride.

"To be sure," said Oscar, "you don't belong to one of the first families of Boston, like our friend, Fitz."

"No, I belong to one of the second families. You can't blame me, for I can't help it."

"No, I won't blame you, but of course I consider you low."

"I am afraid, Tom, I haven't got any cousins in the tin trade, like Fitz."

"Poor Fitz! His little dreams of his impending trial. If he did, I am afraid he wouldn't sleep a wink tonight."

"I wish I thought as much of myself as Fitz does," said Henry Fairbanks. "You can see by his dignified pace, and the way he tosses his head, how well satisfied he is with being Fitzgerald Fletcher, Esq."

"I'll bet five cents he won't strut round so much tomorrow afternoon," said Tom, "after his interview with his new cousin. But hush, boys! Not a word more of this. There's Fitz coming up the hill. I wouldn't have him suspect what's going on, or he might defeat our plans by staying away."

CHAPTER XI

FITZ AND HIS COUSIN

The next morning at eight the boys began to gather in the field beside the Seminary. They began to play ball, but took little interest in the game, compared with the "tragedy in real life," as Tom jocosely called it, which was expected soon to come off.

Fitz appeared upon the scene early. In fact one of the boys called for him, and induced him to come round to school earlier than usual. Significant glances were exchanged when he made his appearance, but Fitz suspected nothing, and was quite unaware that he was attracting more attention than usual.

Punctually at half-past eight, Abner Bickford with his tin-cart appeared in the street, and with a twitch of the rein began to ascend the Academy Hill.

"Look there," said Tom Carver, "the tin-peddler's coming up the hill. Wonder if he expects to sell any of his wares to us boys. Do you know him, Fitz?"

"I!" answered Fitzgerald with a scornful look, "what should I know of a tin-peddler?"

Tom's mouth twitched, and his eyes danced with the anticipation of fun.

By this time Mr. Bickford had brought his horse to a halt, and jumping from his box, approached the group of boys, who suspended their game.

"We don't want any tinware," said one of the boys, who was not in the secret.

"Want to know! Perhaps you haven't got tin enough to pay for it. Never mind, I'll buy you for old rags, at two cents a pound."

"He has you there, Harvey," said Tom Carver. "Can I do anything for you, sir?"

"Is your name Fletcher?" asked Abner, not appearing to recognize Tom.

"Why, he wants you, Fitz!" said Harvey, in surprise.

"This gentleman's name is Fletcher," said Tom, placing his hand on the shoulder of the astonished Fitzgerald.

"Not Fitz Fletcher?" said Abner, interrogatively.

"My name is Fitzgerald Fletcher," said the young Bostonian, haughtily, "but I am at a loss to understand why you should desire to see me."

Abner advanced with hand extended, his face lighted up with an expansive grin.

"Why, Cousin Fitz," he said heartily, "do you mean to say you don't know me?"

"Sir," said Fitzgerald, drawing back, "you are entirely mistaken in the person. I don't know you."

"I guess it's you that are mistaken, Fitz," said the peddler, familiarly; "why, don't you remember Cousin Abner, that used to trot you on his knee when you was a baby? Give us your hand, in memory of old times."

"You must be crazy," said Fitzgerald, his cheeks red with indignation, and all the more exasperated because he saw significant smiles on the faces of his school-companions.

"I s'pose you was too young to remember me," said Abner. "I hain't seen you for ten years."

"Sir," said Fitz, wrathfully, "you are trying to impose upon me. I am a native of Boston."

"Of course you be," said the imperturbable peddler. "Cousin Jim—that's your father—went to Boston when he was a boy, and they do say he's worked his way up to be a mighty rich man. Your father is rich, ain't he?"

"My father is wealthy, and always was," said Fitzgerald.

"No he wasn't, Cousin Fitz," said Abner. "When he was a boy, he used to work in grandfather's store up in Hampton; but he got sort of discontented and went to Boston. Did you ever hear him tell of his cousin Roxanna? That's my mother."

"I see that you mean to insult me, fellow," said Fitz, pale with passion. "I don't know what your object is, in pretending that I am your relation. If you want any pecuniary help—"

"Hear the boy talk!" said the peddler, bursting into a horse laugh. "Abner Bickford don't want no pecuniary help, as you call it. My tin-cart'll keep me, I guess."

"You needn't claim relationship with me," said Fitzgerald, scornfully; "I haven't any low relations."

"That's so," said Abner, emphatically; "but I ain't sure whether I can say that for myself."

"Do you mean to insult me?"

"How can I? I was talkin' of my relations. You say you ain't one of 'em."

"I am not."

"Then you needn't go for to put on the coat. But you're out of your reckoning, I guess. I remember your mother very well. She was Susan Baker."

"Is that true, Fitz?"

"Ye—es," answered Fitz, reluctantly.

"I told you so," said the peddler, triumphantly.

"Perhaps he is your cousin, after all," said Henry Fairbanks.

"I tell you he isn't," said Fletcher, impetuously.

"How should he know your mother's name, then, Fitz?" asked Tom.

"Some of you fellows told him," said Fitzgerald.

"I can say, for one, that I never knew it," said Tom.

"Nor I."

"Nor I."

"We used to call her Sukey Baker," said Abner. "She used to go to the deestrict school along of Mother. They was in the same class. I haven't seen your mother since you was a baby. How many children has she got?"

"I must decline answering your impertinent questions," said Fitzgerald, desperately. He began to entertain, for the first time, the horrible suspicion that the peddler's story might be true—that he might after all be his cousin. But he resolved that he never would admit it—NEVER! Where would be his pretentious claims to aristocracy—where his pride—if this humiliating discovery were made? Judging of his schoolfellows and himself, he feared that they would look down upon him.

"You seem kind o' riled to find that I am your cousin," said Abner. "Now, Fitz, that's foolish. I ain't rich, to be sure, but I'm respectable. I don't drink nor chew, and I've got five hundred dollars laid away in the bank."

"You're welcome to your five hundred dollars," said Fitz, in what was meant to be a tone of withering sarcasm.

"Am I? Well, I'd orter be, considerin' I earned it by hard work. Seems to me you've got high notions, Fitz. Your mother was kind of flighty, and I've heard mine say Cousin Jim—that's your father—was mighty sot up by gettin' rich. But seems to me you ought not to deny your own flesh and blood."

221

"I don't know who you refer to, sir."

"Why, you don't seem to want to own me as your cousin."

"Of course not. You're only a common tin-peddler."

"Well, I know I'm a tin-peddler, but that don't change my bein' your cousin."

"I wish my father was here to expose your falsehood."

"Hold on there!" said Abner. "You're goin' a leetle too far. I don't let no man, nor boy neither, charge me with lyin', if he is my cousin, I don't stand that, nohow."

There was something in Abner's tone which convinced Fitzgerald that he was in earnest, and that he himself must take care not to go too far.

"I don't wish to have anything more to say to you," said Fitz."

"I say, boys," said Abner, turning to the crowd who had now formed a circle around the cousins, "I leave it to you if it ain't mean for Fitz to treat me in that way. If he was to come to my house, that ain't the way I'd treat him."

"Come, Fitz," said Tom, "you are not behaving right. I would not treat my cousin that way."

"He isn't my cousin, and you know it," said Fitz, stamping with rage.

"I wish I wasn't," said Abner. "If I could have my pick, I'd rather have him," indicating Tom. "But blood can't be wiped out. We're cousins, even if we don't like it."

"Are you quite sure you are right about this relationship?" asked Henry Fairbanks, gravely. "Fitz, here, says he belongs to one of the first families of Boston."

"Well, I belong to one of the first families of Hampton," said Abner, with a grin. "Nobody don't look down on me, I guess."

"You hear that, Fitz," said Oscar. "Be sensible, and shake hands with your cousin."

"Yes, shake hands with your cousin!" echoed the boys.

"You all seem to want to insult me," said Fitz, sullenly.
"Not I," said Oscar, "and I'll prove it—will you shake hands with me, sir?"

"That I will," said Abner, heartily. "I can see that you're a young gentleman, and I wish I could say as much for my cousin, Fitz."

Oscar's example was followed by the rest of the boys, who advanced in turn, and shook hands with the tin-peddler.

"Now, Fitz, it's your turn," said Tom.

"I decline," said Fitz, holding his hands behind his back.

"How much he looks like his marm did when she was young," said Abner. "Well, boys, I can't stop no longer. I didn't think Cousin Fitz would be so stuck up, just because his father's made some money. Good-mornin'!"

"Three cheers for Fitz's cousin!" shouted Tom.

They were given with a will, and Mr. Bickford made acknowledgment by a nod and a grin.

"Remember me to your mother when you write, Cousin Fitz," he said at parting.

Fitz was too angry to reply. He walked off sullenly, deeply mortified and humiliated, and for weeks afterward nothing would more surely throw him into a rage than any allusion to his cousin the tin-peddler. One good effect, however, followed. He did not venture to allude to the social position of his family in presence of his school-mates, and found it politic to lay aside some of his airs of superiority.

CHAPTER XII

HARRY JOINS THE

CLIONIAN SOCIETY

A week later Harry Walton received the following note:—
"Centreville, May 16th, 18—,

"Dear Sir: At the last meeting of the Clionian Society you were elected a member. The next meeting will be held on Thursday evening, in the Academy building.

"Yours truly,

"GEORGE SANBORN,

"Secretary.

"MR. HARRY WALTON."

Our hero read this letter with satisfaction. It would be pleasant for him to become acquainted with the Academy students, but he thought most of the advantages which his membership would afford him in the way of writing and speaking. He had never attempted to debate, and dreaded attempting it for the first time; but he knew that nothing desirable would be accomplished without effort, and he was willing to make that effort.

"What have you there, Walton?" asked Clapp, noticing the letter which he held in his hand.

"You can read it if you like," said Harry.

"Humph!" said Clapp; "so you are getting in with the Academy boys?"

"Why shouldn't he?" said Ferguson.

"Oh, they're a stuck-up set."

"I don't find them so—that is, with one exception," said Harry.

"They are mostly the sons of rich men, and look down on those who have to work for a living."

Clapp was of a jealous and envious disposition, and he was always fancying slights where they were not intended.

"If I thought so," said Harry, "I would not join the Society, but as they have elected me, I shall become a member, and see how things turn out."

"It is a good plan, Harry," said Ferguson. "It will be a great advantage to you."

"I wish I had a chance to attend the Academy for a couple of years," said our hero, thoughtfully.

"I don't," said Clapp. "What's the good of studying Latin and Greek, and all that rigmarole? It won't bring you money, will it?"

"Yes," said Ferguson. "Education will make a man more competent to earn money, at any rate in many cases. I have a cousin, who used to go to school with me, but his father was able to send him to college. He is now a lawyer in Boston, making four or five times my income. But it isn't for the money alone that an education is worth having. There is a pleasure in being educated."

"So I think," said Harry.

"I don't see it," said Clapp. "I wouldn't be a bookworm for anybody. There's Walton learning French. What good is it ever going to do him?"

"I can tell you better by and by, when I know a little more," said Harry. "I am only a beginner now."

"Dr. Franklin would never have become distinguished if he had been satisfied with what he knew as an apprentice," said Ferguson.

"Oh, if you're going to bring up Franklin again, I've got through," said Clapp with a sneer. "I forgot that Walton was trying to be a second Franklin."

"I don't see much chance of it," said Harry, good-humoredly. "I should like to be if I could."

Clapp seemed to be in an ill-humor, and the conversation was not continued. He had been up late the night before with Luke Harrison, and both had drunk more than was good for them. In consequence, Clapp had a severe headache, and this did not improve his temper.

"Come round Thursday evening, Harry," said Oscar Vincent, "and go to the Society with me. I will introduce you to the fellows. It will be less awkward, you know."

"Thank you, Oscar. I shall be glad to accept your escort."

When Thursday evening came, Oscar and Harry entered the Society hall arm in arm. Oscar led his companion up to the Secretary and introduced him.

"I am glad to see you, Mr. Walton," said he. "Will you sign your name to the Constitution? That is all the formality we require."

"Except a slight pecuniary disbursement," added Oscar.

"How much is the entrance fee?" asked Harry.

"One dollar. You win pay that to the Treasurer."

Oscar next introduced our hero to the President, and some of the leading members, all of whom welcomed him cordially.

"Good-evening, Mr. Fletcher," said Harry, observing that young gentleman near him.

"Good-evening, sir," said Fletcher stiffly, and turned on his heel without offering his hand.

"Fletcher don't feel well," whispered Oscar. "He had a visit from a poor relation the other day—a tin-peddler—and it gave such a shock to his sensitive system that he hasn't recovered from it yet."

"I didn't imagine Mr. Fletcher had such a plebeian relative," said Harry.

"Nor did any of us. The interview was rich. It amused us all, but what was sport to us was death to poor Fitz. You have only to make the most distant allusion to a tin-peddler in his hearing, and he will become furious."

"Then I will be careful."

"Oh, it won't do any harm. The fact was, the boy was getting too overbearing, and putting on altogether too many airs. The lesson will do him good, or ought to."

Here the Society was called to order, and Oscar and Harry took their seats.

The exercises proceeded in regular order until the President announced a declamation by Fitzgerald Fletcher.

"Mr. President," said Fletcher, rising, "I must ask to be excused. I have not had time to prepare a declamation."

"Mr. President," said Tom Carver, "under the circumstances I hope you will excuse Mr. Fletcher, as during the last week he has had an addition to his family."

There was a chorus of laughter, loud and long, at this sally. All were amused except Fletcher himself, who looked flushed and provoked.

"Mr. Fletcher is excused," said the President, unable to refrain from smiling. "Will any member volunteer to speak in his place? It will be a pity to have our exercises incomplete."

Fletcher was angry, and wanted to be revenged on somebody. A bright idea came to him. He would place the "printer's devil," whose admission to the Society he resented, in an awkward position. He rose with a malicious smile upon his face.

"Mr. President," he said, "doubtless Mr. Walton, the new member who has done us the honor to join our society, will be willing to supply my place."

"We shall certainly be glad to hear a declamation from Mr. Walton, though it is hardly fair to call upon him at such short notice."

"Can't you speak something, Harry?" whispered Oscar. "Don't do it, unless you are sure you can get through."

Harry started in surprise when his name was first mentioned, but he quickly resolved to accept his duty. He had a high reputation at home for speaking, and he had recently learned a spirited poem, familiar, no doubt, to many of my young readers, called "Shamus O'Brien." It is the story of an Irish volunteer, who was arrested for participating in the Irish rebellion of '98, and is by turns spirited and pathetic. Harry had rehearsed it to himself only the night before, and he had confidence in a strong and retentive memory. At the President's invitation he rose to his feet, and said, "Mr. President, I will do as well as I can, but I hope the members of the Society will make allowance for me, as I have had no time for special preparation."

"Shamus O'Brien" is the story that Harry tells at his first Clionian Society meeting.

All eyes were fixed with interest upon our hero, as he advanced to the platform, and, bowing composedly, commenced his declamation. It was not long before that interest increased, as Harry proceeded in his recitation. He lost all diffidence, forgot the audience, and entered thoroughly into the spirit of the piece. Especially when, in the trial scene, Shamus is called upon to plead guilty or not guilty, Harry surpassed himself, and spoke with a spirit and fire which brought down the house. This is the passage:

"My lord, if you ask me, if in my life-time
I thought any treason, or did any crime,
That should call to my cheek, as I stand alone here,
The hot blush of shame, or the coldness of fear,
Though I stood by the grave to receive my death-blow,
Before God and the world I would answer you, no!
But if you would ask me, as I think it like,

If in the rebellion I carried a pike,
An' fought for ould Ireland from the first to the close,
An' shed the heart's blood of her bitterest foes,
I answer you, yes; and I tell you again,
Though I stand here to perish, it's my glory that then
In her cause I was willing my veins should run dhry,
An' that now for her sake I am ready to die."

After the applause had subsided, Harry proceeded, and at the conclusion of the declamation, when he bowed modestly and left the platform, the hall fairly shook with the stamping, in which all joined except Fletcher, who sat scowling with dissatisfaction at a result so different from his hopes. He had expected to bring discomfiture to our hero. Instead, he had given him an opportunity to achieve a memorable triumph.

"You did yourself credit, old boy!" said Oscar, seizing and wringing the hand of Harry, as the latter resumed his seat. "Why, you ought to go on the stage!"

"Thank you," said Harry; "I am glad I got through well."

"Isn't Fitz mad, though? He thought you'd break down. Look at him!"

Harry looked over to Fletcher, who, with a sour expression, was sitting upright, and looking straight before him.

"He don't look happy, does he?" whispered Oscar, comically.

Harry came near laughing aloud, but luckily for Fletcher's peace of mind, succeeded in restraining himself.

"He won't call you up again in a hurry; see if he does," continued Oscar.

"I am sure we have all been gratified by Mr. Walton's spirited declamation," said the President, rising. "We congratulate ourselves upon adding so fine a speaker to our society, and hope often to have the pleasure of hearing him declaim."

There was a fresh outbreak of applause, after which the other exercises followed. When the meeting was over the members of the Society crowded around Harry, and congratulated him on his success. These congratulations he received so modestly, as to confirm the favorable impression he had made by his declamation.

"By Jove, old fellow," said Oscar, as they were walking home, "I am beginning to be proud of you. You are doing great credit to your teacher."

"Thank you, Professor," said Harry. "Don't compliment me too much, or I may become vain, and put on airs."

"If you do, I'll get Fitz to call, and remind you that you are only a printer's devil, after all."

CHAPTER XIII

VACATION BEGINS

AT THE ACADEMY

Not long after his election as a member of the Clionian Society, the summer term of the Prescott Academy closed. The examination took place about the tenth of June, and a vacation followed, lasting till the first day of September. Of course, the Clionian Society, which was composed of Academy students, suspended its meetings for the same length of time. Indeed, the last meeting for the season took place during the first week in June, as the evenings were too short and too warm, and the weather was not favorable to oratory. At the last meeting, an election was held of officers to serve for the following term. The same President and Vice-President were chosen; but as the Secretary declined to serve another term, Harry Walton, considerably to his surprise, found himself elected in his place.

Fitzgerald Fletcher did not vote for him. Indeed, he expressed it as his opinion that it was a shame to elect a "printer's devil" Secretary of the Society.

"Why is it?" said Oscar. "Printing is a department of literature, and the Clionian is a literary society, isn't it?"

"Of course it is a literary society, but a printer's devil is not literary."

"He's as literary as a tin-peddler," said Tom Carver, maliciously.

Fletcher turned red, but managed to say, "And what does that prove?"

"We don't object to you because you are connected with the tin business."

"Do you mean to insult me?" demanded Fletcher, angrily. "What have I to do with the tin business?"

"Oh, I beg pardon, it's your cousin that's in it."

"I deny the relationship," said Fletcher, "and I will thank you not to refer again to that vulgar peddler."

"Really, Fitz, you speak rather roughly, considering he's your cousin. But as to Harry Walton, he's a fine fellow, and he has an excellent handwriting, and I was very glad to vote for him."

Fitzgerald walked away, not a little disgusted, as well at the allusion to the tin-peddler, as at the success of Harry Walton in obtaining an office to which he had himself secretly aspired. He had fancied that it would sound well to put "Secretary of the Clionian Society" after his name, and would give him increased consequence at home. As to the tin-peddler, it would have relieved his mind to hear that Mr. Bickford had been carried off suddenly by an apoplectic fit, and notwithstanding the tie of kindred, he would not have taken the trouble to put on mourning in his honor.

Harry Walton sat in Oscar Vincent's room, on the last evening of the term. He had just finished reciting the last French lesson in which he would have Oscar's assistance for some time to come.

"You have made excellent progress," said Oscar. "It is only two months since you began French, and now you take a long lesson in translation."

"That is because I have so good a teacher. But do you think I can get along without help during the summer?"

"No doubt of it. You may find some difficulties, but those you can mark, and I will explain when I come back. Or I'll tell you what is still better. Write to me, and I'll answer. Shall I write in French?"

"I wish you would, Oscar."

"Then I will. I'm rather lazy with the pen, but I can find time for you. Besides, it will be a good way for me to keep up my French."

"Shall you be in Boston all summer, Oscar?"

"No; our family has a summer residence at Nahant, a sea-shore place twelve miles from Boston. Then I hope father will let me travel about a little on my own account. I want to go to Saratoga and Lake George."

"That would be splendid."

"I wish you could go with me, Harry."

"Thank you, Oscar, but perhaps you can secure Fletcher's company. That will be much better than that of a 'printer's devil' like myself."

"It may show bad taste, but I should prefer your company, notwithstanding your low employment."

"Thank you, Oscar. I am much obliged."

"Fitz has been hinting to me how nice it would be for us to go off somewhere together, but I don't see it in that light. I asked him why he didn't secure board with his cousin, the tin-peddler, but that made him angry, and he walked away in disgust. But I can't help

232

pitying you a little, Harry."

"Why? On account of my occupation?"

"Partly. All these warm summer days, you have got to be working at the case, while I can lounge in the shade, or travel for pleasure. Sha'n't you have a vacation?"

Printers working at a newspaper office. The man in the middle of the picture is working at "the case," which is what Harry did.

"I don't expect any. I don't think I could well be spared. However, I don't mind it. I hope to do a good deal of studying while you are gone."

"And I sha'n't do any."

"Neither would I, perhaps, in your position. But there's a good deal of difference between us. You are a Latin and Greek scholar, and can talk French, while I am at the bottom of the ladder. I have no time to lose."

"You have begun to mount the ladder, Harry. Don't be discouraged. You can climb up."

"But I must work for it. I haven't got high enough up to stop and rest. But there is one question I want to ask you, before you go."

"What is it?"

"What French book would you recommend after I have finished this Reader? I am nearly through now."

"Telemaque will be a good book to take next. It is easy and interesting. Have you got a French dictionary?"

"No; but I can buy one."

"You can use mine while I am gone. You may as well have it as not. I have no copy of Telemaque, but I will send you one from Boston."

"Agreed, provided you will let me pay you for it."

"So I would, if I had to buy one. But I have got an old copy, not very ornamental, but complete. I will send it through the mail."

"Thank you, Oscar. How kind you are!"

"Don't flatter me, Harry. The favors you refer to are but trifles. I will ask a favor of you in return."

"I wish you would."

"Then help me pack my trunk. There's nothing I detest so much. Generally I tumble things in helter-skelter, and get a good scolding from mother for doing it, when she inspects my trunk."

"I'll save you the trouble, then. Bring what you want to carry home, and pile it on the floor, and I'll do the packing."

"A thousand thanks, as the French say. It takes a load off my mind. By the way, here is a lot of my photographs. Would you like one to remember your professor by?"

"Very much, Oscar."

"Then take your choice. They don't do justice to my beauty, which is of a stunning description, as you are aware, nor do they convey an idea of the lofty intellect which sits enthroned behind my classic brow; but such as they are, you are welcome to one."

"Any one would think, to hear you, that you had no end of self-conceit, Oscar," said Harry, laughing.

"How do you know that I haven't? Most people think they are beautiful. A photographer told my sister that he was once visited by a frightfully homely man from the country, who wanted his 'picter took.' When the result was placed before him, he seemed dissatisfied. 'Don't you think it like?' said the artist.b'Well, ye-es,' he answered slowly, 'but it hasn't got my sweet expression about the mouth!'"

"Very good," said Harry, laughing; "that's what's the matter with your picture."

"Precisely. I am glad your artistic eye detects what is wanting. But, hold! There's a knock. It's Fitz, I'll bet a hat."

"Come in!" he cried, and Fletcher walked in.

"Good-evening, Fletcher," said Oscar. "You see I'm packing, or rather Walton is packing. He's a capital packer."

"Indeed!" sneered Fletcher. "I was not aware that Mr. Walton was in that line of business. What are his terms?"

"I refer you to him."

"What do you charge for packing trunks, Mr. Walton?"

"I think fifty cents would be about right," answered Harry, with perfect gravity. "Can you give me a job, Mr. Fletcher?"

"I might, if I had known it in time, though I am particular who handles my things."

"Walton is careful, and I can vouch for his honesty," said Oscar, carrying out the joke. "His wages in the printing office are not large, and he would be glad to make a little extra money."

"It must be very inconvenient to be poor," said Fletcher, with a supercilious glance at our hero, who was kneeling before Oscar's trunk.

"It is," answered Harry, quietly, "but as long as work is to be had I shall not complain."

"To be sure!" said Fletcher. "My father is wealthy, and I shall not have to work."

"Suppose he should fail?" suggested Oscar.

"That is a very improbable supposition," said Fletcher, loftily.

"But not impossible?"

"Nothing is impossible."

"Of course. I say, Fitz, if such a thing should happen, you've got something to fall back upon."

"To what do you refer?"

"Mr. Bickford could give you an interest in the tin business."

"Good-evening!" said Fletcher, not relishing the allusion.

"Good-evening! Of course I shall see you in the city."

"I suppose I ought not to tease Fitz," said Oscar, after his visitor had departed, "but I enjoy seeing how disgusted he looks."

In due time the trunk was packed, and Harry, not without regret, took leave of his friend for the summer.

CHAPTER XIV

HARRY BECOMES AN AUTHOR

The closing of the Academy made quite a difference in the life of Centreville. The number of boarding scholars was about thirty, and these, though few in number, were often seen in the street and at the post office, and their withdrawal left a vacancy. Harry Walton felt quite lonely at first; but there is no cure for loneliness like occupation, and he had plenty of that. The greater part of the day was spent in the printing office, while his evenings and early mornings were occupied in study and reading. He had become very much interested in French, in which he found himself advancing rapidly. Occasionally he took tea at Mr. Ferguson's, and this he always enjoyed; for, as I have already said, he and Ferguson held very similar views on many important subjects. One evening, at the house of the latter, he saw a file of weekly papers, which proved, on examination, to be back numbers of the Weekly Standard, a literary paper issued in Boston.

"I take the paper for my family," said Ferguson. "It contains quite a variety of reading matter, stories, sketches and essays."

"It seems quite interesting," said Harry.

"Yes, it is. I will lend you some of the back numbers, if you like."

"I would like it. My father never took a literary paper; his means were so limited that he could not afford it."

"I think it is a good investment. There are few papers from which you cannot obtain in a year more than the worth of the subscription. Besides, if you are going to be an editor, it will be useful for you to become familiar with the manner in which such papers are conducted."

When Harry went home he took a dozen copies of the paper, and sat up late reading them. While thus engaged an idea struck him. It was this: Could not he write something which would be accepted for publication in the Standard? It was his great ambition to learn to write for the press, and he felt that he was old enough to commence.

"If I don't succeed the first time, I can try again," he reflected.

The more he thought of it, the more he liked the plan. It is very possible that he was influenced by the example of Franklin, who, while yet a boy in his teens, contributed articles to his brother's paper though at the time the authorship was not suspected. Finally he decided to commence writing as soon as he could think of a suitable subject. This he found was not easy. He could think of plenty of subjects of which he was not qualified to write, or in which he felt little interest; but he rightly decided that he could succeed better with something that had a bearing upon his own experience or hopes for the future.

Finally he decided to write on Ambition.

I do not propose to introduce Harry's essay in these pages, but will give a general idea of it, as tending to show his views of life.

He began by defining ambition as a desire for superiority, by which most men were more or less affected, though it manifested itself in very different ways, according to the character of him with whom it was found. Here I will quote a passage, as a specimen of Harry's style and mode of expression.

"There are some who denounce ambition as wholly bad and to be avoided by all; but I think we ought to make a distinction between true and false ambition. The desire of superiority is an honorable motive, if it leads to honorable exertion. I will mention Napoleon as an illustration of false ambition, which is selfish in itself, and has brought misery and ruin, to prosperous nations. Again, there are some who are ambitious to dress better than their neighbors, and their principal thoughts are centered upon the tie of their cravat, or the cut of their coat, if young men; or upon the richness and style of their dresses, if they belong to the other sex. Beau Brummel is a noted instance of this kind of ambition. It is said that fully half of his time was devoted to his toilet, and the other half to displaying it in the streets, or in society. Now this is a very low form of ambition, and it is wrong to indulge it, because it is a waste of time which could be much better employed."

Harry now proceeded to describe what he regarded as a true and praiseworthy ambition. He defined it as a desire to excel in what would be of service to the human race, and he instanced his old Franklin, who, induced by an honorable ambition, worked his way up to a high civil station, as well as a commanding position in the scientific world. He mentioned Columbus as ambitious to extend the limits of geographical knowledge, and made a brief reference to the difficulties and discouragements over which he triumphed on the way to success. He closed by an appeal to boys and young men to direct their ambition into worthy channels, so that even if they could not leave behind a great name, they might at least lead useful lives, and in dying have the satisfaction of thinking that they had done some service to the race.

This will give a very fair idea of Harry's essay. There was nothing remarkable about it, and no striking originality in the ideas, but it was very creditably expressed for a boy of his years, and did even more credit to his good judgment, since it was an unfolding of the principles by which he meant to guide his own life.

It must not be supposed that our hero was a genius, and that he wrote his essay without difficulty. It occupied him two evenings to write it, and he employed the third in revising and copying it. It covered about five pages of manuscript, and, according to his estimate, would fill about two-thirds of a long column in the Standard.

After preparing it, the next thing was to find a nom de plume, for he shrank from signing his own name. After long consideration, he at last decided upon Franklin, and this was the name he signed to his maiden contribution to the press.

He carried it to the post office one afternoon, after his work in the printing office was over, and dropped it unobserved into the letterbox. He did not want the postmaster to learn his secret, as he would have done had he received it directly from him, and noted the address on the envelope.

For the rest of the week, Harry went about his work weighed down with his important secret—a secret which he had not even shared with Ferguson. If the essay was declined, as he thought it might very possibly be, he did not want any one to know it. If it were accepted, and printed, it would be time enough then to make it known. But there were few minutes in which his mind was not on his literary venture. His preoccupation was observed by his fellow-workmen in the office, and he was rallied upon it, good-naturedly, by Ferguson, but in a different spirit by Clapp.

"It seems to me you are unusually silent, Harry," said Ferguson.

"You're not in love, are you?"

"Not that I know of," said Harry, smiling. "It's rather too early yet."

"I've known boys of your age to fancy themselves in love."

"He is more likely thinking up some great discovery," said Clapp, sneering. "You know he's a second Franklin."

"Thank you for the compliment," said our hero, good-humoredly, "but I don't deserve it. I don't expect to make any great discovery at present."

"I suppose you expect to set the river on fire, some day," said Clapp, sarcastically.

"I am afraid it wouldn't do much good to try," said Harry, who was too sensible to take offense. "It isn't so easily done."

"I suppose some day we shall be proud of having been in the same office with so great a man," pursued Clapp.

"Really, Clapp, you're rather hard on our young friend," said Ferguson. "He doesn't put on any airs of superiority, or pretend to anything uncommon."

"He's very kind—such an intellect as he's got, too!" said Clapp.

"I'm glad you found it out," said Harry. "I haven't a very high idea of my intellect yet. I wish I had more reason to do so."

Finding that he had failed in his attempt to provoke Harry by his ridicule, Clapp desisted, but he disliked him none the less.

The fact was, that Clapp was getting into a bad way. He had no high aim in life, and cared chiefly for the pleasure of the present moment. He had found Luke Harrison a congenial companion, and they had been associated in more than one excess. The morning previous, Clapp had entered the printing office so evidently under the influence of liquor, that he had been sharply reprimanded by Mr. Anderson.

"I don't choose to interfere with your mode of life, unwise and ruinous as I may consider it," he said, "as long as it does not interfere with your discharge of duty. But today you are clearly incapacitated for labor, and I have a right to complain. If it happens again, I shall be obliged to look for another journeyman."

Clapp did not care to leave his job just at present, for he had no money saved up, and was even somewhat in debt, and it might be some time before he got another job. So he rather sullenly agreed to be more careful in the future, and did not go to work till the afternoon. But though circumstances compelled him to submit, it put him in bad humor, and made him more disposed to sneer than ever. He had an unreasoning prejudice against Harry, which was stimulated by Luke Harrison, who had this very sufficient reason for hating our hero, that he had succeeded in injuring him. As an old proverb has it "We are slow to forgive those whom we have injured."

CHAPTER XV

A LITERARY DEBUT

Harry waited eagerly for the next issue of the Weekly Standard. It was received by Mr. Anderson in exchange for the Centreville Gazette, and usually came to hand on Saturday morning. Harry was likely to obtain the first chance of examining the paper, as he was ordinarily sent to the post office on the arrival of the morning mail.

His hands trembled as he unfolded the paper and hurriedly scanned the contents. But he looked in vain for his essay on Ambition. There was not even a reference to it. He was disappointed, but he soon became hopeful again.

"I couldn't expect it to appear so soon," he reflected. "These city weeklies have to be printed some days in advance. It may appear yet."

So he was left in suspense another week, hopeful and doubtful by turns of the success of his first offering for the press. He was rallied from time to time on his silence in the office, but he continued to keep his secret. If his contribution was slighted, no one should know it but himself.

At last another Saturday morning came around and again he set out for the post office. Again he opened the paper with trembling fingers, and eagerly scanned the well-filled columns. This time his search was rewarded. There, on the first column of the last page, in all the glory of print, was his treasured essay!

A flash of pleasure tinged his cheek, and his heart beat rapidly, as he read his first printed production. It is a great event in the life of a literary novice, when he first sees himself. Even Byron says, "'Tis pleasant, sure, to see one's self in print."

To our young hero the essay read remarkably well—better than he had expected; but then, very likely he was prejudiced in its favor. He read it through three times on his way back to the printing office, and each time felt better satisfied.

"I wonder if any of the readers will think it was written by a boy?" thought Harry. Probably many did so suspect, for, as I have said, though the thoughts were good and sensible, the article was only moderately well expressed. A practiced critic would readily have detected marks of immaturity, although it was a very creditable production for a boy of sixteen.

"Shall I tell Ferguson?" thought Harry.

On the whole he concluded to remain silent just at present. He knew Ferguson took the paper, and waited to see if he would make any remark about it.

"I should like to hear him speak of it, without knowing that I was the writer," thought our hero.

Just before he reached the office, he discovered with satisfaction the following editorial reference to his article:

"We print in another column an essay on 'ambition' by a new contributor. It contains some good ideas, and we especially commend it to the perusal of our young readers. We hope to hear from 'Franklin' again."

"That's good," thought Harry. "I am glad the editor likes it. I shall write again as soon as possible."

"What makes you look so bright, Harry?" asked Ferguson, as he re-entered the office. "Has any one left you a fortune?"

"Not that I know of," said Harry. "Do I look happier than usual?"

"So it seems to me."

Harry was spared answering this question, for Clapp struck in, grumbling, as usual: "I wish somebody'd leave me a fortune. You wouldn't see me here long."

"What would you do?" asked his fellow-workman.

"Cut work to begin with. I'd go to Europe and have a jolly time."

"You can do that without a fortune."

"I should like to know how?"

"Be economical, and you can save enough in three years to pay for a short trip. Bayard Taylor was gone two years, and only spent five hundred dollars."

"Oh, hang economy!" drawled Clapp. "It don't suit me. I should like to know how a feller's going to economize on fifteen dollars a week."

"I could."

"Oh, no doubt," sneered Clapp, "but a man can't starve."

"Come round and take dinner with me, some night," said Ferguson, good-humoredly, "and you can judge for yourself whether I believe in starving."

Clapp didn't reply to this invitation. He would not have enjoyed a quiet evening with his fellow-workman. An evening at billiards or cards, accompanied by bets on the games, would have been much more to his mind.

"Who is Bayard Taylor, that made such a cheap tour in Europe?" asked Harry, soon afterward.

"A young journalist who had a great desire to travel. He has lately published an account of his tour. I don't buy many books, but I bought that. Would you like to read it?"

"Very much."

"You can have it any time."

"Thank you."

On Monday, a very agreeable surprise awaited Harry.

"I am out of copy," he said, going up to Mr. Anderson's table.

"Here's a selection for the first page," said Mr. Anderson. "Cut it in two, and give part of it to Clapp."

Could Harry believe his eyes! It was his own article on ambition, and it was to be reproduced in the Gazette. Next to the delight of seeing one's self in print for the first time, is the delight of seeing that first article copied. It is a mark of appreciation which cannot be mistaken.

Still Harry said nothing, but, with a manner as unconcerned as possible, handed the lower half of the essay to Clapp to set up. The signature "Franklin" had been cut off, and the name of the paper from which the essay had been cut was substituted.

"Wouldn't Clapp feel disgusted," thought Harry, "if he knew that he was setting up an article of mine. I believe he would have a fit."

He was too considerate to expose his fellow-workman to such a contingency, and went about his work in silence.

That evening he wrote to the publisher of the Standard, inclosing the price of two copies of the last number, which he desired should be sent to him by mail. He wished to keep one himself, and the other he intended to forward to his father, who, he knew, would sympathize with him in his success as well as his aspirations. He accompanied the paper by a letter in which he said, "I want to improve in writing as much as I can. I want to be something more than a printer, sometime. I shall try to qualify myself for an editor; for an editor can exert a good deal of influence in the community. I hope you will approve my plans."

In due time Harry received the following reply:

"My dear son: I am indeed pleased and proud to hear of your success, not that it is a great matter in itself, but because I think it shows that you are in earnest in your determination to win an honorable position by honorable labor. I am sorry that my narrow means have not permitted me to give you those advantages which wealthy fathers can bestow upon their sons. I should like to have sent you to college and given you an opportunity afterward of studying for a profession. I think your natural abilities would have justified such an outlay. But, alas! Poverty has always held me back. It shuts out you, as it has shut out me, from the chance of culture. Your college, my boy, must be the printing office. If you make the best of that, you will find that it is no mean instructor. Not Franklin alone, but many of our most eminent and influential men have graduated from it.

"You will be glad to hear that we are all well. I have sold the cow which I bought of Squire Green, and got another in her place that proves to be much better. We all send much love, and your mother wishes me to say that she misses you very much, as indeed we all do. But we know that you are better off in Centreville than you would be at home, and that helps to make us contented. Don't forget to write every week.

"Your affectionate father,

"HIRAM WALTON.

"P. S.—If you print any more articles, we shall be interested to read them."

Harry read this letter with eager interest. He felt glad that his father was pleased with him, and it stimulated him to increased exertions.

"Poor father!" he said to himself. "He has led a hard life, cultivating that rocky little farm. It has been hard work and poor pay with him. I hope there is something better in store for him. If I ever get rich, or even well off, I will take care that he has an easier time."

After the next issue of the Gazette had appeared, Harry informed Ferguson in confidence that he was the author of the article on Ambition.

"I congratulate you, Harry," said his friend. "It is an excellent essay, well thought out, and well expressed. I don't wonder, now you tell me of it. It sounds like you. Without knowing the authorship, I asked Clapp his opinion of it."

"What did he say?"

"Are you sure it won't hurt your feelings?"

"It may; but I shall get over it. Go ahead."

"He said it was rubbish."

Harry laughed.

"He would be confirmed in his decision, if he knew that I wrote it," he said.

"No doubt. But don't let that discourage you. Keep on writing by all means, and you'll become an editor in time."

CHAPTER XVI

FERDINAND B. KENSINGTON

It has already been mentioned that John Clapp and Luke Harrison were close. Though their occupations differed, one being a printer and the other a shoemaker, they had similar tastes, and took similar views of life. Both were discontented with the lot which Fortune had assigned them. To work at the case, or the shoe-bench, seemed equally irksome, and they often lamented to each other the hard necessity which compelled them to it. Suppose we listen to their conversation, as they walked up the village street, one evening about this time, smoking cigars.

"I say, Luke," said John Clapp, "I've got tired of this kind of life. Here I've been in the office a year, and I'm not a cent richer than when I entered it, besides working like a dog all the while."

"Just my case," said Luke. "I've been shoe-makin' ever since I was fourteen, and I'll be blest if I can show five dollars, to save my life."

"What's worse," said Clapp, "there isn't any prospect of anything better in my case. What's a feller to do on fifteen dollars a week?"

"Won't old Anderson raise your wages?"

"Not he! He thinks I ought to get rich on what he pays me now," and Clapp laughed scornfully. "If I were like Ferguson, I might. He never spends a cent without taking twenty-four hours to think it over beforehand."

My readers, who are familiar with Mr. Ferguson's views and ways of life, will at once see that this was unjust, but justice cannot be expected from an angry and discontented man.

"Just so," said Luke. "If a feller was to live on bread and water, and get along with one suit of clothes a year, he might save something, but that ain't my style."

"Nor mine."

"It's strange how lucky some men are," said Luke. "They get rich without tryin'. I never was lucky. I bought a ticket in a lottery once, but of course I didn't draw anything. Just my luck!"

"So did I," said Clapp, "but I fare no better. It seemed as if Fortune had a spite against me. Here I am twenty-five years old, and all I'm worth is two dollars and a half, and I owe more than that to the tailor."

"You're as rich as I am," said Luke. "I only get fourteen dollars a week. That's less than you do."

"A dollar more or less don't amount to much," said Clapp. "I'll tell you what it is, Luke," he resumed after a pause, "I'm getting sick of Centreville."

"So am I," said Luke, "but it don't make much difference. If I had fifty dollars, I'd go off and try my luck somewhere else, but I'll have to wait till I'm gray-headed before I get as much as that."

"Can't you borrow it?"

"Who'd lend it to me?"

"I don't know. If I did, I'd go in for borrowing myself. I wish there was some way of my getting to California."

"California!" repeated Luke with interest. "What would you do there?"

"I'd go to the mines."

"Do you think there's money to be made there?"

"I know there is," said Clapp, emphatically.

"How do you know it?"

"There's an old school-mate of mine—Ralph Smith—went out there two years ago. Last week he returned home—I heard it in a letter—and how much do you think he brought with him?"

"How much?"

"Eight thousand dollars!"

"Eight thousand dollars! He didn't make it all at the mines, did he?"

"Yes, he did. When he went out there, he had just money enough to pay his passage. Now, after only two years, he can lay off and live like a gentleman."

"He's been lucky, and no mistake."

"You bet he has. But we might be as lucky if we were only out there."

"Ay, there's the rub. A fellow can't travel for nothing."

At this point in their conversation, a well-dressed young man, evidently a stranger in the village, met them, and stopping, asked politely for a light.

This Clapp afforded him.

"You are a stranger in the village?" he said, with some curiosity.

"Yes, I was never here before. I come from New York."

"Indeed! If I lived in New York I'd stay there, and not come to such a beastly place as Centreville."

"Do you live here?" asked the stranger.

"Yes."

"I wonder you live in such a beastly place," he said, with a smile.

"You wouldn't, if you knew the reason."

"What is the reason?"

"I can't get away."

The stranger laughed.

"Cruel parents?" he asked.

"Not much," said Clapp. "The plain reason is, that I haven't got money enough to get me out of town."

"It's the same with me," said Luke Harrison.

"Gentlemen, we are well met," said the stranger. "I'm hard up myself."

"You don't look like it," said Luke, glancing at his rather flashy attire.

"These clothes are not paid for," said the stranger, laughing; "and what's more, I don't think they are likely to be. But, I take it, you gentlemen are better off than I in one respect. You've got situations—something to do."

"Yes, but on starvation pay," said Clapp. "I'm in the office of the Centreville Gazette."

"And I'm in a shoemaker's shop. It's a beastly business for a young man of spirit," said Luke.

"Well, I'm a gentleman at large, living on my wits, and pretty poor living it is sometimes," said the stranger. "As I think we'll agree together pretty well, I'm glad I've met you. We ought to know each other better. There's my card."

He drew from his pocket a highly glazed piece of pasteboard, bearing the name,

FREDERICK B. KENSINGTON.

"I haven't any cards with me," said Clapp, "but my name is John Clapp."

"And mine is Luke Harrison," said the bearer of that appellation.

"I'm proud to know you, gentlemen. If you have no objection, we'll walk on together."

To this Clapp and Luke acceded readily. Indeed, they were rather proud of being seen in company with a young man so dashing in manner, and fashionably dressed, though in a pecuniary way their new acquaintance, by his own confession, was scarcely as well off as themselves.

"Where are you staying, Mr. Kensington?" said Clapp.

"At the hotel. It's a poor place. No style."

"Of course not. I can't help wondering, Mr. Kensington, what can bring you to such a one-horse place as this."

"I don't mind telling you, then. The fact is, I've got an old aunt living about two miles from here. She's alone in the world—got neither chick nor child—and is worth at least ten thousand dollars. Do you see?"

"I think I do," said Clapp. "You want to come in for a share of the stamps."

"Yes; I want to see if I can't get something out of the old girl," said Kensington, carelessly.

"Do you think the chance is good?"

"I don't know. I hear she's pretty tight-fisted. But I've run on here on the chance of doing something. If she will only make me her heir, and give me five hundred dollars in hand, I'll go to California, and see what'll turn up."

"California!" repeated John Clapp and Luke in unison.

"Yes; were you ever there?"

"No; but we were talking of going there just as you came up," said John. "An old school-mate of mine has just returned from there with eight thousand dollars in gold."

"Lucky fellow! That's the kind of haul I'd like to make."

"Do you know how much it costs to go out there?"

"The prices are down just at present. You can go for a hundred dollars—second cabin."

"It might as well be a thousand!" said Luke. "Clapp and I can't raise a hundred dollars apiece to save our lives."

"I'll tell you what," said Kensington. "You two fellows are just the company I'd like. If I can raise five hundred dollars out of the old girl, I'll take you along with me, and you can pay me after you get out there."

John Clapp and Luke Harrison were astounded at this liberal offer from a perfect stranger, but they had no motives of delicacy about accepting it. They grasped the hand of their new friend, and assured him that nothing would suit them so well.

"All right!" said Kensington. "Then it's agreed. Now, boys, suppose we go round to the tavern, and ratify our compact by a drink."

"I say amen to that," answered Clapp, "but I insist on standing treat."

"Just as you say," said Kensington. "Come along."

It was late when the three parted company. Luke and John Clapp were delighted with their new friend, and, as they staggered home with uncertain steps, they indulged in bright visions of future prosperity.

CHAPTER XVII

AUNT DEBORAH

Miss Deborah Kensington sat in an old-fashioned rocking-chair covered with a cheap print, industriously engaged in footing a stocking. She was a maiden lady of about sixty, with a thin face, thick seamed with wrinkles, a prominent nose, bridged by spectacles, sharp gray eyes, and thin lips. She was a shrewd New England woman, who knew very well how to take care of and increase the property which she had inherited. Her nephew had been correctly informed as to her being close-fisted. All her establishment was carried on with due regard to economy, and though her income in the eyes of a city man would be counted small, she saved half of it every year, thus increasing her accumulations.

As she sat placidly knitting, an interruption came in the shape of a knock at the front door.

"I'll go myself," she said, rising, and laying down the stocking. "Hannah's out in the back room, and won't hear. I hope it ain't Mrs. Smith, come to borrow some butter. She ain't returned that last half-pound she borrowed. She seems to think her neighbors have got to support her."

These thoughts were in her mind as she opened the door. But no Mrs. Smith presented her figure to the old lady's gaze. She saw instead, with considerable surprise, a stylish young man with a book under his arm. She jumped to the conclusion that he was a book-peddler, having been annoyed by several persistent specimens of that class of travelling merchants.

"If you've got books to sell," she said, opening the attack, "you may as well go away. I ain't got no money to throw away."

Mr. Ferdinand B. Kensington—for he was the young man in question—laughed heartily, while the old lady stared at him half amazed, half angry.

"I don't see what there is to laugh at," said she, offended.

"I was laughing at the idea of my being taken for a book-peddler."

"Well, ain't you one?" she retorted. "If you ain't, what be you?"

"Aunt Deborah, don't you know me?" asked the young man, familiarly.

"Who are you that calls me aunt?" demanded the old lady, puzzled.

"I'm your brother Henry's son. My name is Ferdinand."

"You don't say so!" exclaimed the old lady. "Why, I'd never 'ave thought it. I ain't seen you since you was a little boy."

"This don't look as if I was a little boy, aunt," said the young man, touching his luxuriant whiskers.

"How time passes, I do declare!" said Deborah. "Well, come in, and we'll talk over old times. Where did you come from?"

"From the city of New York. That's where I've been living for some time."

"You don't say! Well, what brings you this way?"

"To see you, Aunt Deborah. It's so long since I've seen you that I thought I'd like to come."

"I'm glad to see you, Ferdinand," said the old lady, flattered by such a degree of dutiful attention from a fine-looking young man. "So your poor father's dead?"

"Yes, aunt, he's been dead three years."

"I suppose he didn't leave much. He wasn't very forehanded."

"No, aunt; he left next to nothing."

"Well, it didn't matter much, seein' as you was the only child, and big enough to take care of yourself."

"Still, aunt, it would have been comfortable if he had left me a few thousand dollars."

"Ain't you doin' well? You look as if you was," said Deborah, surveying critically her nephew's good clothes.

"Well, I've been earning a fair salary, but it's very expensive living in a great city like New York."

"Humph! That's accordin' as you manage. If you live snug, you can get along there cheap as well as anywhere, I reckon. What was you doin'?"

"I was a salesman for A. T. Stewart, our leading dry-goods merchant."

"What pay did you get?"

"A thousand dollars a year."

"Why, that's a fine salary. You'd ought to save up a good deal."

"You don't realize how much it costs to live in New York, aunt. Of course, if I lived here, I could live on half the sum, but I have to pay high prices for everything in New York."

"You don't need to spend such a sight on dress," said Deborah, disapprovingly.

"I beg your pardon, Aunt Deborah; that's where you are mistaken. The store-keepers in New York expect you to dress tip-top and look genteel, so as to do credit to them. If it hadn't been for that, I shouldn't have spent half so much for dress. Then, board's very expensive."

"You can get boarded here for two dollars and a half a week," said Aunt Deborah.

"Two dollars and a half! Why, I never paid less than eight dollars a week in the city, and you can only get poor board for that."

"The boarding-houses must make a great deal of money," said Deborah.

"If I was younger, I'd maybe go to New York, and keep one myself."

"You're rich, aunt. You don't need to do that."

"Who told you I was rich?" said the old lady, quickly.

"Why, you've only got yourself to take care of, and you own this farm, don't you?"

"Yes, but farmin' don't pay much."

"I always heard you were pretty comfortable."

"So I am," said the old lady, "and maybe I save something; but my income ain't as great as yours."

"You have only yourself to look after, and it is cheap living in Centreville."

"I don't fling money away. I don't spend quarter as much as you on dress."

Looking at the old lady'a faded bombazine dress, Ferdinand was very ready to believe this.

"You don't have to dress here, I suppose," he answered. "But, aunt, we won't talk about money matters just yet. It was funny you took me for a book-peddler."

"It was that book you had, that made me think so."

"It's a book I brought as a present to you, Aunt Deborah."

"You don't say!" said the old lady, gratified. "What is it? Let me look at it."

"It's a copy of 'Pilgrim's Progress,' illustrated. I knew you wouldn't like the trashy books they write nowadays, so I brought you this."

"Really, Ferdinand, you're very considerate," said Aunt Deborah, turning over the leaves with manifest pleasure. "It's a good book, and I shall be glad to have it. Where are you stoppin'?"

"At the hotel in the village."

"You must come and stay here. You can get 'em to send round your things any time."

"Thank you, aunt, I shall be delighted to do so. It seems so pleasant to see you again after so many years. You don't look any older than when I saw you last."

Miss Deborah knew very well that she did look older, but still she was pleased by the compliment. Is there any one who does not like to receive the same assurance?

"I'm afraid your eyes ain't very sharp, Ferdinand," she said. "I feel I'm gettin' old. Why, I'm sixty-one, come October."

"Are you? I shouldn't call you over fifty, from your looks, aunt. Really I shouldn't."

"I'm afraid you tell fibs sometimes," said Aunt Deborah, but she said it very graciously, and surveyed her nephew very kindly. "Heigh ho! It's a good while since your poor father and I were children together, and went to the school-house on the hill. Now he's gone, and I'm left alone."

"Not alone, aunt. If he is dead, you have got a nephew."

"Well, Ferdinand, I'm glad to see you, and I shall be glad to have you pay me a good long visit. But how can you be away from your job so long? Did Mr. Stewart give you a vacation?"

"No, aunt; I left him."

"For good?"

"Yes."

"Left a job where you was gettin' a thousand dollars a year!" said the old lady in accents of strong disapproval.

"Yes, aunt."

"Then I think you was very foolish," said Deborah with emphasis.

"Perhaps you won't, when you know why I left it."

"Why did you?"

"Because I could do better."

"Better than a thousand dollars a year!" said Deborah with surprise.

"Yes, I am offered two thousand dollars in San Francisco."

253

"You don't say!" exclaimed Deborah, letting her stocking drop in sheer amazement.

"Yes, I do. It's a positive fact."

"You must be a smart clerk!"

"Well, it isn't for me to say," said Ferdinand, laughing.

"When be you goin' out?"

"In a week, but I thought I must come and bid you good-bye first."

"I'm real glad to see you, Ferdinand," said Aunt Deborah, the more warmly because she considered him so prosperous that she would have no call to help him. But here she was destined to find herself mistaken.

CHAPTER XVIII

AUNT AND NEPHEW

"I don't think I can come here till tomorrow, Aunt Deborah," said Ferdinand, a little later. "I'll stay at the hotel tonight, and come round with my baggage in the morning."

"Very well, nephew, but now you're here, you must stay to tea."

"Thank you, aunt, I will."

"I little thought this mornin', I should have Henry's son to tea," said Aunt Deborah, half to herself. "You don't look any like him, Ferdinand."

"No, I don't think I do."

"It's curis too, for you was his very picter when you was a boy."

"I've changed a good deal since then, Aunt Deborah," said her nephew, a little uneasily.

"So you have, to be sure. Now there's your hair used to be almost black, now it's brown. Really I can't account for it," and Aunt Deborah surveyed the young man over her spectacles.

"You've got a good memory, aunt," said Ferdinand with a forced laugh.

"Now ef your hair had grown darker, I shouldn't have wondered," pursued Aunt Deborah; "but it ain't often black turns to brown."

"That's so, aunt, but I can explain it," said Ferdinand, after a slight pause.

"How was it?"

"You know the French barbers can change your hair to any shade you want."

"Can they?"

"Yes, to be sure. Now—don't laugh at me, aunt—a young lady I used to like didn't fancy dark hair, so I went to a French barber, and he changed the color for me in three months."

"You don't say!"

"Fact, aunt; but he made me pay him well too."

"How much did you give him?"

"Fifty dollars, aunt."

"That's what I call wasteful," said Aunt Deborah, disapprovingly.

"Couldn't you be satisfied with the nat'ral color of your hair? To my mind black's handsomer than brown."

"You're right, aunt. I wouldn't have done it if it hadn't been for Miss Percival."

"Are you engaged to her?"

"No, Aunt Deborah. The fact was, I found she wasn't domestic, and didn't know anything about keeping house, but only cared for dress, so I drew off, and she's married to somebody else now."

"I'm glad to hear it," said Deborah, emphatically. "The jade! She wouldn't have been a proper wife for you. You want some good girl that's willin' to go into the kitchen, and look after things, and not carry all she's worth on her back."

"I agree with you, aunt," said Ferdinand, who thought it politic, in view of the request he meant to make by and by, to agree with his aunt in her views of what a wife should be.

Aunt Deborah began to regard her nephew as quite a sensible young man, and to look upon him with complacency.

"I wish, Ferdinand," she said, "you liked farmin'."

"Why, aunt?"

"You could stay here, and manage my farm for me."

"Heaven forbid!" thought the young man with a shudder. "I should be bored to death. Does the old lady think I would put on a frock and overalls, and go out and plough, or hoe potatoes?"

"It's a good, healthy business," pursued Aunt Deborah, unconscious of the thoughts which were passing through her nephew's mind, "and you wouldn't have to spend much for dress. Then I'm gittin' old, and though I don't want to make no promises, I'd very likely will it to you, ef I was satisfied with the way you managed."

"You're very kind, aunt," said Ferdinand, "but I'm afraid I wasn't cut out for farming. You know I never lived in the country."

"Why, yes, you did," said the old lady. "You was born in the country, and lived there till you was ten years old."

"To be sure," said Ferdinand, hastily, "but I was too young then to take notice of farming. What does a boy of ten know of such things?"

"To be sure. You're right there."

"The fact is, Aunt Deborah, some men are born to be farmers, and some are born to be traders. Now, I've got a talent for trading. That's the reason I've got such a good offer from San Francisco."

"How did you get it? Did you know the man?"

"He used to be in business in New York. He was the first man I worked for, and he knew what I was. San Francisco is full of money, and traders make more than they do here. That's the reason he can afford to offer me so large a salary."

"When did he send for you?"

"I got the letter last week."

"Have you got it with you?"

"No, aunt; I may have it at the hotel," said the young man, hesitating, "but I am not certain."

"Well, it's a good offer. There isn't nobody in Centreville gets so large a salary."

"No, I suppose not. They don't need it, as it is cheap living here."

"I hope when you get out there, Ferdinand, you'll save up money. You'd ought to save two-thirds of your pay."

"I will try to, aunt."

"You'll be wantin' to get married bimeby, and then it'll be convenient to have some money to begin with."

"To be sure, aunt. I see you know how to manage."

"I was always considered a good manager," said Deborah, complacently. "Ef your poor father had had my faculty, he wouldn't have died as poor as he did, I can tell you."

"What a conceited old woman she is, with her faculty!" thought Ferdinand, but what he said was quite different.

"I wish he had had, aunt. It would have been better for me."

"Well, you ought to get along, with your prospects."

"Little the old woman knows what my real prospects are!" thought the young man.

"Of course I ought," he said.

"Excuse me a few minutes, nephew," said Aunt Deborah, gathering up her knitting and rising from her chair. "I must go out and see about tea. Maybe you'd like to read that nice book you brought."

"No, I thank you, aunt. I think I'll take a little walk round your place, if you'll allow me."

"Sartin, Ferdinand. Only come back in half an hour; tea'll be ready then."

"Yea, aunt, I'll remember."

So while Deborah was in the kitchen, Ferdinand took a walk in the fields, laughing to himself from time to time, as if something amused him.

He returned in due time, and sat down to dinner. Aunt Deborah had provided her best, and, though the dishes were plain, they were quite palatable.

When dinner was over, the young man said, "Now, aunt, I think I will be getting back to the hotel."

"You'll come over in the morning, Ferdinand, and fetch your trunk?"

"Yes, aunt. Good-night."

"Good-night."

"Well," thought the young man, as he tramped back to the hotel. "I've opened the campaign, and made, I believe, a favorable impression. But what a pack of lies I have had to tell, to be sure! The old lady came near catching me once or twice, particularly about the color of my hair. It was a lucky thought, that about the French barber. It deceived the poor old soul. I don't think she could ever have been very pretty. If she was she must have changed fearfully."

In the evening, John Clapp and Luke Harrison came round to the hotel to see him.

"Have you been to see your aunt?" asked Clapp.

"Yes, I took tea there."

"Have a good time?"

"Oh, I played the dutiful nephew to perfection. The old lady thinks a sight of me."

"How did you do it?"

"I agreed with all she said, told her how young she looked, and humbugged her generally."

Clapp laughed.

"The best part of the joke is—will you promise to keep dark?"

"Of course."

"Don't breathe it to a living soul, you two fellows. She isn't my aunt at all!"

"Isn't your aunt?"

"No, her true nephew is in New York—I know him—but I know enough of family matters to gull the old lady, and, I hope, raise a few hundred dollars out of her."

This was a joke which Luke and Clapp could appreciate, and they laughed heartily at the deception which was being practiced on simple Aunt Deborah, particularly when Ferdinand explained how he got over the difficulty of having different colored hair from the real owner of the name he assumed.

"We must have a drink on that," said Luke. "Walk up, gentlemen."

"I'm agreeable," said Ferdinand.

"And I," said Clapp. "Never refuse a good offer, say I."

Poor Aunt Deborah! She little dreamed that she was the dupe of a designing adventurer who bore no relationship to her.

CHAPTER XIX

THE ROMANCE OF A RING

Ferdinand B. Kensington, as he called himself, removed the next morning to the house of Aunt Deborah. The latter received him very cordially, partly because it was a pleasant relief to her solitude to have a lively and active young man in the house, partly because she was not forced to look upon him as a poor relation in need of pecuniary assistance. She even felt considerable respect for the prospective recipient of an income of two thousand dollars, which in her eyes was a magnificent salary.

Ferdinand, on his part, spared no pains to make himself agreeable to the old lady, whom he had a mercenary object in pleasing. Finding that she was curious to hear about the great city, which to her was as unknown as London or Paris, he gratified her by long accounts, chiefly of as imaginative character, to which she listened greedily. These included some personal adventures, in all of which he figured very creditably.

Here is a specimen.

"By the way, Aunt Deborah," he said, casually, "have you noticed this ring on my middle finger?"

"No, I didn't notice it before, Ferdinand. It's very handsome."

"I should think it ought to be, Aunt Deborah," said the young man.

"Why?"

"It cost enough to be handsome."

"How much did it cost?" asked the old lady, not without curiosity.

"Guess."

"I ain't no judge of such things; I've only got this plain gold ring. Yours has got some sort of a stone in it."

"That stone is a diamond, Aunt Deborah!"

"You don't say so! Let me look at it. It ain't got no color. Looks like glass."

"It's very expensive, though. How much do you think it cost?"

"Well, maybe five dollars."

"Five dollars!" exclaimed the young man. "Why, what can you be thinking of, Aunt Deborah?"

260

"I shouldn't have guessed so much," said the old lady, misunderstanding him, "only you said it was expensive."

"So it is. Five dollars would be nothing at all."

"You don't say it cost more?"

"A great deal more."

"Did it cost ten dollars?"

"More."

"Fifteen?"

"I see, aunt, you have no idea of the cost of diamond rings! You may believe me or not, but that ring cost six hundred and fifty dollars."

"What!" almost screamed Aunt Deborah, letting fall her knitting in her surprise.

"It's true."

"Six hundred and fifty dollars for a little piece of gold and glass!" exclaimed the old lady.

"Diamond, aunt, not glass."

"Well, it don't look a bit better'n glass, and I do say," proceeded Deborah, with energy, "that it's a sin and a shame to pay so much money for a ring. Why, it was more than half your year's salary, Ferdinand."

"I agree with you, aunt; it would have been very foolish and wrong for a young man on a small salary like mine to buy so expensive a ring as this. I hope, Aunt Deborah, I have inherited too much of your good sense to do that."

"Then where did you get it?" asked the old lady, moderating her tone.

"It was given to me."

"Given to you! Who would give you such a costly present?"

"A rich man whose life I once saved, Aunt Deborah."

"You don't say so, Ferdinand!" said Aunt Deborah, interested. "Tell me all about it."

"So I will, aunt, though I don't often speak of it," said Ferdinand, modestly. "It seems like boasting, you know, and I never like to do that. But this is the way it happened.

"Now for a good tough lie!" said Ferdinand to himself, as the old lady suspended her work, and bent forward with eager attention.

"You know, of course, that New York and Brooklyn are on opposite sides of the river, and that people have to go across in ferryboats."

261

"Yes, I've heard that, Ferdinand."

"I'm glad of that, because now you'll know that my story is correct. Well, one summer I boarded over in Brooklyn—on the Heights—and used to cross the ferry morning and night. It was the Wall Street ferry, and a great many bankers and rich merchants used to cross daily also. One of these was a Mr. Clayton, a wholesale dry-goods merchant, immensely rich, whom I knew by sight, though I had never spoken to him. It was one Thursday morning—I remember even the day of the week—when the boat was unusually full. Mr. Clayton was leaning against the side-railing talking to a friend, when all at once the railing gave way, and he fell backward into the water, which immediately swallowed him up."

"Merciful man!" exclaimed Aunt Deborah, intensely interested. "Go on, Ferdinand."

"Of course there was a scene of confusion and excitement," continued Ferdinand, dramatically. 'Man overboard! Who will save him?' said more than one. 'I will,' I exclaimed, and in an instant I had sprang over the railing into the boiling current."

"Weren't you frightened to death?" asked the old lady. "Could you swim?"

"Of course I could. More than once I have swum all the way from New York to Brooklyn. I caught Mr. Clayton by the collar, as he was sinking for the third time, and shouted to a boatman nearby to come to my help. Well, there isn't much more to tell. We were taken on board the boat, and rowed to shore. Mr. Clayton recovered his senses so far as to realize that I had saved his life.

"'What is your name, young man?' he asked, grasping my hand.

"'Ferdinand B. Kensington,' I answered modestly.

"'You have saved my life,' he said warmly.

"'I am very glad of it,' said I.

"'You have shown wonderful bravery.'

"'Oh no,' I answered. 'I know how to swim, and I wasn't going to see you drown before my eyes.'

"'I shall never cease to be grateful to you.'

"'Oh, don't think of it,' said I.

"'But I must think of it,' he answered. 'But for you I should now be a senseless corpse lying in the bottom of the river,' and he shuddered.

"'Mr. Clayton,' said I, 'let me advise you to get home as soon as possible, or you will catch your death of cold.'

"'So will you,' he said. 'You must come with me.'

"He insisted, so I went, and was handsomely treated, you may depend. Mr. Clayton gave me a new suit of clothes, and the next morning he took me to Tiffany's—that's the best jeweler in New York—and bought me this diamond ring. He first offered me money, but I felt delicate about taking money for such a service, and told him so. So he bought me this ring."

"Well, I declare!" exclaimed Aunt Deborah.

"That was an adventure. But it seems to me, Ferdinand, I would have taken the money."

"As to that, aunt, I can sell this ring, if ever I get hard up, but I hope I sha'n't be obliged to."

"You certainly behaved very well, Ferdinand. Do you ever see Mr. Clayton now?"

"Sometimes, but I don't seek his society, for fear he would think I wanted to get something more out of him."

"How much money do you think he'd have given you?" asked Aunt Deborah, who was of a practical nature.

"A thousand dollars, perhaps more."

"Seems to me I would have taken it."

"If I had, people would have said that's why I jumped into the water, whereas I wasn't thinking anything about getting a reward. So now, aunt, you won't think it very strange that I wear such an expensive ring."

"Of course it makes a difference, as you didn't buy it yourself. I don't see how folks can be such fools as to throw away hundreds of dollars for such a trifle."

"Well, aunt, everybody isn't as sensible and practical as you. Now I agree with you; I think it's very foolish. Still I'm glad I've got the ring, because I can turn it into money when I need to. Only, you see, I don't like to part with a gift, although I don't think Mr. Clayton would blame me."

"Of course he wouldn't, Ferdinand. But I don't see why you should need money when you're goin' to get such a handsome salary in San Francisco."

"To be sure, aunt, but there's something else. However, I won't speak of it today. Tomorrow I may want to ask your advice on a matter of business."

"I'll advise you the best I can, Ferdinand," said the flattered spinster.

"You see, aunt, you're so clear-headed, I shall place great dependence on your advice. But I think I'll take a little walk now, just to stretch my limbs."

"I've made good progress," said the young man to himself, as he lounged over the farm. "The old lady swallows it all. Tomorrow must come my grand stroke. I thought I wouldn't propose it today, for fear she'd suspect the ring story."

CHAPTER XX

A BUSINESS TRANSACTION

Ferdinand found life at the farmhouse rather slow, nor did he particularly enjoy the society of the spinster whom he called aunt. But he was playing for a valuable stake, and meant to play out his game.

"Strike while the iron is hot!" said he to himself. "That's a good rule; but how shall I know when it is hot? However, I must risk something, and take my chances with the old lady."

Aunt Deborah herself hastened his action. Her curiosity had been aroused by Ferdinand's intimation that he wished her advice on a matter of business, and the next morning, after breakfast, she said, "Ferdinand, what was that you wanted to consult me about? You may as well tell me now as any time."

"Here goes, then!" thought the young man.

"I'll tell you, aunt. You know I am offered a large salary in San Francisco?"

"Yes, you told me so."

"And, as you said the other day, I can lay up half my salary, and in time become a rich man."

"To be sure you can."

"But there is one difficulty in the way."

"What is that?"

"I must go out there."

"Of course you must," said the old lady, who did not yet see the point.

"And unfortunately it costs considerable money."

"Haven't you got enough money to pay your fare out there?"

"No, aunt; it is very expensive living in New York, and I was unable to save anything from my salary."

"How much does it cost to go out there?"

"About two hundred and fifty dollars."

"That's a good deal of money."

"So it is; but it will be a great deal better to pay it than to lose so good a job."

"I hope," said the old lady, sharply, "you don't expect me to pay your expenses out there."

"My dear aunt," said Ferdinand, hastily, "how can you suspect such a thing?"

"Then what do you propose to do?" asked the spinster, somewhat relieved.

"I wanted to ask your advice."

"Sell your ring. It's worth over six hundred dollars."

"Very true; but I should hardly like to part with it. I'll tell you what I have thought of. It cost six hundred and fifty dollars. I will give it as security to any one who will lend me five hundred dollars, with permission to sell it if I fail to pay up the note in six months. By the way, aunt, why can't you accommodate me in this matter? You will lose nothing, and I will pay handsome interest."

"How do you know I have the money?"

"I don't know; but I think you must have. But, although I am your nephew, I wouldn't think of asking you to lend me money without security. Business is business, so I say."

"Very true, Ferdinand."

"I ask nothing on the score of relationship, but I will make a business proposal."

"I don't believe the ring would fetch over six hundred dollars."

"It would bring just about that. The other fifty dollars represent the profit. Now, aunt, I'll make you a regular business proposal. If you'll lend me five hundred dollars, I'll give you my note for five hundred and fifty, bearing interest at six percent, payable in six months, or, to make all sure, say in a year. I place the ring in your hands, with leave to sell it at the end of that time if I fail to carry out my agreement. But I sha'n't if I keep my health."

The old lady was attracted by the idea of making a bonus of fifty dollars, but she was cautious, and averse to parting with her money.

"I don't know what to say, Ferdinand," she replied. "Five hundred dollars is a good deal of money."

"So it is, aunt. Well, I don't know but I can offer you a little better terms. Give me four hundred and seventy-five, and I'll give you a note for five hundred and fifty. You can't make as much interest anywhere else."

"I'd like to accommodate you," said the old lady, hesitating, for, like most avaricious persons, she was captivated by the prospect of making extra-legal interest.

"I know you would. Aunt Deborah, but I don't want to ask the money as a favor. It is a strictly business transaction."

"I am afraid I couldn't spare more than four hundred and fifty."

"Very well, I won't dispute about the extra twenty-five dollars. Considering how much income I'm going to get, it isn't of any great importance."

"And you'll give me a note for five hundred and fifty?"

"Yes, certainly."

"I don't know as I ought to take so much interest."

"It's worth that to me, for though, of course, I could raise it by selling the ring, I don't like to do that."

"Well, I don't know but I'll do it. I'll get some ink, and you can write me the due bill."

"Why, Aunt Deborah, you haven't got the money here, have you?"

"Yes, I've got it in the house. A man paid up a mortgage last week, and I haven't yet invested the money. I meant to put it in the savings bank."

"You wouldn't get but six percent there. Now the bonus I offer you will be equal to about twenty percent."

"And you really feel able to pay so much?"

"Yes, aunt; as I told you, it will be worth more than that to me."

"Well, Ferdinand, we'll settle the matter now. I'll go and get the money, and you shall give me the note and the ring."

"Triumph!" said the young man to himself, when the old lady had left the room. "You're badly sold, Aunt Deborah, but it's a good job for me. I didn't think I would have so little trouble."

Within fifteen minutes the money was handed over, and Aunt Deborah took charge of the note and the valuable diamond ring.

"Be careful of the ring, Aunt Deborah," said Ferdinand. "Remember, I expect to redeem it again."

"   I'll take good care of it, nephew, never fear!"

"If it were a little smaller, you could wear it, yourself."

"How would Deborah Kensington look with a diamond ring? The neighbors would think I was crazy. No: I'll keep it in a safe place, but I won't wear it."

"Now, Aunt Deborah, I must speak about other arrangements. Don't you think it would be well to start for San Francisco as soon as possible? You know I enter upon my duties as soon as I get there."

"Yes, Ferdinand, I think you ought to."

"I wish I could spare the time to spend a week with you, aunt; but business is business, and my motto is, business before pleasure."

"And very proper, too, Ferdinand," said the old lady, approvingly.

"So I think I had better leave Centreville tomorrow."

"May be you had. You must write and let me know when you get there, and how you like your job."

"So I will, and I shall be glad to know that you take an interest in me. Now, aunt, as I have some errands to do, I will walk to the village and come back about the middle of the afternoon."

"Won't you be back to lunch?"

"No, I think not, aunt."

"Very well, Ferdinand. Come as soon as you can."

Half an hour later, Ferdinand entered the office of the Centreville Gazette.

"How do you do, Mr. Kensington?" said Clapp, eagerly. "Anything new?"

"I should like to speak with you a moment in private, Mr. Clapp."

"All right!"

Clapp put on his coat, and went outside, shutting the door behind him.

"Well," said Ferdinand, "I've succeeded."

"Have you got the money?"

"Yes, but not quite as much as I anticipated."

"Can't you carry out your plan?" asked Clapp, soberly, fearing he was to be left out in the cold.

"I've formed a new one. Instead of going to California, which is very expensive, we'll go out West, say to St. Louis, and try our fortune there. What do you say?"

"I'm agreed. Can Luke go too?"

"Yes. I'll take you both out there, and lend you fifty dollars each besides, and you shall pay me back as soon as you are able. Will you let your friend know?"

"Yes, I'll undertake that; but when do you propose to start?"

"Tomorrow morning."

"Whew! That's short notice."

"I want to get away as soon as possible, for fear the old lady should change her mind, and want her money back."

"That's where you're right."

"Of course you must give up your situation at once, as there is short time to get ready."

"No trouble about that," said Clapp. "I've hated the business for a long time, and shall be only too glad to leave. It's the same with Luke. He won't shed many tears at leaving Centreville."

"Well, we'll all meet this evening at the hotel. I depend upon your both being ready to start in the morning."

"All right, I'll let Luke know."

It may be thought singular that Ferdinand should have made so liberal an offer to two comparative strangers; but, to do the young man justice, though he had plenty of faults, he was disposed to be generous when he had money, though he was not particular how he obtained it. Clapp and Luke Harrison he recognized as congenial spirits, and he was willing to sacrifice something to obtain their companionship. How long his fancy was likely to last was perhaps doubtful; but for the present he was eager to associate them with his own plans.

CHAPTER XXI

HARRY IS PROMOTED

Clapp re-entered the printing office highly elated.

"Mr. Anderson," said he to the editor, "I am going to leave you."

Ferguson and Harry Walton looked up in surprise, and Mr. Anderson asked, "Have you got another job?"

"No; I am going West."

"Indeed! How long have you had that in view?"

"Not long. I am going with Mr. Kensington."

"The one who just called on you?"

"Yes."

"How soon do you want to leave?"

"Now."

"That is rather short notice."

"I know it, but I leave town tomorrow morning."

"Well, I wish you success. Here is the money I owe you."

"Sha'n't we see you again, Clapp?" asked Ferguson.

"Yes; I'll just look in and say good-bye. Now I must go home and get ready."

"Well, Ferguson," said Mr. Andersen, after Clapp's departure, "that is rather sudden."

"So I think."

"How can we get along with only two hands?"

"Very well, sir. I'm willing to work a little longer, and Harry here is a pretty quick compositor now. The fact is, there isn't enough work for three."

"Then you think I needn't hire another journeyman?"

"No."

"If you both work harder I must increase your wages, and then I shall save money."

"I sha'n't object to that," said Ferguson, smiling.

"Nor I," said Harry.

"I was intending at any rate to raise Harry's wages, as I find he does nearly as much as a journeyman. Hereafter I will give you five dollars a week besides your board."

"Oh, thank you, sir!" said Harry, overjoyed at his good fortune.

"As for you, Ferguson, if you will give me an hour more daily, I will add three dollars a week to your pay."

"Thank you, sir. I think I can afford now to give Mrs. Ferguson the new bonnet she was asking for this morning."

"I don't want to overwork you two, but if that arrangement proves satisfactory, we will continue it."

"I suppose you will be buying your wife a new bonnet too; eh, Harry?" said Ferguson.

"I may buy myself a new hat. Luke Harrison turned up his nose at my old one the other day."

"What will Luke do without Clapp? They were always together."

"Perhaps he is going too."

"I don't know where he will raise the money, nor Clapp either, for that matter."

"Perhaps their new friend furnishes the money."

"If he does, he is indeed a friend."

"Well, it has turned out to our advantage, at any rate, Harry. Suppose you celebrate it by coming round and taking dinner with me?"

"With the greatest pleasure."

Harry was indeed made happy by his promotion. Having been employed for some months on board-wages, he had been compelled to trench upon the small stock of money which he had saved up when in the employ of Prof. Henderson, and he had been unable to send any money to his father, whose circumstances were straitened, and who found it very hard to make both ends meet. That evening he wrote a letter to his father, in which he enclosed ten dollars remaining to him from his fund of savings, at the same time informing him of his promotion. A few days later, he received the following reply:

"MY DEAR SON:

"Your letter has given me great satisfaction, for I conclude from your promotion that you have done your duty faithfully, and won the approbation of your employer. The wages you now earn will amply pay your expenses, while you may reasonably hope that they will be still further increased, as you become more skillful and experienced. I am glad to hear that you are using your leisure hours to such good purpose, and are trying daily to improve your education. In this way you may hope in time to qualify yourself for the position of an editor, which is an honorable and influential profession, to which I should be proud to have you belong.

"The money which you so considerately enclose comes at the right time. Your brother needs some new clothes, and this will enable me to provide them. We all send love, and hope to hear from you often.

"Your affectionate father,

"HIRAM WALTON."

Harry's promotion took place just before the beginning of September. During the next week the fall term of the Prescott Academy commenced, and the village streets again became lively with returning students. Harry was busy at the case, when Oscar Vincent entered the printing office, and greeted him warmly.

"How are you, Oscar?" said Harry, his face lighting up with pleasure. "I am glad to see you back. I would shake hands, but I am afraid you wouldn't like it," and Harry displayed his hands soiled with printer's ink.

"Well, we'll shake hands in spirit, then, Harry. How have you passed the time?"

"I have been very busy, Oscar."

"And I have been very lazy. I have scarcely opened a book, that is, a study-book, during the vacation. How much have you done in French?"

"I have nearly finished Telemachus."

"You have! Then you have done splendidly. By the way, Harry, I received the paper you sent, containing your essay. It does you credit, my boy."

Mr. Anderson, who was sitting at his desk, caught the last words.

"What is that, Harry?" he asked. "Have you been writing for the papers?"

Harry blushed.

"Yes, sir," he replied. "I have written two or three articles for the Boston Weekly Standard."

"Indeed! I should like to see them."

"You republished one of them in the Gazette, Mr. Anderson," said Ferguson.

"What do you refer to?"

"Don't you remember an article on 'Ambition,' which you inserted some weeks ago?"

"Yes, it was a good article. Did you write it, Walton?"

"Yes, sir."

"Why didn't you tell me of it?"

"He was too bashful," said Ferguson.

"I am glad to know that you can write," said the editor. "I shall call upon you for assistance, in getting up paragraphs occasionally."

"I shall be very glad to do what I can," said Harry, gratified.

"Harry is learning to be an editor," said Ferguson.

"I will give him a chance for practice, then," and Mr. Anderson returned to his exchanges.

"By the way, Oscar," said Harry, "I am not a printer's devil any longer. I am promoted to be a journeyman."

"I congratulate you, Harry, but what will Fitz do now? He used to take so much pleasure in speaking of you as a printer's devil."

"I am sorry to deprive him of that pleasure. Did you see much of him on vacation, Oscar?"

"I used to meet him almost every day walking down Washington Street, swinging a light cane, and wearing a stunning necktie, as usual."

"Is he coming back this term?"

"Yes, he came on the same train with me. Hasn't he called to pay his respects to you?"

"No," answered Harry, with a smile. "He hasn't done me that honor. He probably expects me to make the first call."

"Well, Harry, I suppose you will be on hand next week, when the Clionian holds its first meeting?"

"Yes, I will be there."

"And don't forget to call at my room before that time. I want to examine you in French, and see how much progress you have made."

"Thank you, Oscar."

"Now I must be going. I have got a tough Greek lesson to prepare for tomorrow. I suppose it will take me twice as long as usual. It is always hard to get to work again after a long vacation. So good-morning, and don't forget to call at my room soon—say tomorrow evening."

"I will come."

"What a gentlemanly fellow your friend is!" said Ferguson.

"What is his name, Harry?" asked Mr. Anderson.

"Oscar Vincent. His father is an editor in Boston."

"What! The son of John Vincent?" said Mr. Anderson, surprised.

"Yes, sir; do you know his father?"

"Only by reputation. He is a man of great ability."

"Oscar is a smart fellow, too, but not a hard student."

"I shall be glad to have you bring him round to the house some evening, Harry. I shall be glad to become better acquainted with him."

"Thank you, sir. I will give him the invitation."

It is very possible that Harry rose in the estimation of his employer, from his relationship with the son of a man who stood so high in his own profession. At all events, Harry found himself from this time treated with greater respect and consideration than before, and Mr. Anderson often called upon him to write paragraphs upon local matters, so that his position might be regarded except as to pay, as that of an assistant editor.

CHAPTER XXII

MISS DEBORAH'S EYES ARE OPENED

Aunt Deborah felt that she had done a good stroke of business. She had lent Ferdinand four hundred and fifty dollars, and received in return a note for five hundred and fifty, secured by a diamond ring worth even more. She plumed herself on her shrewdness, though at times she felt a little twinge at the idea of the exorbitant interest which she had exacted from so near a relative.

"But he said the money was worth that to him," she said to herself in extenuation, "and he's goin' to get two thousand dollars a year. I didn't want to lend the money, I'd rather have had it in the savings bank, but I did it to obleege him."

By such casuistry Aunt Deborah quieted her conscience, and carefully put the ring away among her bonds and mortgages.

"Who'd think a little ring like that should be worth so much?" she said to herself. "It's a clear waste of money. But then Ferdinand didn't buy it. It was given to him, and a very foolish gift it was too. Railly, it makes me nervous to have it to take care of. It's so little it might get lost easy."

Aunt Deborah plumed herself upon her shrewdness. It was not easy to get the advantage of her in a bargain, and yet she had accepted the ring as security for a considerable loan without once questioning its genuineness. She relied implicitly upon her nephew's assurance of its genuineness, just as she had relied upon his assertion of relationship. But the time was soon coming when she was to be undeceived.

One day, a neighbor stopped his horse in front of her house, and jumping out of his wagon, walked up to the door and knocked.

"Good-morning, Mr. Simpson," said the old lady, answering the knock herself; "won't you come in?"

"Thank you, Miss Deborah, I can't stop this morning. I was at the post office just now, when I saw there was a letter for you, and thought I'd bring it along."

"A letter for me!" said Aunt Deborah in some surprise, for her correspondence was very limited. "Who's it from?"

"It is post-marked New York," said Mr. Simpson.

"I don't know no one in New York," said the old lady, fumbling in her pockets for her spectacles.

"Maybe it's one of your old beaux," said Mr. Simpson, humorously, a joke which brought a grim smile to the face of the old spinster. "But I must be goin'. If it's an offer of marriage, don't forget to invite me to the wedding."

Aunt Deborah went into the house, and seating herself in her accustomed place, carefully opened the letter. She turned over the page, and glanced at the signature. To her astonishment it was signed,

"Your affectionate nephew,

"FERDINAND B. KENSINGTON."

"Ferdinand!" she exclaimed in surprise. "Why, I thought he was in Californy by this time. How could he write from New York? I s'pose he'll explain. I hope he didn't lose the money I lent him."

The first sentence in the letter was destined to surprise Miss Deborah yet more.

"Dear aunt," it commenced, "it is so many years since we have met, that I am afraid you have forgotten me."

"So many years!" repeated Miss Deborah in bewilderment. "What on earth can Ferdinand mean? Why, it's only five weeks yesterday since he was here. He must be crazy."

She resumed reading.

"I have often had it in mind to make you a little visit, but I have been so engrossed by business that I have been unable to get away. I am a salesman for A. T. Stewart, whom you must have heard of, as he is the largest retail dealer in the city. I have been three years in his employ, and have been promoted by degrees, till I now receive quite a good salary, until—and that is the news I have to write you—I have felt justified in getting married. My wedding is fixed for next week, Thursday. I should be very glad if you could attend, though I suppose you would consider it a long journey. But at any rate I can assure you that I should be delighted to see you present on the occasion, and so would Maria. If you can't come, write to me, at any rate, in memory of old times. It is just possible that during our bridal tour—we are to go to the White Mountains for a week—we shall call on you. Let me know if it will be convenient for you to receive us for a day.

"Your affectionate nephew,

"FERDINAND B. KENSINGTON."

Miss Deborah read this letter like one dazed. She had to read it a second time before she could comprehend its purport.

276

"Ferdinand going to be married! He never said a word about it when he was here. And he don't say a word about Californy. Then again he says he hasn't seen me for years. Merciful man! I see it now—the other fellow was an impostor!" exclaimed Miss Deborah, jumping to her feet in excitement. "What did he want to deceive an old woman for?"

It flashed upon her at once. He came after money, and he had succeeded only too well. He had carried away four hundred and fifty dollars with him. True, he had left a note, and security. But another terrible suspicion had entered the old lady's mind; the ring might not be genuine.

"I must know at once," exclaimed the disturbed spinster. "I'll go over to Brandon, to the jeweler's, and inquire. If it's paste, then, Deborah Kensington, you're the biggest fool in Centreville."

Miss Deborah summoned Abner, her farm servant from the field, and ordered him instantly to harness the horse, as she wanted to go to Brandon.

"Do you want me to go with you?" asked Abner.

"To be sure, I can't drive so fur, and take care of the horse."

"It'll interrupt the work," objected Abner.

"Never mind about the work," said Deborah, impatiently. "I must go right off. It's on very important business."

"Wouldn't it be best to go after lunch?"

"No, we'll get some lunch over there, at the tavern."

"What's got into the old woman?" thought Abner. "It isn't like her to spend money at a tavern for lunch, when she might as well dine at home. Interruptin' the work, too! However, it's her business!"

Deborah was ready and waiting when the horse drove up to the door. She got in, and they set out. Abner tried to open a conversation, but he found Miss Deborah strangely unsocial. She appeared to take no interest in the details of farm work of which he spoke.

"Something's on her mind, I guess," thought Abner; and, as we know, he was right.

In her hand Deborah clutched the ring, of whose genuineness she had come to entertain such painful doubts. It might be genuine, she tried to hope, even if it came from an impostor; but her hope was small. She felt a presentiment that it would prove as false as the man from whom she received it. As for the story of the manner in which he became possessed of it, doubtless that was as false as the rest.

"How blind I was!" groaned Deborah in secret. "I saw he didn't look like the family. What a goose I was to believe that story about his changin' the color of his hair! I was an old fool, and that's all about it."

"Drive to the jeweler's," said Miss Deborah, when they reached Brandon.

In some surprise, Abner complied.

Deborah got out of the wagon hastily and entered the store.

"What can I do for you, Miss Kensington?" asked the jeweler, who recognized the old lady.

"I want to show you a ring," said Aunt Deborah, abruptly. "Tell me what it's worth."

She produced the ring which the false Ferdinand had entrusted to her.

The jeweler scanned it closely.

"It's a good imitation of a diamond ring," he said.

"Imitation!" gasped Deborah.

"Yes; you didn't think it was genuine?"

"What's it worth?"

"The value of the gold. That appears to be genuine. It may be worth three dollars."

"Three dollars!" exclaimed Deborah. "He told me it cost six hundred and fifty."

"Whoever told you that was trying to deceive you."

"You're sure about its being imitation, are you?"

"There can be no doubt about it."

"That's what I thought," muttered the old lady, her face pale and rigid. "Is there anything to pay?"

"Oh, no; I am glad to be of service to you."

"Good-afternoon, then," said Deborah, abruptly, and she left the store.

"Drive home, Abner, as quick as you can," she said.

"I haven't had any lunch," Abner remarked. "You said you'd get some at the tavern."

"Did I? Well, drive over there. I'm not hungry myself, but I'll pay for some lunch for you."

Poor Aunt Deborah! It was not the loss alone that troubled her, though she was fond of money; but it was humiliating to think that she had fallen such an easy prey to a designing adventurer. In her present bitter mood, she would gladly have ridden fifty miles to see the false Ferdinand hanged.

CHAPTER XXIII

THE PLOT AGAINST FLETCHER

The closeness between Harry and Oscar Vincent continued, and, as during the former term, the latter volunteered to continue giving French lessons to our hero. These were now partly of a conversational character, and, as Harry was thoroughly in earnest, it was not long before he was able to speak quite creditably.

About the first of November, Fitzgerald Fletcher left the Prescott Academy, and returned to his home in Boston. It was not because he had finished his education, but because he felt that he was not appreciated by his fellow-students. He had been ambitious to be elected to an official position in the Clionian Society, but his aspirations were not gratified. He might have accepted this disappointment, and borne it as well as he could, had it not been aggravated by the elevation of Harry Walton to the presidency. To be only a common member, while a boy so far his social inferior was President, was more than Fitzgerald could stand. He was so incensed that upon the announcement of the vote he immediately rose to a point of order.

"Mr. President," he said warmly, "I must protest against this election. Walton is not a member of the Prescott Academy, and it is unconstitutional to elect him President."

"Will the gentleman point out the constitutional clause which has been violated by Walton's election?" said Oscar Vincent.

"Mr. President," said Fletcher, "this Society was founded by students of the Prescott Academy; and the offices should be confined to the members of the school."

Harry Walton rose and said: "Mr. President, my election has been a great surprise to myself. I had no idea that any one had thought of me for the position. I feel highly complimented by your kindness, and deeply grateful for it; but there is something in what Mr. Fletcher says. You have kindly allowed me to share in the benefits of the Society, and that satisfies me. I think it will be well for you to make another choice as President."

"I will put it to vote," said the presiding officer. "Those who are ready to accept Mr. Walton's resignation will signify it in the usual way."

Fletcher raised his hand, but he was alone.

"Those who are opposed," said the President.

Every other hand except Harry's was now raised.

"Mr. Walton, your resignation is not accepted," said the presiding officer. "I call upon you to assume the duties of your new position."

Harry rose, and, modestly advanced to the chair. "I have already thanked you, gentlemen," he said, "for the honor you have conferred upon me in selecting me as your presiding officer. I have only to add that I will discharge its duties to the best of my ability."

All applauded except Fletcher. He sat with an unpleasant scowl upon his face, and waited for the result of the balloting for Vice-President and Secretary. Had he been elected to either position, the Clionian would probably have retained his illustrious name upon its roll. But as these honors were conferred upon other members, he formed the heroic resolution no longer to remain a member.

"Mr. President," he said, when the last vote was announced, "I desire to terminate my connection with this Society."

"I hope Mr. Fletcher will reconsider his determination," said Harry from the chair.

"I would like to inquire the gentleman's reasons," said Tom Carver.

"I don't like the way in which the Society is managed," said Fletcher. "I predict that it will soon disband."

"I don't see any signs of it," said Oscar. "If the gentleman is really sincere, he should not desert the Clionian in the hour of danger."

"I insist upon my resignation," said Fletcher.

"I move that it be accepted," said Tom Carver.

"Second the motion," said the boy who sat next him.

The resignation was unanimously accepted. Fletcher ought to have felt gratified at the prompt granting of his request, but he was not. He had intended to strike dismay into the Society by his proposal to withdraw, but there was no consternation visible. Apparently they were willing to let him go.

He rose from his seat mortified and wrathful.

"Gentlemen," he said, "you have complied with my request, and I am deeply grateful. I no longer consider it an honor to belong to the Clionian. I trust your new President may succeed as well in his new office as he has in the capacity of a printer's devil."

Fletcher was unable to proceed, being interrupted by a storm of hisses, in the midst of which he hurriedly made his exit.

"He wanted to be President himself—that's what's the matter," said Tom Carver in a whisper to his neighbor. "But he couldn't blame us for not wanting to have him."

Other members of the Society came to the same conclusion, and it was generally said that Fletcher had done himself no good by his undignified resentment. His parting taunt leveled at Harry was regarded as mean and ungenerous, and only strengthened the sentiment in favor of our hero, who bore his honors modestly. In fact Tom Carver, who was fond of fun, conceived a project for mortifying Fletcher, and readily obtained the cooperation of his classmates.

It must be premised that Fitz was vain of his reading and declamation. He had a secret suspicion that, if he should choose to devote his talents to the stage, he would make a second Booth. This self-conceit of his made it the more easy to play the following joke upon him.

A fortnight later, the young ladies of the village proposed to hold a Fair to raise funds for some public object. At the head of the committee of arrangements was a sister of the doctor's wife, named Pauline Clinton. This will explain the following letter, which Fletcher received the succeeding day:

"FITZGERALD FLETCHER, ESQ.—Dear Sir: Understanding that you are a superior reader, we should be glad of your assistance in lending eclat to the Fair which we propose to hold on the evening of the 29th. Will you be kind enough to occupy twenty minutes by reading such selections as in your opinion will be of popular interest? It is desirable that you should let me know as soon as possible what pieces you have selected, that they may be printed on the program.

"Yours respectfully,
"PAULINE CLINTON,
"(for the Committee)."

This note reached Fletcher at a time when he was still smarting from his disappointment in obtaining promotion from the Clionian Society. He read it with a flushed and triumphant face. He never thought of questioning its genuineness. Was it not true that he was a superior reader? What more natural than that he should be invited to give eclat to the Fair by the exercise of his talents! He felt it to be a deserved compliment. It was a greater honor to be solicited to give a public reading than to be elected President of the Clionian Society.

"They won't laugh at me now," thought Fletcher.

He immediately started for Oscar's room to make known his new honors.

"How are you, Fitz?" said Oscar, who was in the secret, and guessed the errand on which he came.

"Very well, thank you, Oscar," answered Fletcher, in a stately manner.

"Anything new with you?" asked Oscar, carelessly.

"Not much," said Fletcher. "There's a note I just received."

"Whew!" exclaimed Oscar, in affected astonishment. "Are you going to accept?"

"I suppose I ought to oblige them," said Fletcher. "It won't be much trouble to me, you know."

"To be sure; it's in a good cause. But how did they hear of your reading?"

"Oh, there are no secrets in a small village like this," said Fletcher.

"It's certainly a great compliment. Has anybody else been invited to read?"

"I think not," said Fletcher, proudly. "They rely upon me."

"Couldn't you get a chance for me? It would be quite an honor, and I should like it for the sake of the family."

"I shouldn't feel at liberty to interfere with their arrangements," said Fletcher, who didn't wish to share the glory with any one. "Besides, you don't read well enough."

"Well, I suppose I must give it up," said Oscar, in a tone of resignation. "By the way, what have you decided to read?"

"I haven't quite made up my mind," said Fletcher, in a tone of importance. "I have only just received the invitation, you know."

"Haven't you answered it yet?"

"No; but I shall as soon as I go home. Good-night, Oscar."

"Good-night, Fitz."

"How mad Fitz will be when he finds he has been sold!" said Oscar to himself. "But he deserves it for treating Harry so meanly."

283

CHAPTER XXIV

READING UNDER DIFFICULTIES

On reaching home, Fletcher looked over his "Speaker," and selected three poems which he thought he could read with best effect. The selection made, he sat down to his desk, and wrote a reply to the invitation, as follows:

"MISS PAULINE CLINTON: I hasten to acknowledge your polite invitation to occupy twenty minutes in reading choice selections at your approaching Fair. I have paid much attention to reading, and hope to be able to give pleasure to the large numbers who will doubtless honor the occasion with their presence. I have selected three poems—Poe's Raven, the Battle of Ivry, by Macaulay, and Marco Bozarris, by Halleck. I shall be much pleased if my humble efforts add eclat to the occasion.

"Yours, very respectfully,

"FITZGERALD FLETCHER."

"There," said Fletcher, reading his letter through with satisfaction. "I think that will do. It is high-toned and dignified, and shows that I am highly cultured and refined. I will copy it off, and mail it."

Fletcher saw his letter deposited in the post office, and returned to his room.

"I ought to practice reading these poems, so as to do it up handsomely," he said. "I suppose I shall get a good notice in the Gazette. If I do, I will buy a dozen papers, and send to my friends. They will see that I am a person of consequence in Centreville, even if I didn't get elected to any office in the high and mighty Clionian Society."

I am sorry that I cannot reproduce the withering sarcasm which Fletcher put into his tone in the last sentence.

When Demosthenes was practicing oratory, he sought the seashore; but Fitzgerald repaired instead to a piece of woods about half a mile distant. It was rather an unfortunate selection, as will appear.

It so happened that Tom Carver and Hiram Huntley were strolling about the woods, when they spied Fletcher approaching with an open book in his hand.

284

"Hiram," said Tom, "there's fun coming. There's Fitz Fletcher with his 'Speaker' in his hand. He's going to practice reading in the woods. Let us hide, and hear the fun."

"I'm in for it," said Hiram, "but where will be the best place to hide?"

"Here in this hollow tree. He'll be very apt to halt here."

"All right! Go ahead, I'll follow."

They quickly concealed themselves in the tree, unobserved by Fletcher, whose eyes were on his book.

About ten feet from the tree he paused.

"I guess this'll be a good place," he said aloud. "There's no one to disturb me here. Now, which shall I begin with? I think I'll try The Raven. But first it may be well to practice an appropriate little speech. Something like this:

Fletcher made a low bow to the assembled trees, cleared his throat, and commenced.

"Ladies and Gentlemen: It gives me great pleasure to appear before you this evening, in compliance with the request of the committee, who have thought that my humble efforts would give eclat to the Fair. I am not a professional reader, but I have ever found pleasure in reciting the noble productions of our best authors, and I hope to give you pleasure."

"That'll do, I think," said Fletcher, complacently. "Now I'll try The Raven."

**Fitzgerald Fletcher was practicing The Raven,
by Edgar Allan Poe, when his two classmates
scared him from inside the hollow tree.**

In a deep, sepulchral tone, Fletcher read the first verse, which is quoted below:

"Once upon a midnight dreary, while I pondered weak and weary,
Over many a quaint and curious volume of forgotten lore,
While I nodded, nearly napping, suddenly there came a tapping,
As of some one gently rapping, rapping at my chamber door.
"Tis some visitor,' I muttered, 'tapping at my chamber door—
Only this and nothing more.'"

Was it fancy, or did Fletcher really hear a slow, measured tapping near him—upon one of the trees, as it seemed? He started, and looked nervously; but the noise stopped, and he decided that he had been deceived, since no one was visible.

The boys within the tree made no other demonstration till Fletcher had read the following verse:

"Back into the chamber turning, all my soul within me burning,
Soon again I heard a tapping, something louder than before.
'Surely,' said I, 'surely that is something at my window lattice;
Let me see then what thereat is, and this mystery explore—
Let my heart be still a moment, and this mystery explore;
'Tis the wind, and nothing more.'"

Here an indescribable, unearthly noise was heard from the interior of the tree, like the wailing of some discontented ghost.

"Good heavens! What's that?" exclaimed Fletcher, turning pale, and looking nervously around him.

It was growing late, and the branches above him, partially stripped of their leaves, rustled in the wind. Fletcher was somewhat nervous, and the weird character of the poem probably increased this feeling, and made him very uncomfortable. He summoned up courage enough, however, to go on, though his voice shook a little. He was permitted to go on without interruption to the end. Those who are familiar with the poem know that it becomes more and more wild and weird as it draws to the conclusion. This, with his gloomy surroundings, had its effect upon the mind of Fletcher. Scarcely had he uttered the last words, when a burst of wild and sepulchral laughter was heard within a few feet of him. A cry of fear proceeded from Fletcher, and, clutching his book, he ran at wild speed from the enchanted spot, not daring to look behind him. Indeed, he never stopped running till he passed out of the shadow of the woods, and was well on his way homeward.

Tom Carver and Hiram crept out from their place of concealment. They threw themselves on the ground, and roared with laughter.

"I never had such fun in my life," said Tom.

"Nor I."

"I wonder what Fitz thought."

"That the wood was enchanted, probably; he left in a hurry."

"Yes; he stood not on the order of his going, but went at once."

"I wish I could have seen him. We must have made a fearful noise."

"I was almost frightened myself. He must be almost home by this time."

"When do you think he'll find out about the trick?"

"About the invitation? Not till he gets a letter from Miss Clinton, telling him it is all a mistake. He will be terribly mortified."

Meanwhile Fletcher reached home, tired and out of breath. His temporary fear was over, but he was quite at sea as to the cause of the noises he had heard. He could not suspect any of his school-fellows, for no one was visible, nor had he any idea that any were in the wood at the time.

"I wonder if it was an animal," he reflected. "It was a fearful noise. I must find some other place to practice reading in. I wouldn't go to that wood again for fifty dollars."

But Fletcher's readings were not destined to be long continued. When he got home from school the next day, he found the following note, which had been left for him during the morning:

"MR. FITZGERALD FLETCHER,—Dear Sir: I beg to thank you for your kind proposal to read at our Fair; but I think there must be some mistake in the matter, as we have never contemplated having any readings, nor have I written to you on the subject, as you intimate. I fear that we shall not have time to spare for such a feature, though under other circumstances, it might be attractive. In behalf of the committee, I beg to tender thanks for your kind proposal.

"Yours respectfully,

"PAULINE CLINTON."

Fletcher read this letter with feelings which can better be imagined than described. He had already written home in the most boastful manner about the invitation he had received, and he knew that before he could contradict it, it would have been generally reported by his gratified parents to his city friends. And now he would be compelled to explain that he had been duped, besides enduring the jeers of those who had planned the trick.

This was more than he could endure. He formed a sudden resolution. He would feign illness, and go home the next day. He could let it be inferred that it was sickness alone which had compelled him to give up the idea of appearing as a public reader.

Fitz immediately acted upon his decision, and the next day found him on the way to Boston. He never returned to the Prescott Academy as a student.

CHAPTER XXV

AN INVITATION TO BOSTON

Harry was doubly glad that he was now in receipt of a moderate salary. He welcomed it as evidence that he was rising in the estimation of his employer, which was of itself satisfactory, and also because in his circumstances the money was likely to be useful.

"Five dollars a week!" said Harry to himself. "Half of that ought to be enough to pay for my clothes and miscellaneous expenses, and the rest I will give to father. It will help him take care of the rest of the family."

Our hero at once made this proposal by letter. This is a paragraph from his father's letter in reply:

"I am glad, my dear son, to find you so considerate and dutiful, as your offer indicates. I have indeed had a hard time in supporting my family, and have not always been able to give them the comforts I desired. Perhaps it is my own fault in part. I am afraid I have not the faculty of getting along and making money that many others have. But I have had an unexpected stroke of good fortune. Last evening a letter reached your mother, stating that her cousin Nancy had recently died at St. Albans, Vermont, and that, in accordance with her will, your mother is to receive a legacy of four thousand dollars. With your mother's consent, one-fourth of this is to be devoted to the purchase of the ten acres adjoining my little farm, and the balance will be so invested as to yield us an annual income of one hundred and eighty dollars. Many would think this a small addition to an income, but it will enable us to live much more comfortably. You remember the ten-acre lot to the east of us, belonging to the heirs of Reuben Todd. It is excellent land, well adapted for cultivation, and will fully double the value of my farm.

"You see, therefore, my dear son, that a new era of prosperity has opened for us. I am now relieved from the care and anxiety which for years have oppressed me, and feel sure of a comfortable support. Instead of accepting the half of your salary, I desire you, if possible, to save it, depositing in some reliable savings institution. If you do this every year till you are twenty-one, you will have a little capital to start you in business, and will be able to lead a more prosperous career than your father. Knowing you as well as I do, I

---

do not feel it necessary to caution you against unnecessary expenditures. I will only remind you that extravagance is comparative, and that what would be only reasonable expenditure for one richer than yourself would be imprudent in you."

Harry read this letter with great joy. He was warmly attached to the little home circle, and the thought that they were comparatively provided for gave him fresh courage. He decided to adopt his father's suggestion, and the very next week deposited three dollars in the savings bank.

"That is to begin an account," he thought. "If I can only keep that up, I shall feel quite rich at the end of a year."

Several weeks rolled by, and Thanksgiving approached.

Harry was toiling at his case one day, when Oscar Vincent entered the office.

"Hard at work, I see, Harry," he said.

"Yes," said Harry; "I can't afford to be idle."

"I want you to be idle for three days," said Oscar.

Harry looked up in surprise.

"How is that?" he asked.

"You know we have a vacation from Wednesday to Monday at the Academy."

"Over Thanksgiving?"

"Yes."

"Well, I am going home to spend that time, and I want you to go with me."

"What, to Boston?" asked Harry, startled, for to him, inexperienced as he was, that seemed a very long journey.

"Yes. Father and mother gave me permission to invite you. Shall I show you the letter?"

"I'll take it for granted, Oscar, but I am afraid I can't go."

"Nonsense! What's to prevent?"

"In the first place, Mr. Anderson can't spare me."

"Ask him."

"What's that?" asked the editor, hearing his name mentioned.

"I have invited Harry to spend the Thanksgiving vacation with me in Boston, and he is afraid you can't spare him."

"Does your father sanction your invitation?"

"Yes, he wrote me this morning—that is, I got the letter this morning—telling me to ask Harry to come."

Now the country editor had a great respect for the city editor, who was indeed known by reputation throughout New England as a man of influence and ability, and he felt disposed to accede to any request of his.

So he said pleasantly, "Of course, Harry, we shall miss you, but if Mr. Ferguson is disposed to do a little additional work, we will get along till Monday. What do you say, Mr. Ferguson?"

"I shall be very glad to oblige Harry," said the older workman, "and I hope he will have a good time."

"That settles the question, Harry," said Oscar, joyfully. "So all you've got to do is to pack up and be ready to start tomorrow morning. It's Tuesday, you know, already."

Harry hesitated, and Oscar observed it.

"Well, what's the matter now?" he said; "out with it."

"I'll tell you, Oscar," said Harry, coloring a little. "Your father is a rich man, and lives handsomely. I haven't any clothes good enough to wear on a visit to your house."

"Oh, hang your clothes!" said Oscar, impetuously. "It isn't your clothes we invite. It's yourself."

"Still, Oscar—"

"Come, I see you think I am like Fitz Fletcher, after all. Say you think me a snob, and done with it."

"But I don't," said Harry, smiling.

"Then don't make any more ridiculous objections. Don't you think they are ridiculous, Mr. Ferguson?"

"They wouldn't be in some places," said Ferguson, "but here I think they are out of place. I feel sure you are right, and that you value Harry more than the clothes he wears."

"Well, Harry, do you surrender at discretion?" said Oscar. "You see Ferguson is on my side."

"I suppose I shall have to," said Harry, "as long as you are not ashamed of me."

"None of that, Harry."

"I'll go."

"The first sensible words you've spoken this morning."

"I want to tell you how much I appreciate your kindness, Oscar," said Harry, earnestly.

"Why shouldn't I be kind to my friend?"

"Even if he was once a printer's devil."

292

"Very true. It is a great objection, but still I will overlook it. By the way, there is one inducement I didn't mention."

"What is that?"

"We may very likely see Fitz in the city. He is studying at home now, I hear. Who knows but he may get up a great party in your honor?"

"Do you think it likely?" asked Harry, smiling.

"It might not happen to occur to him, I admit. Still, if we made him a ceremonious call—"

"I am afraid he might send word that he was not at home."

"That would be a loss to him, no doubt. However, we will leave time to settle that question. Be sure to be on hand in time for the morning train."

"All right, Oscar."

Harry had all the love of new scenes natural to a boy of sixteen. He had heard so much of Boston that he felt a strong curiosity to see it. Besides, was not that the city where the Weekly Standard was printed, the paper in which he had already appeared as an author? In connection with this, I must here divulge a secret of Harry's. He was ambitious not only to contribute to the literary papers, but to be paid for his contributions. He judged that essays were not very marketable, and he had therefore in his leisure moments written a humorous sketch, entitled "The Tin-Peddler's Daughter." I shall not give any idea of the plot here; I will only say that it was really humorous, and did not betray as much of the novice as might have been expected. Harry had copied it out in his best hand, and resolved to carry it to Boston, and offer it in person to the editor of the Standard with an effort, if accepted, to obtain compensation for it.

———

CHAPTER XXVI

THE VINCENTS AT HOME

When Harry rather bashfully imparted to Oscar his plans respecting the manuscript, the latter entered enthusiastically into them, and at once requested the privilege of reading the story. Harry awaited his judgment with some anxiety.

"Why, Harry, this is capital," said Oscar, looking up from the perusal.

"Do you really think so, Oscar?"

"If I didn't think so, I wouldn't say so."

"I thought you might say so out of friendship."

"I don't say it is the best I ever read, mind you, but I have read a good many that are worse. I think you managed the denouement (you're a French scholar, so I'll venture on the word) admirably."

"I only hope the editor of the Standard will think so."

"If he doesn't, there are other papers in Boston; the Argus for instance."

"I'll try the Standard first, because I have already written for it."

"All right. Don't you want me to go to the office with you?"

"I wish you would. I shall be bashful."

"I am not troubled that way. Besides, my father's name is well known, and I'll take care to mention it. Sometimes influence goes farther than merit, you know."

"I should like to increase my income by writing for the city papers. Even if I only made fifty dollars a year, it would all be clear gain."

Harry's desire was natural. He had no idea how many shared it. Every editor of a successful weekly could give information on this subject. Certainly there is no dearth of aspiring young writers—Scotts and Shakspeares in embryo—in our country, and if all that were written for publication succeeded in getting into print, the world would scarcely contain the books and papers which would pour in uncounted thousands from the groaning press.

Beacon Street in Boston is where Oscar Vincent's family lives.

When the two boys arrived in Boston they took a carriage to Oscar's house. It was situated on Beacon Street, not far from the Common—a handsome brick house with a swell front, such as they used to build in Boston. No one of the family was in, and Oscar and Harry went up at once to the room of the former, which they were to share together. It was luxuriously furnished, so Harry thought, but then our hero had been always accustomed to the plainness of a country home.

"Now, old fellow, make yourself at home," said Oscar. "You can get yourself up for lunch. There's water and towels, and a brush."

"I don't expect to look very magnificent," said Harry. "You must tell your mother I am from the country."

"I would make you an offer if I dared," said Oscar.

"I am always open to a good offer."

"It's this: I'm one size larger than you, and my last year's suits are in that wardrobe. If any will fit you, they are yours."

"Thank you, Oscar," said Harry; "I'll accept your offer tomorrow."

"Why not today?"

"You may not understand me, but when I first appear before your family, I don't want to wear false colors."

"I understand," said Oscar, with instinctive delicacy.

An hour later, the bell rang for lunch.

Harry went down, and was introduced to his friend's mother and sister. The former was a true lady, refined and kindly, and her smile made our hero feel quite at home.

295

"I am glad to meet you, Mr. Walton," she said. "Oscar has spoken of you frequently."

With Oscar's sister Maud—a beautiful girl two years younger than himself—Harry felt a little more bashful; but the young lady soon entered into an animated conversation with him.

"Do you often come to Boston, Mr. Walton?" she asked.

"This is my first visit," said Harry.

"Then I dare say Oscar will play all sorts of tricks upon you. We had a cousin visit us from the country, and the poor fellow had a hard time."

"Yes," said Oscar, laughing, "I used to leave him at a street corner, and dodge into a doorway. It was amusing to see his perplexity when he looked about, and couldn't find me."

"Shall you try that on me?" asked Harry.

"Very likely."

"Then I'll be prepared."

"You might tie him with a rope, Mr. Walton," said Maud, "and keep firm hold."

"I will, if Oscar consents."

"I will see about it. But here is my father. Father, this is my friend, Harry Walton."

"I am glad to see you, Mr. Walton," said Mr. Vincent. "Then you belong to my profession?"

"I hope to, some time, sir; but I am only a printer as yet."

"You are yet to rise from the ranks. I know all about that. I was once a compositor."

Harry looked at the editor with great respect. He was stout, squarely built, with a massive head and a thoughtful expression. His appearance was up to Harry's anticipations. He felt that he would be prouder to be Mr. Vincent than any man in Boston. He could hardly believe that this man, who controlled so influential an organ, and was so honored in the community, was once a printer boy like himself.

"What paper are you connected with?" asked Mr. Vincent.

"The Centreville Gazette."

"I have seen it. It is quite a respectable paper."

"But how different," thought Harry, "from a great city daily!"

"Let us go out to lunch," said Mr. Vincent, consulting his watch. "I have an engagement immediately afterward."

At the table Harry sat between Maud and Oscar. If at first he felt a little bashful, the feeling soon wore away. The lunch hour passed very pleasantly. Mr. Vincent chatted very agreeably about men and things. There is no one better qualified to shine in this kind of conversation than the editor of a city daily, who is compelled to be exceptionally well informed. Harry listened with such interest that he almost forgot to eat, till Oscar charged him with want of appetite.

"I must leave in haste," said Mr. Vincent, when lunch was over. "Oscar, I take it for granted that you will take care of your friend."

"Certainly, father. I shall look upon myself as his guardian, adviser and friend."

"You are not very well fitted to be a mentor, Oscar," said Maud.

"Why not, young lady?"

"You need a guardian yourself. You are young and frivolous."

"And you, I suppose, are old and judicious."

"Thank you. I will own to the last, and the first will come in time."

"Isn't it singular, Harry, that my sister should have so much conceit, whereas I am remarkably modest?"

"I never discovered it, Oscar," said Harry, smiling.

"That is right, Mr. Walton," said Maud. "I see you are on my side. Look after my brother, Mr. Walton. He needs an experienced friend."

"I am afraid I don't answer the description, Miss Maud."

"I don't doubt you will prove competent. I wish you a pleasant walk."

"My sister's a jolly girl, don't you think so?" asked Oscar, as Maud left the room.

"That isn't exactly what I should say of her, but I can describe her as even more attractive than her brother."

"You couldn't pay her a higher compliment. But come; we'll take a walk on the Common."

Boston Common is where they meet up with Fitzgerald Fletcher in Boston.

They were soon on the Common, dear to every Bostonian, and sauntered along the walks, under the pleasant shade of the stately elms.

"Look there," said Oscar, suddenly; "isn't that Fitz Fletcher?"

"Yes," said Harry, "but he doesn't see us."

"We'll join him. How are you, Fitz?"

"Glad to see you, Oscar," said Fletcher, extending a gloved hand, while in the other he tossed a light cane. "When did you arrive?"

"Only this morning; but you don't see Harry Walton."

Fletcher arched his brows in surprise, and said coldly, "Indeed, I was not aware Mr. Walton was in the city."

"He is visiting me," said Oscar.

Fletcher looked surprised. He knew the Vincents stood high socially, and it seemed extraordinary that they should receive a printer's devil as a guest.

"Have you given up the printing business?" he asked superciliously.

"No; I only have a little vacation from it."

"Ah, indeed! It's a very dirty business. I would as soon be a chimney-sweep."

"Each to his taste, Fitz," said Oscar. "If you have a taste for chimneys, I hope your father won't interfere."

"I haven't a taste for such a low business," said Fletcher, haughtily. "I should like it as well as being a printer's devil though."

"Would you? At any rate, if you take it up, you'll be sure to be well sooted."

Fletcher did not laugh at the joke. He never could see any wit in jokes directed at himself.

"How long are you going to stay at that beastly school?" he asked.

"I am not staying at any beastly school."

"I mean the Academy."

"Till I am ready for college. Where are you studying?"

"I recite to a private tutor."

"Well, we shall meet at Harvard if we are lucky enough to get in."

Fletcher rather hoped Oscar would invite him to call at his house, for he liked to visit a family of high social position; but he waited in vain.

"What a fool Oscar makes of himself about that country clod-hopper!" thought the stylish young man, as he walked away. "The idea of associating with a printer's devil! I hope I know what is due to myself better."

CHAPTER XXVII

THE OFFICE OF THE "STANDARD"

On the day after Thanksgiving, Harry brought out from his carpet-bag his manuscript story, and started with Oscar for the office of the Weekly Standard. He bought the last copy of the paper, and thus ascertained the location of the office.

Oscar turned the last page, and ran through a sketch of about the same length as Harry's.

"Yours is fully as good as this, Harry," he said.

"The editor may not think so."

"Then he ought to."

"This story is by one of his regular contributors, Kenella Kent."

"You'll have to take a name yourself—a nom de plume, I mean."

"I have written so far over the name of Franklin."

"That will do very well for essays, but is not appropriate for stories."

"Suppose you suggest a name, Oscar."

"How will 'Fitz Fletcher' do?"

"Mr. Fletcher would not permit me to take such a liberty."

"And you wouldn't want to take it."

"Not much."

"Let me see. I suppose I must task my invention, then. How will Old Nick do?"

"People would think you wrote the story."

"A fair hit. Hold on, I've got just the name. Frank Lynn."

"I thought you objected to that name."

"You don't understand me. I mean two names, not one. Frank Lynn! Don't you see?"

"Yes, it's a good plan. I'll adopt it."

"Who knows but you may make the name illustrious, Harry?"

"If I do, I'll dedicate my first boot to Oscar Vincent."

"Shake hands on that. I accept the dedication with mingled feelings of gratitude and pleasure."

"Better wait till you get it," said Harry, laughing. "Don't count your chickens before they're hatched."

"The first egg is laid, and that's something. But here we are at the office."

It was a building containing a large number of offices. The names of the respective occupants were printed on slips of black tin at the entrance. From this, Harry found that the office of the Weekly Standard was located at No. 6.

"My heart begins to beat, Oscar," said Harry, naturally excited in anticipation of an interview with one who could open the gates of authorship to him.

"Does it?" asked Oscar. "Mine has been beating for a number of years."

"You are too matter-of-fact for me, Oscar. If it was your own story, you might feel differently."

"Shall I pass it off as my own, and make the negotiation?"

Harry was half tempted to say yes, but it occurred to him that this might prove an embarrassment in the future, and he declined the proposal.

They climbed rather a dark, and not very elegant staircase, and found themselves before No. 6.

Harry knocked, or was about to do so, when a young lady with long ringlets, and a roll of manuscript in her hand, who had followed them upstairs advanced confidently, and, opening the door, went in. The two boys followed, thinking the ceremony of knocking needless.

They found themselves in a large room, one corner of which was partitioned off for the editor's sanctum. A middle-aged man was directing papers in the larger room, while piles of papers were ranged on shelves at the sides of the apartment.

The two boys hesitated to advance, but the young lady in ringlets went on, and entered the office through the open door.

"We'll wait till she is through," said Harry.

It was easy to hear the conversation that passed between the young lady and the editor, whom they could not see.

"Good-morning, Mr. Houghton," she said.

"Good-morning. Take a seat, please," said the editor, pleasantly. "Are you one of our contributors?"

"No, sir, not yet," answered the young lady, "but I would become so."

"We are not engaging any new contributors at present, but still if you have brought anything for examination you may leave it."

"I am not wholly unknown to fame," said the young lady, with an air of consequence. "You have probably heard of Prunella Prune."

"Possibly, but I don't at present recall it. We editors meet with so many names, you know. What is the character of your articles?"

"I am a poetess, sir, and I also write stories."

"Poetry is a drug in the market. We have twice as much offered us as we can accept. Still we are always glad to welcome really meritorious poems."

"I trust my humble efforts will please you," said Prunella. "I have here some lines to a nightingale, which have been very much praised in our village. Shall I read them?"

"If you wish," said the editor, by no means cheerfully.

Miss Prune raised her voice, and commenced:

"O star-eyed Nightingale,
How nobly thou dost sail
Through the air!
No other bird can compare
With the tuneful song
Which to thee doth belong.
I sit and hear thee sing,
While with tireless wing
Thou dost fly.
And it makes me feel so sad,
It makes me feel so bad,
I know not why,
And I heave so many sighs,
O warbler of the skies!"

"Is there much more?" asked the editor.

"That is the first verse. There are fifteen more," said Prunella.

"Then I think I shall not have time at present to hear you read it all. You may leave it, and I will look it over at my leisure."

"If it suits you," said Prunella, "how much will it be worth?"

"I don't understand."

"How much would you be willing to pay for it?"

"Oh, we never pay for poems," said Mr. Houghton.

"Why not?" asked Miss Prune, evidently disappointed.

"Our contributors are kind enough to send them gratuitously."

"Is that fostering American talent?" demanded Prunella, indignantly.

"American poetical talent doesn't require fostering, judging from the loads of poems which are sent in to us."

"You pay for stories, I presume?"

———

302

"Yes, we pay for good, popular stories."

"I have one here," said Prunella, untying her manuscript, "which I should like to read to you."

"You may read the first paragraph, if you please. I haven't time to hear more. What is the title?"

"'The Bandit's Bride.' This is the way it opens:

"'The night was tempestuous. Lightnings flashed in the cerulean sky, and the deep-voiced thunder rolled from one end of the firmament to the other. It was a landscape in Spain. From a rocky defile gayly pranced forth a masked cavalier, Roderigo di Lima, a famous bandit chief.

"'"Ha! ha!" he laughed in demoniac glee, "the night is well fitted to my purpose. Ere it passes, Isabella Gomez shall be mine."'"

"I think that will do," said Mr. Houghton, hastily. "I am afraid that style won't suit our readers."

"Why not?" demanded Prunella, sharply. "I can assure you, sir, that it has been praised by excellent judges in our village."

"It is too exciting for our readers. You had better carry it to The Weekly Corsair."

"Do they pay well for contributions?"

"I really can't say. How much do you expect?"

"This story will make about five columns. I think twenty-five dollars will be about right."

"I am afraid you will be disappointed. We can't afford to pay such prices, and the Corsair has a smaller circulation than our paper."

"How much do you pay?"

"Two dollars a column."

"I expected more," said Prunella, "but I will write for you at that price."

"Send us something suited to our paper, and we will pay for it at that price."

"I will write you a story tomorrow. Good-morning, sir."

"Good-morning, Miss Prune."

The young lady with ringlets sailed out of the editor's room, and Oscar, nudging Harry, said, "Now it is our turn. Come along. Follow me, and don't be frightened."

CHAPTER XXVIII

ACCEPTED

The editor of the Standard looked with some surprise at the two boys. As editor, he was not accustomed to receive such young visitors. He was courteous, however, and said, pleasantly:

"What can I do for you, young gentlemen?"

"Are you the editor of the Standard?" asked Harry, diffidently.

"I am. Do you wish to subscribe?"

"I have already written something for your paper," Harry continued.

"Indeed!" said the editor. "Was it poetry or prose?"

Harry felt flattered by the question. To be mistaken for a poet he felt to be very complimentary. If he had known how much trash weekly found its way to the Standard office, under the guise of poetry, he would have felt less flattered.

"I have written some essays over the name of 'Franklin,'" he hastened to say.

"Ah, yes, I remember, and very sensible essays too. You are young to write."

"Yes, sir; I hope to improve as I grow older."

By this time Oscar felt impelled to speak for his friend. It seemed to him that Harry was too modest.

"My friend is assistant editor of a New Hampshire paper, The Centreville Gazette," he announced.

"Indeed!" said the editor, looking surprised. "He is certainly young for an editor."

"My friend is not quite right," said Harry, hastily. "I am one of the compositors on that paper."

"But you write editorial paragraphs," said Oscar.

"Yes, unimportant ones."

"And are you, too, an editor?" asked the editor of the Standard, addressing Oscar with a smile.

"Not exactly," said Oscar; "but I am an editor's son. Perhaps you are acquainted with my father, John Vincent of this city."

"Are you his son?" said the editor, respectfully. "I know your father slightly. He is one of our ablest journalists."

"Thank you, sir."

"I am very glad to receive a visit from you, and should be glad to print anything from your pen."

"I am not sure about that," said Oscar, smiling. "If I have a talent for writing, it hasn't developed itself yet. But my friend here takes to it as naturally as a duck takes to water."

"Have you brought me another essay, Mr. 'Franklin'?" asked the editor, turning to Harry. "I address you by your nom de plume, not knowing your real name."

"Permit me to introduce my friend, Harry Walton," said Oscar.

"Harry, where is your story?"

"I have brought you in a story," said Harry, blushing. "It is my first attempt, and may not suit you, but I shall be glad if you will take the trouble to examine it."

"With pleasure," said the editor. "Is it long?"

"About two columns. It is of a humorous character."

The editor reached out his hand, and, taking the manuscript, unrolled it. He read the first few lines, and they seemed to strike his attention.

"If you will amuse yourselves for a few minutes, I will read it at once," he said. "I don't often do it, but I will break over my custom this time."

"Thank you, sir," said Harry.

"There are some of my exchanges," said the editor, pointing to a pile on the floor. "You may find something to interest you in some of them."

They picked up some papers, and began to read. But Harry could not help thinking of the verdict that was to be pronounced on his manuscript. Upon that a great deal hinged. If he could feel that he was able to produce anything that would command compensation, however small, it would make him proud and happy. He tried, as he gazed furtively over his paper at the editor's face, to anticipate his decision, but the latter was too much accustomed to reading manuscript to show the impression made upon him.

Fifteen minutes passed, and he looked up.

"Well, Mr. Walton," he said, "your first attempt is a success."

Harry's face brightened.

"May I ask if the plot is original?"

"It is so far as I know, sir. I don't think I ever read anything like it."

"Of course there are some faults in the construction, and the dialogue might be amended here and there. But it is very creditable, and I will use it in the Standard if you desire it."

"I do, sir."

"And how much are you willing to pay for it?" Oscar struck in.

The editor hesitated.

"It is not our custom to pay novices just at first," he said. "If Mr. Walton keeps on writing, he would soon command compensation."

Harry would not have dared to press the matter, but Oscar was not so diffident. Indeed, it is easier to be bold in a friend's cause than one's own.

"Don't you think it is worth being paid for, if it is worth printing?" he persisted.

"Upon that principle, we should feel obliged to pay for poetry," said the editor.

"Oh," said Oscar, "poets don't need money. They live on flowers and dew-drops."

The editor smiled.

"You think prose-writers require something more substantial?"

"Yes, sir."

"I will tell you how the matter stands," said the editor. "Mr. Walton is a beginner. He has his reputation to make. When it is made he will be worth a fair price to me, or any of my brother editors."

"I see," said Oscar; "but his story must be worth something. It will fill up two columns. If you didn't print it, you would have to pay somebody for writing these two columns."

"You have some reason in what you say. Still our ordinary rule is based on justice. A distinction should be made between new contributors and old favorites."

"Yes, sir. Pay the first smaller sums."

If the speaker had not been John Vincent's son, it would have been doubtful if his reasoning would have prevailed. As it was, the editor yielded.

"I may break over my rule in the case of your friend," said the editor; "but he must be satisfied with a very small sum for the present."

"Anything will satisfy me, sir," said Harry, eagerly.

"Your story will fill two columns. I commonly pay two dollars a column for such articles, if by practiced writers. I will give you half that."

"Thank you, sir. I accept it," said Harry, promptly.

"In a year or so I may see my way clear to paying you more, Mr. Walton; but you must consider that I give you the opportunity of winning popularity, and regard this as part of your compensation, at present."

"I am quite satisfied, sir," said Harry, his heart fluttering with joy and triumph. "May I write you some more sketches?"

"I shall be happy to receive and examine them; but you must not be disappointed if from time to time I reject your manuscripts."
"No, sir; I will take it as a hint that they need improving."

"I will revise my friend's stories, sir," said Oscar, humorously, "and give him such hints as my knowledge of the world may suggest."

"No doubt such suggestions from so mature a friend will materially benefit them," said the editor, smiling.

He opened his wallet, and, drawing out a two-dollar bill, handed it to Harry.

"I shall hope to pay you often," he said, "for similar contributions."

"Thank you, sir," said Harry.

Feeling that their business was at an end, the boys withdrew. As they reached the foot of the stairs, Oscar took off his cap, and bowed low.

"Mr. Lynn, I congratulate you," he said.

"I can't tell you how glad I feel, Oscar," said Harry, his face radiant.

"Let me suggest that you owe me a commission for impressing upon the editor the propriety of paying you."

"How much do you ask?"

"An ice-cream will be satisfactory."

"All right."

"Come round to Copeland's then. We'll celebrate your success in a becoming manner."

CHAPTER XXIX

MRS. CLINTON'S PARTY

When Oscar and Harry reached home they were met by Maud, who flourished in her hand what appeared to be a note.

"What is it, Maud?" asked Oscar. "A love-letter for me?"

"Don't flatter yourself, Oscar. No girl would be so foolish as to write you a love-letter. It is an invitation to a party on Saturday evening."

"Where?"

"At Mrs. Clinton's."

"I think I will decline," said Oscar. "I wouldn't like to leave Harry alone."

"Oh, he is included too. Mrs. Clinton heard of his being here, and expressly included him in the invitation."

"That alters the case. You'll go, Harry, won't you?"

"I am afraid I shouldn't know how to behave at a fashionable party," said Harry.

"Oh, you've only got to make me your model," said Oscar, "and you'll be all right."

"Did you ever see such conceit, Mr. Walton?" said Maud.

"It reminds me of Fletcher," said Harry.

"Fitz Fletcher? By the way, he will probably be there. His family are acquainted with the Clintons."

"Yes, he is invited," said Maud.

"Good! Then there's promise of fun," said Oscar. "You'll see Fitz with his best company manners on."

"I am afraid he won't enjoy meeting me there," said Harry.

"Probably not."

"I don't see why," said Maud.

"Shall I tell, Harry?"

"Certainly."

"To begin with, Fletcher regards himself as infinitely superior to Walton here, because his father is rich, and Walton's poor. Again, Harry is a printer, and works for a living, which Fitz considers degrading. Besides all this, Harry was elected President of our Debating Society—an office which Fitz wanted."

"I hope," said Maud, "that Mr. Fletcher's dislike does not affect your peace of mind, Mr. Walton."

"Not materially," said Harry, laughing.

"By the way, Maud," said Oscar, "did I ever tell you how Fletcher's pride was mortified at school by our discovering his relationship to a tin-peddler?"

"No, tell me about it."

The story, already familiar to the reader, was graphically told by Oscar, and served to amuse his sister.

"He deserved the mortification," she said. "I shall remember it if he shows any of his arrogance at the party."

"Fletcher rather admires Maud," said Oscar, after his sister had gone out of the room; "but the favor isn't reciprocated. If he undertakes to say anything to her against you, she will take him down, depend upon it."

Saturday evening came, and Harry, with Oscar and his sister, started for the party. Our hero, having confessed his inability to dance, had been diligently instructed in the Lancers by Oscar, so that he felt some confidence in being able to get through without any serious blunder.

"Of course you must dance, Harry," he said. "You don't want to be a wall-flower."

"I may have to be," said Harry. "I shall know none of the young ladies except your sister."

"Maud will dance the first Lancers with you, and I will get you a partner for the second."

"You may dispose of me as you like, Oscar."

"Wisely said. Don't forget that I am your Mentor."

When they entered the brilliantly lighted parlors, they were already half full. Oscar introduced his friend to Mrs. Clinton.

"I am glad to see you here, Mr. Walton," said the hostess, graciously. "Oscar, I depend upon you to introduce your friend to some of the young ladies."

"You forget my diffidence, Mrs. Clinton."

"I didn't know you were troubled in that way.'"

"See how I am misjudged. I am painfully bashful."

"You hide it well," said the hostess, with a smile.

"Escort my sister to a seat, Harry," said Oscar. "By the way, you two will dance in the first Lancers."

"If Miss Maud will accept so awkward a partner," said Harry.

"Oh, yes, Mr. Walton. I'll give you a hint if you are going wrong."

Five minutes later Fletcher touched Oscar on the shoulder.

"Oscar, where is your sister?" he asked.

"There," said Oscar, pointing her out.

Fletcher, who was rather near-sighted, did not at first notice that Harry Walton was sitting beside the young lady. He advanced, and made a magnificent bow, on which he rather prided himself.

"Good-evening, Miss Vincent," he said.

"Good-evening, Mr. Fletcher."

"I am very glad you have favored the party with your presence."

"Thank you, Mr. Fletcher. Don't turn my head with your compliments."

"May I hope you will favor me with your hand in the first Lancers?"

"I am sorry, Mr. Fletcher, but I am engaged to Mr. Walton. I believe you are acquainted with him."

Fletcher for the first time observed our hero, and his face wore a look of mingled annoyance and scorn.

"I have met the gentleman," he said, haughtily.

"Mr. Fletcher and I have met frequently," said Harry, pleasantly.

"I didn't expect to meet you here," said Fletcher with marked emphasis.

"Probably not," said Harry. "My invitation is due to my being a friend of Oscar's."

"I was not aware that you danced," said Fletcher who was rather curious on the subject.

"I don't—much."

"Where did you learn—in the printing office?"

"No, in the city."

"Ah! Indeed!"

Fletcher thought he had wasted time enough on our hero, and turned again to Maud.

"May I have the pleasure of your hand in the second dance?" he asked.

"I will put you down for that, if you desire it."

"Thank you."

**Harry, Oscar and Maud attend a party where people
are doing a dance called the Lancers. This is a
picture of people doing that dance.**

It so happened that when Harry and Maud took the floor, they found Fletcher their vis-a-vis. Perhaps it was this that made Harry more emulous to get through without making any blunders. At any rate, he succeeded, and no one in the set suspected that it was his first appearance in public as a dancer.

Fletcher was puzzled. He had hoped that Harry would make himself ridiculous, and throw the set into confusion. But the dance passed off smoothly, and in due time Fletcher led out Maud. If he had known his own interest, he would have kept silent about Harry, but he had little discretion.

"I was rather surprised to see Walton here," he began.

"Didn't you know he was in the city?

"Yes, I met him with Oscar."

"Then why were you surprised?"

"Because his social position does not entitle him to appear in such a company. When I first knew him, he was only a printer's apprentice."

Fletcher wanted to say printer's devil, but did not venture to do so in the presence of a young lady.

"He will rise higher than that."

"I dare say," said Fletcher, with a sneer, "he will rise in time to be a journeyman with a salary of fifteen dollars a week."

"If I am not mistaken in Mr. Walton, he will rise much higher than that. Many of our prominent men have sprung from beginnings like his."

"It must be rather a trial to him to come here. His father is a day-laborer, I believe, and of course he has never been accustomed to any refinement or polish."

"I don't detect the absence of either," said Maud, quietly.

"Do you believe in throwing down all social distinctions, and meeting the sons of laborers on equal terms?"

"As to that," said Maud, meeting her partner's glance, "I am rather democratic. I could even meet the son of a tin-peddler on equal terms, provided he were a gentleman."

The blood rushed to Fletcher's cheeks.

"A tin-peddler!" he exclaimed.

"Yes! Suppose you were the son, or relation, of a tin-peddler, why should I consider that? It would make you neither better nor worse."

"I have no connection with tin-peddlers," said Fletcher, hastily. "Who told you I had?"

"I only made a supposition, Mr. Fletcher."

But Fletcher thought otherwise. He was sure that Maud had heard of his mortification at school, and it disturbed him not a little, for, in spite of her assurance, he felt that she believed the story, and it annoyed him so much that he did not venture to make any other reference to Harry.

"Poor Fitz!" said Oscar, when on their way home Maud gave an account of their conversation. "I am afraid he will murder the tin-peddler some time, to get rid of such an odious relationship."

CHAPTER XXX

TWO LETTERS FROM THE WEST

The vacation was over all too soon, yet, brief as it was, Harry looked back upon it with great satisfaction. He had been kindly received in the family of a man who stood high in the profession which he was ambitious to enter; he had gratified his curiosity to see the chief city of New England; and, by no means least, he had secured a position as paid contributor for the Standard.

"I suppose you will be writing another story soon," said Oscar.

"Yes," said Harry, "I have got the plan of one already."

"If you should write more than you can get into the Standard, you had better send something to the Weekly Argus."

"I will; but I will wait till the Standard prints my first sketch, so that I can refer to that in writing to the Argus."

"Perhaps you are right. There's one advantage to not presenting yourself. They won't know you're only a boy."

"Unless they judge so from my style."

"I don't think they would infer it from that. By the way, Harry, suppose my father could find an opening for you as a reporter on his paper—would you be willing to accept it?"

"I am not sure whether it would be best for me," said Harry, slowly, "even if I were qualified."

"There is more chance to rise on a city paper."

"I don't know. If I stay here I may before many years control a paper of my own. Then, if I want to go into politics, there would be more chance in the country than in the city."

"Would you like to go into politics?"

"I am rather too young to decide about that; but if I could be of service in that way, I don't see why I should not desire it."

"Well, Harry, I think you are going the right way to work."

"I hope so. I don't want to be promoted till I am fit for it. I am going to work hard for the next two or three years."

"I wish I were as industrious as you are, Harry."

"And I wish I knew as much as you do, Oscar."

Say no more, or we shall be forming a Mutual Admiration Society," said Oscar, laughing.

Harry received a cordial welcome back to the printing office. Mr. Anderson asked him many questions about Mr. Vincent; and our hero felt that his employer regarded him with increased consideration, on account of his acquaintance with the great city editor. This consideration was still farther increased when Mr. Anderson learned our hero's engagement by the Weekly Standard.

Three weeks later, the Standard published Harry's sketch, and accepted another, at the same price. Before this latter was printed, Harry wrote a third sketch, which he called "Phineas Popkin's Engagement." This he enclosed to the Weekly Argus, with a letter in which he referred to his engagement by the Standard. In reply he received the following letter:

"BOSTON, Jan., 18—,

"MR. FRANK LYNN,—Dear Sir: We enclose three dollars for your sketch, 'Phineas Popkin's Engagement.' We shall be glad to receive other sketches, of similar character and length, and, if accepted, we will pay the same price therefor.

"I. B. FITCH & Co."

The Argus is one of the newspapers that buy a story from Harry.

This was highly satisfactory to Harry. He was now an accepted contributor to two weekly papers, and the addition to his income would be likely to reach a hundred dollars a year. All this he would be able to lay up, and as much or more from his salary on the Gazette. He felt on the high road to success. Seeing that his young compositor was meeting with success and appreciation abroad, Mr. Anderson called upon him more frequently to write paragraphs for the Gazette. Though this work was gratuitous, Harry willingly undertook it. He felt that in this way he was preparing himself for the career to which he steadily looked forward. Present compensation, he justly reasoned, was of small importance, compared with the chance of improvement. In this view, Ferguson, who proved to be a very judicious friend, fully concurred. Indeed Harry and he became closer than before, if that were possible, and they felt that Clapp's departure was by no means to be regretted. They were remarking this one day, when Mr. Anderson, who had been examining his mail, looked up suddenly, and said, "What do you think, Mr. Ferguson? I've got a letter from Clapp."

"A letter from Clapp? Where is he?" inquired Ferguson, with interest.

"This letter is dated at St. Louis. He doesn't appear to be doing very well."

"I thought he was going to California."

"So he represented. But here is the letter." Ferguson took it, and, after reading, handed it to Harry.

It ran thus:

"ST. LOUIS, April 4, 18—.

"JOTHAM ANDERSON, ESQ.,—Dear Sir: Perhaps you will be surprised to hear from me, but I feel as if I would like to hear from Centreville, where I worked so long. The man that induced me and Harrison to come out here left us in the lurch three days after we reached St. Louis. He said he was going on to San Francisco, and he had only money enough to pay his own expenses. As Luke and I were not provided with money, we had a pretty hard time at first, and had to pawn some of our clothes, or we should have starved. Finally I got a job in the Democrat office, and a week after, Luke got something to do, though it didn't pay very well. So we scratched along as well as we could. Part of the time since we have been out of work, and we haven't found 'coming West' all that it was cracked up to be.

"Are Ferguson and Harry Walton still working for you? I should like to come back to the Gazette office, and take my old job; but I haven't got five dollars ahead to pay my travelling expenses. If you will send me out thirty dollars, I will come right on, and work it out after I come back. Hoping for an early reply, I am,

"Yours respectfully,
"HENRY CLAPP."

"Are you going to send out the money, Mr. Anderson?" asked Ferguson.

"Not I. Now that Walton has got well learnt, I don't need another workman. I shall respectfully decline his offer."

Both Harry and Ferguson were glad to hear this, for they felt that Clapp's presence would be far from making the office more agreeable.

"Here's a letter for you, Walton, also post-marked St. Louis," said Mr. Anderson, just afterward.

Harry took it with surprise, and opened it at once.

"It's from Luke Harrison," he said, looking at the signature.

"Does he want you to send him thirty dollars?" asked Ferguson.

"Listen and I will read the letter."

"DEAR HARRY," it commenced, "you will perhaps think it strange that I have written to you; but we used to be good friends. I write to tell you that I don't like this place. I haven't got along well, and I want to get back. Now I am going to ask of you a favor. Will you lend me thirty or forty dollars, to pay my fare home? I will pay you back in a month or two months sure, after I get to work. I will also pay you the few dollars which I borrowed some time ago. I ought to have done it before, but I was thoughtless, and I kept putting it off. Now, Harry, I know you have the money, and you can lend it to me just as well as not, and I'll be sure to pay it back before you need it. Just get a post office order, and send it to Luke Harrison, 17 R—— Street, St. Louis, and I'll be sure to get it. Give my respects to Mr. Anderson, and also to Mr. Ferguson.

"Your friend,
"LUKE HARRISON."

"There is a chance for a first-class investment, Harry," said Ferguson.

"Do you want to join me in it?"

"No, I would rather pay the money to have 'your friend' keep away."

"I don't want to be unkind or disobliging," said Harry, "but I don't feel like giving Luke this money. I know he would never pay me back."

"Say no, then."

"I will. Luke will be mad, but I can't help it."

So both Mr. Anderson and Harry wrote declining to lend. The latter, in return, received a letter from Luke, denouncing him as a "mean, miserly hunks"; but even this did not cause him to regret his decision.

CHAPTER XXXI

ONE STEP UPWARD

In real life the incidents that call for notice do not occur daily. Months and years pass, sometimes, where the course of life is quiet and uneventful. So it was with Harry Walton. He went to his daily work with unfailing regularity, devoted a large part of his leisure to reading and study, or writing sketches for the Boston papers, and found himself growing steadily wiser and better informed. His account in the savings-bank grew slowly, but steadily; and on his nineteenth birthday, when we propose to look in upon him again, he was worth five hundred dollars.

Some of my readers who are favored by fortune may regard this as a small sum. It is small in itself, but it was not small for a youth in Harry's position to have saved from his small earnings. But of greater value than the sum itself was the habit of self-denial and saving which our hero had formed. He had started in the right way, and made a beginning which was likely to lead to prosperity in the end. It had not been altogether easy to save this sum. Harry's income had always been small, and he might, without incurring the charge of excessive extravagance, have spent the whole. He had denied himself on many occasions, where most boys of his age would have yielded to the temptation of spending money for pleasure or personal gratification; but he had been rewarded by the thought that he was getting on in the world.

"This is my birthday, Mr. Ferguson," he said, as he entered the printing-office on that particular morning.

"Is it?" asked Ferguson, looking up from his case with interest. "How venerable are you, may I ask?"

"I don't feel very venerable as yet," said Harry, with a smile. "I am nineteen."

"You were sixteen when you entered the office."

"As printer's devil—yes."

"You have learned the business pretty thoroughly. You are as good a workman as I now, though I am fifteen years older."

"You are too modest, Mr. Ferguson."

"No, it is quite true. You are as rapid and accurate as I am, and you ought to receive as high pay."

"That will come in time. You know I make something by writing for the papers."

"That's extra work. How much did you make in that way last year?"

"I can tell you, because I figured it up last night. It was one hundred and twenty-five dollars, and I put every cent into the savings-bank."

"That is quite an addition to your income."

"I shall make more this year. I am to receive two dollars a column, hereafter, for my sketches."

"I congratulate you, Harry—the more heartily, because I think you deserve it. Your recent sketches show quite an improvement over those you wrote a year ago."

"Do you really think so?" said Harry, with evident pleasure.

"I have no hesitation in saying so. You write with greater ease than formerly, and your style is less that of a novice."

"So I have hoped and thought; but of course I was prejudiced in my own favor."

"You may rely upon it. Indeed, your increased pay is proof of it. Did you ask it?"

"The increase? No, the editor of the Standard wrote me voluntarily that he considered my contributions worth the additional amount."

"That must be very pleasant. I tell you what, Harry, I've a great mind to set up opposition to you in the story line."

"Do so," said Harry, smiling.

"I would if I had the slightest particle of imagination; but the fact is, I'm too practical and matter-of-fact. Besides, I never had any talent for writing of any kind. Some time I may become publisher of a village paper like this; but farther than that I don't aspire."

"We are to be partners in that, you know, Ferguson."

"That may be, for a time; but you will rise higher than that, Harry."

"I am afraid you overrate me."

"No; I have observed you closely in the time we have been together, and I have long felt that you are destined to rise from the ranks in which I am content to remain. Haven't you ever felt so, yourself, Harry?"

Harry's cheek flushed, and his eye lighted up.

———

"I won't deny that I have such thoughts sometimes," he said; "but it may end in that."

"It often does end in that; but it is only where ambition is not accompanied by faithful work. Now you are always at work. You are doing what you can to help fortune, and the end will be that fortune will help you."

"I hope so, at any rate," said Harry, thoughtfully. "I should like to fill an honorable position, and do some work by which I might be known in after years."

"Why not? The boys and young men of today are hereafter to fill the highest positions in the community and State. Why may not the lot fall to you?"

"I will try, at any rate, to qualify myself. Then if responsibilities come, I will try to discharge them."

The conversation was here interrupted by the entrance of Mr. Anderson, the editor of the Gazette. He was not as well or strong as when we first made his acquaintance. Then he seemed robust enough, but now he was thinner, and moved with slower gait. It was not easy to say what had undermined his strength, for he had had no severe fit of sickness; but certainly he was in appearance several years older than when Harry entered the office.

"How do you feel this morning, Mr. Anderson?" asked Ferguson.

"I feel weak and languid, and indisposed to exertion of any kind."

"You need some change."

"That is precisely what I have thought myself. The doctor advises change of scene, and this very morning I had a letter from a brother in Wisconsin, asking me to come out and visit him."

"I have no doubt it would do you good."

"So it would. But how can I go? I can't take the paper with me," said Mr. Andersen, rather despondently.

"No; but you can leave Harry to edit it in your absence."

"Mr. Ferguson!" exclaimed Harry, startled by the proposition.

"Harry as editor!" repeated Mr. Anderson.

"Yes; why not? He is a practiced writer. For more than two years he has written for two Boston papers."

"But he is so young. How old are you, Harry?" asked the editor.

"Nineteen today, sir."

"Nineteen. That's very young for an editor."

"Very true; but, after all, it isn't so much the age as the qualifications, is it, Mr. Anderson?"

"True," said the editor, meditatively. "Harry, do you think you could edit the paper for two or three months?"

"I think I could," said Harry, with modest confidence. His heart beat high at the thought of the important position which was likely to be opened to him; and plans of what he would do to make the paper interesting already began to be formed in his mind.

"It never occurred to me before, but I really think you could," said the editor, "and that would remove every obstacle to my going. By the way, Harry, you would have to find a new boarding-place, for Mrs. Anderson would accompany me, and we should shut up the house."

"Perhaps Ferguson would take me in?" said Harry.

"I should be glad to do so; but I don't know that my humble fare would be good enough for an editor."

Harry smiled. "I won't put on airs," he said, "till my commission is made out."

"I am afraid that I can't offer high pay for your services in that capacity," said Mr. Anderson.

"I shall charge nothing, sir," said Harry, "but thank you for the opportunity of entering, if only for a short time, a profession to which it is my ambition to belong."

After a brief consultation with his wife, Mr. Anderson appointed Harry editor pro tem., and began to make arrangements for his journey. Harry's weekly wages were raised to fifteen dollars, out of which he was to pay Ferguson four dollars a week for board.

So our hero found himself, at nineteen, the editor of an old established paper, which, though published in a country village, was not without its share of influence in the county and State.

CHAPTER XXXII

THE YOUNG EDITOR

The next number of the Centreville Gazette contained the following notice from the pen of Mr. Anderson:

"For the first time since our connection with the Gazette, we purpose taking a brief respite from our duties. The state of our health renders a vacation desirable, and an opportune invitation from a brother at the West has been accepted. Our absence may extend to two or three months. In the interim we have committed the editorial management to Mr. Harry Walton, who has been connected with the paper, in a different capacity, for nearly three years. Though Mr. Walton is a very young man, he has already acquired a reputation, as contributor to papers of high standing in Boston, and we feel assured that our subscribers will have no reason to complain of the temporary change in the editorship."

"The old man has given you quite a handsome notice, Harry," said Ferguson.

"I hope I shall deserve it," said Harry; "but I begin now to realize that I am young to assume such responsible duties. It would have seemed more appropriate for you to undertake them."

"I can't write well enough, Harry. I like to read, but I can't produce. In regard to the business management I feel competent to advise."

"I shall certainly be guided by your advice, Ferguson."

As it may interest the reader, we will raise the curtain and show our young hero in the capacity of editor. The time is ten days after Mr. Anderson's absence. Harry was accustomed to do his work as compositor in the morning and the early part of the afternoon. From three to five he occupied the editorial chair, read letters, wrote paragraphs, and saw visitors. He had just seated himself, when a man entered the office and looked about him inquisitively.

"I would like to see the editor," he said.

"I am the editor," said Harry, with dignity.

The visitor looked surprised.

"You are the youngest-looking editor I have met," he said. "Have you filled the office long?"

"Not long," said Harry. "Can I do anything for you?"

"Yes, sir, you can. First let me introduce myself. I am Dr. Theophilus Peabody."

"Will you be seated, Dr. Peabody?"

"You have probably heard of me before," said the visitor.

"I can't say that I have."

"I am surprised at that," said the doctor, rather disgusted to find himself unknown. "You must have heard of Peabody's Unfailing Panacea."

"I am afraid I have not."

"You are young," said Dr. Peabody, compassionately; "that accounts for it. Peabody's Panacea, let me tell you, sir, is the great remedy of the age. It has effected more cures, relieved more pain, soothed more aching bosoms, and done more good, than any other medicine in existence."

"It must be a satisfaction to you to have conferred such a blessing on mankind," said Harry, inclined to laugh at the doctor's magniloquent style.

"It is. I consider myself one of the benefactors of mankind; but, sir, the medicine has not yet been fully introduced. There are thousands, who groan on beds of pain, who are ignorant that for the small sum of fifty cents they could be restored to health and activity."

"That's a pity."

"It is a pity, Mr. ——"

"Walton."

"Mr. Walton—I have called, sir, to ask you to co-operate with me in making it known to the world, so far as your influence extends."

"Is your medicine a liquid?"

"No, sir; it is in the form of pills, twenty-four in a box. Let me show you."

The doctor opened a wooden box, and displayed a collection of very unwholesome-looking brown pills.

"Try one, sir; it won't do you any harm."

"Thank you; I would rather not. I don't like pills. What will they cure?"

"What won't they cure? I've got a list of fifty-nine diseases in my circular, all of which are relieved by Peabody's Panacea. They may cure more; in fact, I've been told of a consumptive patient who was considerably relieved by a single box. You won't try one?"

"I would rather not."

"Well, here is my circular, containing accounts of remarkable cures performed. Permit me to present you a box."

"Thank you," said Harry, dubiously.

"You'll probably be sick before long," said the doctor, cheerfully, "and then the pills will come handy."

"Doctor," said Ferguson, gravely, "I find my hair getting thin on top of the head. Do you think the panacea would restore it?"

"Yes," said the doctor, unexpectedly. "I had a case, in Portsmouth, of a gentleman whose head was as smooth as a billiard-ball. He took the pills for another complaint, and was surprised, in the course of three weeks, to find young hair sprouting all over the bald spot. Can't I sell you half a dozen boxes? You may have half a dozen for two dollars and a half."

Ferguson, who of course had been in jest, found it hard to forbear laughing, especially when Harry joined the doctor in urging him to purchase.

"Not today," he answered. "I can try Mr. Walton's box, and if it helps me I can order some more."

"You may not be able to get it, then," said the doctor, persuasively.

"I may not be in Centreville."

"If the panacea is well known, I can surely get it without difficulty."

"Not so cheap as I will sell it."

"I won't take any today," said Ferguson, decisively.

"You haven't told me what I can do for you," said Harry, who found the doctor's call rather long.

"I would like you to insert my circular to your paper. It won't take more than two columns."

"We shall be happy to insert it at regular advertising rates."

"I thought," said Dr. Peabody, disappointed, "that you might do it gratuitously, as I had given you a box."

"We don't do business on such terms," said Harry. "I think I had better return the box."

"No, keep it," said the doctor. "You will be willing to notice it, doubtless."

Harry rapidly penned this paragraph, and read it aloud:

"Dr. Theophilus Peabody has left with us a box of his Unfailing Panacea, which he claims will cure a large variety of diseases."

"Couldn't you give a list of the diseases?" insinuated the doctor.

"There are fifty-nine, you said?"

"Yes, sir."

"Then I am afraid we must decline."

Harry resumed his writing, and the doctor took his leave, looking far from satisfied.

"Here, Ferguson," said Harry, after the visitor had retired, "take the pills, and much good may they do you. Better take one now for the growth of your hair."

It was fortunate that Dr. Peabody did not hear the merriment that followed, or he would have given up the editorial staff of the Centreville Gazette as maliciously disposed to underrate his favorite medicine.

"Who wouldn't be an editor?" said Harry.

"I notice," said Ferguson, "that pill-tenders and blacking manufacturers are most liberal to the editorial profession. I only wish jewelers and piano manufacturers were as free with their manufactures. I would like a good gold watch, and I shall soon want a piano for my daughter."

"You may depend upon it, Ferguson, when such gifts come in, that I shall claim them as editorial perquisites."

"We won't quarrel about them till they come, Harry."

Our hero here opened a bulky communication.

"What is that?" asked Ferguson.

"An essay on 'The Immortality of the Soul'—covers fifteen pages foolscap. What shall I do with it?"

"Publish it in a supplement with Dr. Peabody's circular."

"I am not sure but the circular would be more interesting reading."

"From whom does the essay come?"

"It is signed 'L. S.'"

"Then it is by Lemuel Snodgrass, a retired schoolteacher, who fancies himself a great writer."

"He'll be offended if I don't print it, won't he?"

"I'll tell you how to get over that. Say, in an editorial paragraph, 'We have received a thoughtful essay from "L. S.," on "The Immortality of the Soul." We regret that its length precludes our publishing it in the Gazette. We would suggest to the author to print it in a pamphlet.' That suggestion will be regarded as complimentary, and we may get the job of printing it."

"I see you are shrewd, Ferguson. I will follow your advice."

CHAPTER XXXIII
AN UNEXPECTED PROPOSAL

During his temporary editorship, Harry did not feel at liberty to make any decided changes in the character or arrangement of the paper; but he was ambitious to improve it, as far as he was able, in its different departments. Mr. Anderson had become rather indolent in the collection of local news, merely publishing such items as were voluntarily contributed. Harry, after his day's work was over, made a little tour of the village, gathering any news that he thought would be of interest to the public. Moreover he made arrangements to obtain news of a similar nature from neighboring villages, and the result was, that in the course of a month he made the Gazette much more readable.

"Really, the Gazette gives a good deal more news than it used to," was a common remark.

It was probably in consequence of this improvement that new subscriptions began to come in, not from Centreville alone, but from towns in the neighborhood. This gratified and encouraged Harry, who now felt that he was on the right tack.

There was another department to which he devoted considerable attention. This was a condensed summary of news from all parts of the world, giving the preference and the largest space, of course, to American news. He aimed to supply those who did not take a daily paper with a brief record of events, such as they would not be likely, otherwise, to hear of. Of course all this work added to his labors as compositor; and his occasional sketches for Boston papers absorbed a large share of his time. Indeed, he had very little left at his disposal for rest and recreation.

"I am afraid you are working too hard, Harry," said Ferguson. "You are doing Mr. Anderson's work better than he ever did it, and your own too."

"I enjoy it," said Harry. "I work hard, I know, but I feel paid by the satisfaction of finding that my labors are appreciated."

"When Mr. Anderson gets back, he will find it necessary to employ you as assistant editor, for it won't do to let the paper get back to its former dullness."

"I will accept," said Harry, "if he makes the offer. I feel more and more that I must be an editor."

"You are certainly showing yourself competent for the position."

"I have only made a beginning," said our hero, modestly. "In time I think I could make a satisfactory paper."

One day, about two months after Mr. Anderson's departure, Ferguson and Harry were surprised, and not altogether agreeably, by the entrance of John Clapp and Luke Harrison. They looked far from prosperous. In fact, both of them were decidedly seedy. Going West had not effected an improvement in their fortunes.

"Is that you, Clapp?" asked Ferguson. "Where did you come from?"

"From St. Louis."

"Then you didn't feel inclined to stay there?"

"Not I. It's a beastly place. I came near starving."

Clapp would have found any place beastly where a fair day's work was required for fair wages, and my young readers in St. Louis, therefore, need not heed his disparaging remarks.

"How was it with you, Luke?" asked Harry. "Do you like the West no better than Clapp?"

"You don't catch me out there again," said Luke. "It isn't what it's cracked up to be. We had the hardest work in getting money enough to get us back."

As Luke did not mention the kind of hard work by which the money was obtained, I may state here that an evening's luck at the faro table had supplied them with money enough to pay the fare to Boston by railway; otherwise another year might have found them still in St. Louis.

"Hard work doesn't suit your constitution, does it?" said Ferguson, slyly.

"I can work as well as anybody," said Luke; "but I haven't had the luck of some people."

"You were lucky enough to have your fare paid to the West for you."

"Yes, and when we got there, the rascal left us to shift for ourselves. That ain't much luck."

"I've always had to shift for myself, and always expect to," was the reply.

"Oh, you're a model!" sneered Clapp. "You always were as sober and steady as a deacon. I wonder they didn't make you one."

"And Walton there is one of the same sort," said Luke. "I say, Harry, it was real mean in you not to send me the money I wrote for. You hadn't it, had you?"

"Yes," said Harry, firmly; "but I worked hard for it, and I didn't feel like giving it away."

"Who asked you to give it away? I only wanted to borrow it."

"That's the same thing—with you. You were not likely to repay it again."

"Do you mean to insult me?" blustered Luke.

"No, I never insult anybody. I only tell the truth. You know, Luke Harrison, whether I have reason for what I say."

"I wouldn't leave a friend to suffer when I had plenty of money in my pocket," said Luke, with an injured air. "If you had been a different sort of fellow I would have asked you for five dollars to keep me along till I can get work. I've come back with empty pockets."

"I'll lend you five dollars if you need it," said Harry, who judged from Luke's appearance that he told the truth.

"Will you?" said Luke, brightening up. "That's a good fellow. I'll pay you just as soon as I can."

Harry did not place much reliance on this assurance; but he felt that he could afford the loss of five dollars, if loss it should prove, and it might prevent Luke's obtaining the money in a more questionable way.

"Where's Mr. Anderson?" asked Clapp, looking round the office.

"He's been in Wisconsin for a couple of months."

"You don't say so! Why, who runs the paper?"

"Ferguson and I," said Harry.

"I mean who edits it?"

"Harry does that," said his fellow-workman.

"Whew!" exclaimed Clapp, in surprise. "Why, but two years ago you was only a printer's devil!"

"He's risen from the ranks," said Ferguson, "and I can say with truth that the Gazette has never been better than since it has been under his charge."

"How much does old Anderson pay you for taking his place?" asked Luke, who was quite as much surprised as Clapp.

"I don't ask anything extra. He pays me fifteen dollars a week as compositor."

"You're doing well," said Luke, enviously. "Got a big pile of money laid up, haven't you?"

"I have something in the bank."

"Harry writes stories for the Boston papers, also," said Ferguson. "He makes a hundred or two that way."

"Some folks are born to luck," said Clapp, discontentedly. "Here am I, six or eight years older, out of a job, and without a cent to fall back upon. I wish I was one of your lucky ones."

"You might have had a few hundred dollars, at any rate," said Ferguson, "if you hadn't chosen to spend all your money when you were earning good wages."

"A man must have a little enjoyment. We can't drudge all the time."

"It's better to do that than to be where you are now."

But Clapp was not to be convinced that he was himself to blame for his present disagreeable position. He laid the blame on fortune, like thousands of others. He could not see that Harry's good luck was the legitimate consequence of industry and frugality.

After a while the two left the office. They decided to seek their old boarding-house, and remain there for a week, waiting for something to turn up.

The next day Harry received the following letter from Mr. Anderson:

"DEAR WALTON: My brother urges me to settle permanently at the West. I am offered a partnership in a paper in this vicinity, and my health has much improved here. The West seems the place for me. My only embarrassment is the paper. If I could dispose of the Gazette for two thousand dollars cash, I could see my way clear to remove. Why can't you and Ferguson buy it? The numbers which you have sent me show that you are quite capable of filling the post of editor; and you and Ferguson can do the mechanical part. I think it will be a good chance for you. Write me at once whether there is any likelihood of your purchasing.

"Your friend,

"JOTHAM ANDERSON."

Harry's face flushed eagerly as he read this letter. Nothing would suit him better than to make this arrangement, if only he could provide the purchase money. But this was likely to present a difficulty.

CHAPTER XXXIV

A FRIEND IN NEED

Harry at once showed Ferguson the letter he had received.

"What are you going to do about it?" asked his friend.

"I should like to buy the paper, but I don't see how I can. Mr. Anderson wants two thousand dollars cash."

"How much have you got?"

"Only five hundred."

"I have seven hundred and fifty," said Ferguson, thoughtfully.

Harry's face brightened.

"Why can't we go into partnership?" he asked.

"That is what we spoke of once," said Ferguson, "and it would suit me perfectly; but there is a difficulty. Your money and mine added together will not be enough."

"Perhaps Mr. Anderson would take a mortgage on the establishment for the balance."

"I don't think so. He says expressly that he wants cash."

Harry looked disturbed.

"Do you think any one would lend us the money on the same terms?" he asked, after a while.

"Squire Trevor is the only man in the village likely to have money to lend. There he is in the street now. Run down, Harry, and ask him to step in a minute."

Our hero seized his hat, and did as requested. He returned immediately, followed by Squire Trevor, a stout, puffy little man, reputed shrewd and a capitalist.

"Excuse our calling you in, Squire Trevor," said Ferguson, "but we want to consult you on a matter of business. Harry, just show the squire Mr. Anderson's letter."

The squire read it deliberately.

"Do you want my advice?" he said, looking up from the perusal. "Buy the paper. It is worth what Anderson asks for it."

"So I think, but there is a difficulty. Harry and I can only raise twelve hundred dollars or so between us."

"Give a note for the balance. You'll be able to pay it off in two years, if you prosper."

"I am afraid that won't do. Mr. Anderson wants cash. Can't you lend us the money, Squire Trevor?" continued Ferguson, bluntly.

The village capitalist shook his head.

"If you had asked me last week I could have obliged you," he said; "but I was in Boston day before yesterday, and bought some railway stock which is likely to enhance in value. That leaves me short."

"Then you couldn't manage it?" said Ferguson, soberly.

"Not at present," said the squire, decidedly.

"Then we must write to Mr. Anderson, offering what we have, and a mortgage to secure the rest."

"That will be your best course."

"He may agree to our terms," said Harry, hopefully, after their visitor had left the office.

"We will hope so, at all events."

A letter was at once dispatched, and in a week the answer was received.

"I am sorry," Mr. Anderson wrote, "to decline your proposals, but, I have immediate need of the whole sum which I ask for the paper. If I cannot obtain it, I shall come back to Centreville, though I would prefer to remain here."

Upon the receipt of this letter, Ferguson gave up his work for the morning, and made a tour of the Village, calling upon all who he thought were likely to have money to lend. He had small expectation of success, but felt that he ought to try everywhere before giving up so good a chance.

While he was absent, Harry had a welcome visitor. It was no other than Professor Henderson, the magician, in whose employ he had spent three months some years before, as related in "Bound to Rise."

"Take a seat, professor," said Harry, cordially. "I am delighted to see you."

"How you have grown, Harry!" said the professor. "Why, I should hardly have known you!"

"We haven't met since I left you to enter this office."

"No; it is nearly three years. How do you like the business?"

"Very much indeed."

"Are you doing well?"

"I receive fifteen dollars a week."

"That is good. What are your prospects for the future?"

"They would be excellent if I had a little more capital."

"I don't see how you need capital, as a journeyman printer."

"I have a chance to buy out the paper."

"But who would edit it?"

"I would."

"You!" said the magician, rather incredulously.

"I have been the editor for the last two months."

"You—a boy!"

"I am nineteen, professor."

"I shouldn't have dreamed of editing a paper at nineteen; or, indeed, as old as I am now."

Harry laughed.

"You are too modest, professor. Let me show you our last two issues."

The professor took out his glasses, and sat down, not without considerable curiosity, to read a paper edited by one who only three years before had been his assistant.

"Did you write this article?" he asked, after a pause, pointing to the leader in the last issue of the Gazette.

"Yes, sir."

"Then, by Jove, you can write. Why, it's worthy of a man of twice your age!"

"Thank you, professor," said Harry, gratified.

"Where did you learn to write?"

Harry gave his old employer some account of his literary experiences, mentioning his connection with the two Boston weekly papers.

"You ought to be an editor," said the professor. "If you can do as much at nineteen, you have a bright future before you."

"That depends a little on circumstances. If I only could buy this paper, I would try to win reputation as well as money."

"What is your difficulty?"

"The want of money."

"How much do you need?"

"Eight hundred dollars."

"Is that all the price such a paper commands?"

"No. The price is two thousand dollars; but Ferguson and I can raise twelve hundred between us."

"Do you consider it good property?"

"Mr. Anderson made a comfortable living out of it, besides paying for office work. We should have this advantage, that we should be our own compositors."

"That would give you considerable to do, if you were editor also."

"I shouldn't mind," said Harry, "if I only had a paper of my own. I think I should be willing to work night and day."

"What are your chances of raising the sum you need?"

"Very small. Ferguson has gone out at this moment to see if he can find any one willing to lend; but we don't expect success."

"Why don't you apply to me?" asked the professor.

"I didn't know if you had the money to spare."

"I might conjure up some. Presto!—change!—you know. We professors of magic can find money anywhere."

"But you need some to work with. I have been behind the scenes," said Harry, smiling.

"But you don't know all my secrets, for all that. In sober earnest, I haven't been practicing magic these twenty-five years for nothing. I can lend you the money you want, and I will."

Harry seized his hand, and shook it with delight.

"How can I express my gratitude?" he said.

"By sending me your paper gratis, and paying me seven percent interest on my money."

"Agreed. Anything more?"

"Yes. I am to give an exhibition in the village tomorrow night. You must give me a good puff."

"With the greatest pleasure. I'll write it now."

"Before it takes place? I see you are following the example of some of the city dailies."

"And I'll print you some handbills for nothing."

"Good. When do you want the money? Will next week do?"

"Yes. Mr. Anderson won't expect the money before."

Here Ferguson entered the efface. Harry made a signal of silence to the professor, whom he introduced. Then he said:

"Well, Ferguson, what luck?"

"None at all," answered his fellow-compositor, evidently dispirited.

"Nobody seems to have any money. We shall have to give up our plan."

"I don't mean to give it up."

"Then perhaps you'll tell me where to find the money."

"I will."

"You don't mean to say—" began Ferguson, eagerly.

"Yes, I do. I mean to say that the money is found."

"Where?"

"Prof. Henderson has agreed to let us have it."

"Is that true?" said Ferguson, bewildered.

"I believe so," said the professor, smiling. "Harry has juggled the money out of me—you know he used to be in the business—and you can make your bargain as soon as you like."

It is hardly necessary to say that Prof. Henderson got an excellent notice in the next number of the Centreville Gazette; and it is my opinion that he deserved it.

CHAPTER XXXV

FLETCHER'S OPINION OF

HARRY WALTON

In two weeks all the business arrangements were completed, and Ferguson and Harry became joint proprietors of the Centreville Gazette, the latter being sole editor. The change was received with favor in the village, as Harry had, as editor pro tem. for two months, shown his competence for the position. It gave him prominence also in town, and, though only nineteen, he already was classed with the minister, the doctor and the lawyer. It helped him also with the weekly papers to which he contributed in Boston, and his pay was once more raised, while his sketches were more frequently printed. Now this was all very pleasant, but it was not long before our hero found himself overburdened with work.

"What is the matter Harry? You look pale," said Ferguson, one morning.

"I have a bad headache, and am feeling out of sorts."

"I don't wonder at it. You are working too hard."

"I don't know about that."

"I do. You do nearly as much as I, as a compositor. Then you do all the editorial work, besides writing sketches for the Boston papers."

"How can I get along with less? The paper must be edited, and I shouldn't like giving up writing for the Boston papers."

"I'll tell you what to do. Take a boy and train him up as a printer. After a while he will relieve you almost wholly, while, by the time he commands good wages, we shall be able to pay them."

"It is a good idea, Ferguson. Do you know of any boy that wants to learn printing?"

"Haven't you got a younger brother?"

"The very thing," said Harry, briskly. "Father wrote to me last week that he should like to get something for —."

"Better write and offer him a place in the office."

"I will."

The letter was written at once. An immediate answer was received, of a favorable nature. The boy was glad to leave home, and the father was pleased to have him under the charge of his older brother.

After he had become editor, and part proprietor of the Gazette, Harry wrote to Oscar Vincent to announce his promotion. Though Oscar had been in college now nearly two years, and they seldom met, the two were as warm friends as ever, and from time to time exchanged letters.

This was Oscar's reply:

"HARVARD COLLEGE, June 10.

"DEAR MR. EDITOR: I suppose that's the proper way to address you now. I congratulate you with all my heart on your brilliant success and rapid advancement. Here you are at nineteen, while I am only a rattle-brained sophomore. I don't mind being called that, by the way, for at least it credits me with the possession of brains. Not that I am doing so very badly. I am probably in the first third of the class, and that implies respectable scholarship here.

"But you—I can hardly realize that you, whom I knew only two or three years ago as a printer's apprentice (I won't use Fletcher's word), have lifted yourself to the responsible position of sole editor. Truly you have risen from the ranks!

"Speaking of Fletcher, by the way, you know he is my classmate. He occupies an honorable position somewhere near the foot of the class, where he is likely to stay, unless he receives from the faculty leave of absence for an unlimited period. I met him yesterday, swinging his little cane, and looking as dandified as he used to.

"'Hallo! Fletcher,' said I, 'I've just got a letter from a friend of yours.'

"'Who is it?' he asked.

"'Harry Walton.'

"'He never was a friend of mine,' said Fitz, turning up his delicately chiseled nose—'the beggarly printer's devil!'

"I hope you won't feel sensitive about the manner in which Fitz spoke of you.

"'You've made two mistakes,' said I. 'He's neither a beggar nor a printer's devil.'

"'He used to be,' retorted Fitz.

"'The last, not the first. You'll be glad to hear that he's getting on well.'

"'Has he had his wages raised twenty-five cents a week?' sneered Fitz.

"'He has lost his job,' said I.

"Fletcher actually looked happy, but I dashed his happiness by adding, 'but he's got a better one.'

"'What's that?' he snarled.

"'He has bought out the paper of Mr. Anderson, and is now sole editor and part proprietor.'

"'A boy like him buy a paper, without a cent of money and no education!'

"'You are mistaken. He had several hundred dollars, and as a writer he is considerably ahead of either of us.'

"'He'll run the paper into the ground,' said Fitz, prophetically.

"'If he does, it'll only be to give it firmer root.'

"'You are crazy about that country lout,' said Fitz. 'It isn't much to edit a little village paper like that, after all.'

"So you see what your friend Fitz thinks about it. As you may be in danger of having your vanity fed by compliments from other sources, I thought I would offset them by the candid opinion of a disinterested and impartial scholar like Fitz.

"I told my father of the step you have taken. 'Oscar,' said he, 'that boy is going to succeed. He shows the right spirit. I would have given him a job on my paper, but very likely he does better to stay where he is.'

"Perhaps you noticed the handsome notice he gave you in his paper yesterday. I really think he has a higher opinion of your talents than of mine; which, of course, shows singular lack of discrimination. However, you're my friend, and I won't make a fuss about it.

"I am cramming for the summer examinations and hot work I find it, I can tell you. This summer I am going to Niagara, and shall return by way of the St. Lawrence and Montreal, seeing the Thousand Islands, the rapids, and so on. I may send you a letter or two for the Gazette, if you will give me a puff in your editorial columns."

These letters were actually written, and, being very lively and readable, Harry felt quite justified in referring to them in a complimentary way. Fletcher's depreciation of him troubled him very little.

"It will make me neither worse nor better," he reflected. "The time will come, I hope, when I shall have risen high enough to be wholly indifferent to such ill-natured sneers."

His brother arrived in due time, and was set to work as Harry himself had been three years before. He was not as smart as Harry, nor was he ever likely to rise as high; but he worked satisfactorily, and made good progress, so that in six months he was able to relieve Harry of half his labors as compositor. This enabled him to give more time to his editorial duties. Both boarded at Ferguson's, where they had a comfortable home and good, plain fare.

Meanwhile, Harry was acknowledged by all to have improved the paper, and the most satisfactory evidence of the popular approval of his efforts came in an increased subscription list, and this, of course, made the paper more profitable. At the end of twelve months, the two partners had paid off the money borrowed from Professor Henderson, and owned the paper without incumbrance.

"A pretty good year's work, Harry," said Ferguson, cheerfully.

"Yes," said Harry; "but we'll do still better next year."

CHAPTER XXXVI

CONCLUSION

I have thus traced in detail the steps by which Harry Walton ascended from the condition of a poor farmer's son to the influential position of editor of a weekly newspaper. I call to mind now, however, that he is no longer a boy, and his future career will be of less interest to my young readers. Yet I hope they may be interested to hear, though not in detail, by what successive steps he rose still higher in position and influence.

Harry was approaching his twenty-first birthday when he was waited upon by a deputation of citizens from a neighboring town, inviting him to deliver a Fourth of July oration. He was at first disposed, out of modesty, to decline; but, on consultation with Ferguson, decided to accept and do his best. He was ambitious to produce a good impression, and his experience in the Debating Society gave him a moderate degree of confidence and self-reliance. When the time came he fully satisfied public expectation. I do not say that his oration was a model of eloquence, for that could not have been expected of one whose advantages had been limited, and one for whom I have never claimed extraordinary genius. But it certainly was well written and well delivered, and very creditable to the young orator. The favor with which it was received may have had something to do in influencing the people of Centreville to nominate and elect him, to the New Hampshire Legislature a few months later.

He entered that body, the youngest member in it. But his long connection with a Debating Society, and the experience he had gained in parliamentary proceedings, enabled him at once to become a useful working Member. He was successively re-elected for several years, during which he showed such practical ability that he obtained a State reputation. At twenty-eight he received a nomination for Congress, and was elected by a close vote. During all this time he remained in charge of the Centreville Gazette, but of course had long relinquished the task of a compositor into his brother's hands. He had no foolish ideas about this work being beneath him; but he felt that he could employ his time more profitably in other ways. Under his judicious management, the Gazette attained a circulation and influence that it had never before reached. The income derived from it was double that which it yielded in the days of his predecessor; and both he and Ferguson were enabled to lay by a few hundred dollars every year. But Harry had never sought wealth. He was content with a comfortable support and a competence. He liked influence and the popular respect, and he was gratified by the important trusts which he received. He was ambitious, but it was a creditable and honorable ambition. He sought to promote the public welfare, and advance the public interests, both as a speaker and as a writer; and though sometimes misrepresented, the people on the whole did him justice.

A few weeks after he had taken his seat in Congress, a young man was ushered into his private room. Looking up, he saw a man of about his own age, dressed with some attempt at style, but on the whole wearing a look of faded gentility.

"Mr. Walton," said the visitor, with some hesitation.

"That is my name. Won't you take a seat?"

The visitor sat down, but appeared ill at ease. He nervously fumbled at his hat, and did not speak.

"Can I do anything for you?" asked Harry, at length.

"I see you don't know me," said the stranger.

"I can't say I recall your features; but then I see a great many persons."

"I went to school at the Prescott Academy, when you were in the office of the Centreville Gazette."

Harry looked more closely, and exclaimed, in astonished recognition, "Fitzgerald Fletcher!"

"Yes," said the other, flushing with mortification, "I am Fitzgerald Fletcher."

"I am glad to see you," said Harry, cordially, forgetting the old antagonism that had existed between them.

He rose and offered his hand, which Fletcher took with an air of relief, for he had felt uncertain of his reception.

"You have prospered wonderfully," said Fletcher, with a shade of envy.

"Yes," said Harry, smiling. "I was a printer's devil when you knew me; but I never meant to stay in that position. I have risen from the ranks."

"I haven't," said Fletcher, bitterly.

"Have you been unfortunate? Tell me about it, if you don't mind," said Harry, sympathetically.

"My father failed three years ago," said Fletcher, "and I found myself adrift with nothing to do, and no money to fall back upon. I have drifted about since then; but now I am out of employment. I came to you today to see if you will exert your influence to get me a government clerkship, even of the lowest class. You may rest assured, Mr. Walton, that I need it."

Was this the proud Fitzgerald Fletcher, suing, for the means of supporting himself, to one whom, as a boy, he had despised and looked down upon? Surely, the world is full of strange changes and mutations of fortune. Here was a chance for Harry to triumph over his old enemy; but he never thought of doing it. Instead, he was filled with sympathy for one who, unlike himself, had gone down in the social scale, and he cordially promised to see what he could do for Fletcher, and that without delay.

On inquiry, he found that Fletcher was qualified to discharge the duties of a clerk, and secured his appointment to a clerkship in the Treasury Department, on a salary of twelve hundred dollars a year. It was an income which Fletcher would once have regarded as wholly insufficient for his needs; but adversity had made him humble, and he thankfully accepted it. He holds the position still, discharging the duties satisfactorily. He is glad to claim the Hon. Harry Walton among his acquaintances, and never sneers at him now as a "printer's devil."

Oscar Vincent spent several years abroad, after graduation, acting as foreign correspondent of his father's paper. He is now his father's junior partner, and is not only respected for his ability, but a general favorite in society, on account of his sunny disposition and cordial good nature. He keeps up his friendship with Harry Walton. Indeed, there is good reason for this, since Harry, four years ago, married his sister Maud, and the two friends are brothers-in-law.

Harry's parents are still living, no longer weighed down by poverty, as when we first made their acquaintance. The legacy which came so opportunely improved their condition, and provided them with comforts to which they had long been strangers. But their chief satisfaction comes from Harry's unlooked-for success in life. Their past life of poverty and privation is all forgotten in their gratitude for this great happiness.

THE END

~ ~ ~

TEACHERS GUIDE QUESTIONS FOR
RISEN FROM THE RANKS

1. We catch up with Harry Walton on his first day at the offices of the Centreville Gazette. What got him here up to this point?
2. Describe Harry's friend Oscar Vincent, and his classmate Fitzgerald Fletcher. Both of them have different feelings about Harry. What are they?
3. Who are the two men who work with Harry at the Gazette? What are their personalities?
4. What name does Fitzgerald Fletcher use to describe Harry? What does that name mean?
5. Ferguson has an opinion about Harry's future. What is his opinion, and why does he feel this way?
6. What title does Harry aspire to attain? Why does he wish to do this?
7. What is the Clionian Society? Why does Harry join, and how does it help him in his life?
8. Why does Fitzgerald Fletcher oppose Harry in his application to the Clionian Society? How does he try to keep Harry out? What happens to him as a result of his efforts?
9. Harry writes about "ambition" to the Weekly Standard. How does Harry define Ambition?
10. What situation allows Harry to be promoted at the Gazette? What is the outcome for the person who left the paper? What lesson is being taught with their story?
11. What does Harry have in common with Oscar Vincent's father?
12. What circumstances allow Harry to attain his goal?
13. How far has Harry risen? How has he risen so far? What happens to Fitzgerald Fletcher, and what lesson does this teach?

TEACHERS GUIDE ANSWERS FOR RISEN FROM THE RANKS

1.   Harry left the family farm to help earn money to help his father pay for a cow. Inspired by Benjamin Franklin, he knew he had to go out into the world to make his way. He worked as a shoemaker's apprentice and as an assistant to a ventriloquist. When he went to get advertisements printed for the magician, he met the owner of the Gazette, and in his desire to follow in Benjamin Franklin's footsteps, he asked for a job as a printer.

2.   Both Oscar Vincent and Fitzgerald Fletcher are students at the local academy. They're both sons of rich Boston-area businessmen. Oscar treats Harry with respect while Fitz looks down upon Harry because of his social standing.

3.   Harry works with Clapp and Ferguson at the gazette. Clapp runs in the same social group as Harry's old acquaintance Luke, and he is wasteful with his money, and therefore can't move ahead. He attributes this to his own bad luck. Ferguson is an older man with a wife and two children. He is very frugal with his money, and manages to put together a large savings account.

4.   Fitz repeatedly calls Harry a "Printer's Devil." He means it as an insult, but it's a term for a printer's apprentice.

5.   Ferguson believes that Harry is going to be a great man someday. He believes this because of his hardworking nature and financial sensibility.

6.   Harry wishes to become an editor of a newspaper someday. He desires this because an editor can be a person of great influence, and it's also a position that was once held by Benjamin Franklin.

7.   The Clionian Society is a debate club at the local academy. Harry joins at the recommendation of Oscar Vincent, and he eventually rises to be president of the organization. He later credits his experience with the Clionian Society in making him a much better public speaker.

8.   Fitz wishes to keep Harry out of the Clionian Society because he feels that Harry's social status doesn't make him worthy of membership. He tries to keep Harry out by proposing increases in membership fees that would make it too expensive for Harry to join. His efforts fail, and in retaliation, the other boys from the Clionian Society manage to prove that he has a relative with much lower social standing, which greatly embarrasses Fitz.

9.   Harry defines ambition as the desire to excel in order to benefit the human race.

10. Harry gets a promotion at the paper when Clapp leaves to move to St. Louis. The person he moves with is a dishonest man who stole money from a local old woman by pretending to be his nephew. Soon after arriving in St. Louis, Clapp's partner abandons him and moves to San Francisco, leaving Clapp in serious financial trouble. The author is trying to teach about people who come into their money dishonestly, and how bad things always seem to happen to them.

11. Both Harry and Oscar Vincent's father started out as Printer's Devils.

12. Harry becomes an editor when the owner of the Gazette leaves town for health reasons, and eventually sells the paper to Harry and Ferguson.

13. At the end of the story we find that Harry has risen from farm boy to United States Congressman. He's managed to rise far through hard work and continuing to educate himself. Fitzgerald Fletcher's father goes out of business, leaving him broke and begging Harry for a job, which Harry gets for him. The lesson is not to look down on someone because of their present social standing, because it may not always be that way.

BOUND TO RISE, RISEN FROM THE RANKS COMMENTARY

By Stefan Kanfer

Horatio Alger wrote 108 novels, and every one of them could have been published under the same title: Bound to Rise. No matter what the vicissitudes, protagonists from Ragged Dick Hunter to Mark the Match Boy to Phil the Fiddler to Harry Walton eventually triumph over economic and emotional hardship.

In Alger's heyday—c. 1880 to WW I—his heroes were considered role models by a majority of American youths. They bought the books by the millions, at a time when a sale of ten thousand was considered phenomenal. This was because a) the novels were page-turners with emotionally satisfying endings, and b) they reflected the true stories of many up-from-under American political, artistic and business leaders, ranging from Abraham Lincoln to Mark Twain to Andrew Carnegie and Jacob Astor.

The hero of Bound to Rise, Alger's 23rd novel, is first among equals. One epochal day, Harry Walton, an impoverished New Hampshire farm boy, is given the Autobiography of Benjamin Franklin. Inspired by the story of an obscure printer's son who rose to become a Founding Father, Harry sets out for Massachusetts and an exalted new vocation: journalism. En route, thieves take what little money he has. But in the midst of despair, opportunity appears in the person of Professor Henderson, a traveling magician and potential mentor. The professor hires Harry as a ticket-taker.

The resemblance to Charles Dickens' show business novel, Nicholas Nickleby, is more than coincidental. But Harry is not content with the roar of greasepaint and the smell of the crowd. Ben Franklin has made too deep an impression, and he aims to be nothing less than a newspaper editor—and then, somehow, to serve his country.

Risen From The Ranks, the second volume of Harry's story, covers his rise from ticket-taker to printer's assistant to editor and publisher of the Centerville (Massachusetts) Gazette. From there, he runs for Congress, echoing the career of his ideal.

Fanciful? Absurd? Alger fans didn't think so; success stories like Harry's were all around them. They agreed with Franklin's observation, "God helps those who help themselves." And Tom Paine's, "When we are planning for posterity, we ought to remember that virtue is not hereditary." And Ralph Waldo Emerson's, "Discontent is the want of self-reliance; it is an infirmity of will." Alger's novels aimed to instill the idea behind those phrases into America's children, and they did their job.

Today, more than eight decades after Alger fell out of favor, his works are back in style. As social critics have noted, the attitude of victimization inevitably leads downward to dependence and despair, never upward to freedom and achievement. Browsers with open minds can see what the author so vigorously promoted in Bound to Rise and Risen From The Ranks. Then as now, independence, forbearance and square dealing can be life changing for the young— and well worth the price of admission for every reader, regardless of age or circumstance.

Stefan Kanfer is an award-winning writer for City Journal and the author of numerous best-selling books.

THE LIFE AND THEMES OF
HORATIO ALGER, JR.

By Stefan Kanfer

The Merriam-Webster Dictionary devotes one sentence to him: "Of, relating to, or resembling the fiction of Horatio Alger in which success is achieved through self-reliance and hard work."

True as far as it goes, but that sentence reveals nothing about the man or his accomplishment. Then again, other contemporary reference books are just as terse. Not one acknowledges that Alger in his day (circa 1880-1920) was a publishing phenomenon. During those decades, when a sale of 10,000 volumes was deemed a triumph, readers bought more than 200 million copies of Alger's works, placing him in a league with J.K. Rowling and Stephen King.

Alas, today most of his novels—and there are more than 100—are out of print. But not for long. Thanks to the resuscitation efforts of Sumner Books, a division of Creators Syndicate, Alger's best literary productions are being furnished with fresh covers, new fonts and energetic promotion.

Seldom has there been a more relevant illustration of the maxim that what goes around comes around. At the turn of the 19th century, Alger was the standard-bearer of a phenomenally successful experiment in social reform and personal improvement. That movement inspired disadvantaged kids to move on up, leading juvenile delinquents into productive, significant lives. Men as different as Groucho Marx and Ernest Hemingway were fans.

"Horatio Alger's books conveyed a powerful message to me," wrote Marx, "and to many of my young friends as well—that if you worked hard at your trade, the big chance would eventually come. As a child I didn't regard it as a myth, and as an old man I think of it as the story of my life."

Hemingway's sister Marcelline recalled that during their childhood, "There was one summer when Ernest couldn't get enough of Horatio Alger." Not that Alger's boys' books influenced Papa's prose style. But there must have been something in the writer's stress on grit and self-reliance that affected young Ernest, as it did so many of his contemporaries.

By the end of the Roaring Twenties, though, Horatio Alger had become as passé as the Ford Model T. During the Depression he fared no better; Nathaniel West's satirical 1934 novel, A Cool Million, sent Alger's plots in reverse, as the naïve protagonist loses limb after limb seeking success among rapacious capitalists. Decades later, the film adaptation of Hunter Thompson's 1971 novel, Fear and Loathing in Las Vegas, presented the antihero as "Horatio Alger gone mad on drugs in Las Vegas."

What lay behind Alger's ability to enchant so many Americans—and to enrage so many others? The author's story furnishes a trove of clues:

The sickly child of a Unitarian minister in Marlborough, Massachusetts, Horatio, born in 1832, was always the smallest in his class and far from an academic star. Still, his report cards were good enough for admission to Harvard. There his academic prowess was in inverse proportion to his size (5 feet 2 inches). He won prizes, published verse and fiction in undergraduate magazines, and labeled the entire four years a period of "unmixed happiness."

Decades would pass before he found such contentment again. Upon graduation, Horatio attempted to make his way as a writer. After five unsuccessful years, he returned to Harvard, this time to study at the Divinity School. In 1860 the Reverend Horatio Alger was named minister of the First Parish Unitarian Church of Brewster on Cape Cod. Salary: $800 per year. To supplement his meager income, he turned once again to writing. This time, his stories were well-received, and he allowed himself to dream of a dual career of preacher and writer. That's when catastrophe struck.

It was of his own making, if one historian is to be believed. According to this claim, a 13-year-old told his parents that the new parson had made advances to him. An investigation began. Another lad made a similar complaint. Faced with charges of behaving inappropriately, the accused was allowed to resign—with the proviso that he leave town at once.

Sometime later, Horatio wrote a poem about one Friar Anselmo, who had committed an unspecified crime. Melancholy and remorseful, he comes across a wounded traveler and gives him aid. Whereupon an angel materializes and offers salvation:
Thy guilty stains shall be washed white again
By noble service done thy fellow man.

The fugitive repaired to New York City in the spring of 1866, resolved to live out the Christian ideal, expiating his sin by saving others. The Manhattan he entered was the epicenter of the Gilded Age, a magnet for millions of ambitious climbers, drawn by the post-Civil War boom. Out of sight of the glittering prosperity, the mansions and carriages, however, was another New York, a squalid night town that travelers compared to Calcutta, India.

In The Good Old Days, They Were Terrible, historian Otto Bettmann reports that there was scarcely a slum that pedestrians could negotiate "without climbing over a heap of trash or, in rain, wading through a bed of slime." Many streets were so dangerous that policemen hesitated to walk them alone. A Gramercy Park resident noted in his diary, "Most of my friends are investing in revolvers and carry them about at night"—and the Park was one of the city's better neighborhoods.

The New York City street urchin entered the national consciousness in those years. More than 60,000 neglected or abandoned kids ran unsupervised in the street, partly because of the fallout from the tidal waves of immigration from Europe and partly because of families broken by the Civil War.

What was to be done about these juveniles likely to die on the streets or to end up behind bars? The Reverend Charles Loring Brace founded the Children's Aid Society, designed to take homeless or abused kids away from their corrosive environments. At the same time, John Hughes, New York's first Roman Catholic archbishop, set up parochial schools and a residential institution called the Catholic Protectory, which brought up abandoned or orphaned children to be useful members of society.

Horatio Alger joined these efforts at reclamation. He, too, asked himself what could be done about homeless children. Seeking answers, he wandered through the city's worst neighborhoods. He interviewed "street arabs" who spoke of broken homes, violent confrontations with parents, doomed futures. He observed how their cocky attitudes masked a profound despair. He advised them to get real jobs instead of hanging about, squandering whatever came their way from shining shoes or picking pockets. A handful nodded in agreement, expressing the desire to change their lives; most were content to take life as they found it.

Why, he pondered, did individuals subjected to the same conditions turn out so differently? One boy might become a thief, a sociopath, even a killer. His neighbor, perhaps his brother, might aim to be an upright citizen. What was the difference between them?

What saved certain boys, he came to believe, was a quality that gave them the strength to resist sloth and temptation. In a word, character. But was this inborn? In that case determinism won the day, and change was out of the question. Or, given the right opportunity and attitude, could a dispossessed youth win his share of the American dream? The latter, Alger believed—but only if the boy stopped regarding himself as a victim.

As Alger meditated upon the worst crime of the slums—the stealing of childhood from children—an idea came to him. He would be Brother Anselmo redivivus. He had sinned against youths; now he would rescue them—and in the process save himself. As the novelist put it, by depicting the situation of city waifs, he would "excite a deeper and more widespread sympathy in the public mind, as well as exert a salutary influence upon the class of whom he is writing, by setting before them inspiring examples of what energy, ambition, and an honest purpose may achieve."

Ragged Dick became the template of the fiction to follow. Subtitled Street Life in New York with the Boot Blacks, it charted the rise of a 14-year-old boy from poverty to prosperity. Dick Hunter is an adolescent with all odds against him. He has no family, he smokes, drinks alcohol when he can afford it—not very often on the small change he gets from shining gentlemen's shoes—and sleeps on gratings in the winter.

Yet something separates him from his fellow waifs. He refuses to pick pockets like the others, won't mock his elders, and yearns to "grow up 'spectable.'" His bearing and his innate decency attract the attention of upright New Yorkers. One introduces him to his church; another presents Dick with a few dollars.

The earnest youth resolves to become literate to save his money and live a clean life. One day on a walk near South Ferry he sees a toddler fall in the water. Without hesitation, Dick jumps in and saves the drowning child. In gratitude, the father, an affluent businessman, offers the rescuer a job in his office. Gainfully employed, the onetime vagabond Dick Hunter becomes Richard Hunter Esq., and shuts the door forever on the "old vagabond life which he hoped never to resume."

Naïve? Simplistic? To the jaded, the cynical and the ignorant, yes. But not to thousands of children trapped in the real world of poverty and early death. They got the message of Ragged Dick and demanded more Horatio Alger novels with more moral lessons for them to absorb. Those books changed—and in many cases saved—lives a century before Dr. Martin Luther King Jr. stated his belief that what mattered was not the color of one's skin but the content of one's character.

Today, if you listen closely you can hear, amid the jeers, the escalating sound of the last laugh. In 1947, the Horatio Alger Association was founded. It attracts more prominent men and women now than it did then. The group is dedicated to recognizing American leaders who rose, like Alger's young heroes, from humble origins "through honesty, hard work, self-reliance and perseverance." With grants to U.S. high-school students who have "faced and overcome great obstacles in their young lives," the association encourages them to emulate such enterprising and disparate members as Oprah Winfrey and Ray Kroc, Tom Brokaw and Maya Angelou, Stan Musial and Colin Powell.

They can all testify to the truths that lie between the covers of this volume. Turn the first few pages, and you'll understand why so many followed Horatio Alger's breathless, cliff-hanging chapters leading the way from skid row to success. And why so many more are about to read that map in a world where everything has changed—except the basic truths of life.

Stefan Kanfer is an award-winning writer for City Journal and the author of numerous best-selling books.

ABOUT HORATIO ALGER, JR.

Horatio Alger was born in 1832 in Chelsea, Massachusetts. He spent his early years in the small town and under the guidance of the church and his father, the town pastor, before the family moved just west of Boston to the town of Marlborough. As a shy young boy, Alger poured himself into books and soon became a distinguished student. He studied at Harvard and Harvard Divinity School before becoming a minister. He practiced ministry for a few years near Boston and on Cape Cod, but he was distracted by his true passion: writing. He loved to write, and by 1865 Alger had written a handful of stories, including Frank's Campaign and Paul Prescott's Charge. The latter was the first in a series of stories that would eventually lead to his great success. In 1866, Alger moved to New York to write poetry, newspaper stories and magazine articles. However, he was shocked to find so many homeless and forgotten children among the streets, an unfortunate consequence of the Civil War. He made it his duty to aid the condition of these lost children, both through his stories and by his continuous acts of benevolence.

Horatio Alger became a household name shortly after the Civil War when he began publishing stories in the form of serializations. These serializations were featured in magazines such as Student and Schoolmate and were later compiled as books. Alger's books became enormously popular, especially among teenage boys across the country, and they soon reached millions and millions of readers. Alger continued to produce several stories a year, and, in later years, wrote novels in and of themselves instead of novels from magazine serials.

The years immediately following the Civil War were the same years when the United States emerged as one nation on the road to becoming a worldwide empire. The years between 1865 and 1900 were the years of the empire builders, with the rags-to-riches stories of John D. Rockefeller, Andrew Carnegie, Cornelius Vanderbilt and Thomas Edison. They were the years that laid the foundation for Henry Ford and other business titans and for the spectacular growth of the American economy throughout the 20th century and through today. During these years, Alger published well over 100 stories, poems and novels that spoke to the timeless themes and successes of this era.

The theme of Alger's books is consistent: If you work hard, go the extra mile, are faithful and honest, show kindness and generosity, and maintain a cheerful, positive and optimistic attitude, you will succeed in creating financial security and happiness. On the other hand, if you lie, cheat, steal, are lazy or envious, and try to take advantage of other people, you will be doomed to failure and misery. Despite his background as a preacher, Alger does not make these points in a self-righteous or pontificating way. What he does instead -- just like the parables that Jesus told -- is to create stories that illustrate the virtues that lead to success. And the stories that Alger creates are no ordinary stories. Each one is filled with lively plots and twists and turns, ones that are always unexpected and keep the reader wanting to know what's going to happen next.

As Alger grew older, he continuously strived to write the Great American Novel, little realizing that the rags-to-riches stories he created were more influential than any other novelists'. He travelled out west in early 1877 searching for new material and returned near the end of the year, producing similar stories with a new western backdrop. By 1897, Alger was suffering from asthma, bronchitis and slight short-term memory loss. He moved in with his sister in South Natick, Massachusetts where he spent the last two years of his life.

Most people have never heard of Horatio Alger while some are vaguely familiar with the term "rags-to-riches." In the Alger family, it was the norm to burn correspondence and manuscripts, and this, coupled with Alger's shyness, has greatly kept him from history's limelight. Though too often forgotten today, Alger's works and the themes within them still affect the American psyche. Many assert that there is a lagging spirit in present American culture, that these inspiring stories are irrelevant. Young people are bombarded with external stimuli that make it difficult for them to get to know themselves. Wide-eyed innocence and childlike enthusiasm, once revered as admirable qualities, are sources of mockery and disdain, which makes cynicism and pessimism inevitable. Video games, television shows, movies and music are all aimed at titillating and at seeing who can be the most gritty, violent or shocking. More than a few commentators have used the word "degrading" to describe the assault that children encounter today.

This is unfortunate. Young people need heroes and role models today just as much as they did in the 1870s and '80s, when Alger was creating them at a feverish pace from his New York City apartment, writing as many as four books at a time. Publisher A.K. Loring asserted that Alger's books "captured the spirits of reborn America" for "above all you can hear the cry of triumph of the oppressed over the oppressor ... What Alger has done is to portray the soul – the ambitious soul – of the country." Years later, biographer Edwin P. Hoyt concludes that Alger is "a writer whose influence on the American scene has been so profound that it is hard to measure." Indeed, Alger's works made an overwhelming impression on American culture and society that are still alive with us today. It is for this reason that these classics must be brought to a new generation of readers.

OUR COMMITMENT TO
HORATIO ALGER

By Rick Newcombe

Sumner Books is totally committed to reviving interest in Horatio Alger, one of the best-selling authors of all time yet someone who has been all but forgotten today. I'd like to tell you how this project came about.

Probably the best starting point is to tell you a little about myself. I grew up in suburban Chicago, and my parents were religious and fundamentally optimistic in their outlook on life. They encouraged all eight of their children to be positive in our thinking and hope and pray for the best in all situations. In my adolescence, I discovered many of the self-help authors from the 20th century, including Dale Carnegie, Napoleon Hill and Norman Vincent Peale. I remember reading a small magazine in the 1970s, when I was in my 20s, called Success Unlimited and being inspired each month to work hard and stay positive. The publisher of this magazine was W. Clement Stone, who started his career selling insurance policies door to door and who went on to build Combined Insurance, which became part of Aon, one of the largest insurance companies in the world.

By the time Mr. Stone died in 2002, he was a very successful businessman, an extremely generous philanthropist and totally committed to spreading the gospel of positive thinking. I remember reading one of his books, The Success System That Never Fails, which was both an autobiography and a blueprint for achieving success. Stone told the story of spending a summer on a farm in Michigan when he was 12, getting fresh air, helping on the farm and enjoying picnics, carnivals and camping out.

W. Clement Stone

"But I'll never forget the first day I went upstairs to the attic," he wrote, "for there I met Horatio Alger. At least 50 of his books, dusty and weather-worn, were piled in the corner. I took one down to the hammock in the front yard and started to read."

Stone said he was so enthralled he couldn't stop. "I read through all of them that summer," he wrote.

He said the principle in each book was that "the hero became a success because he was a man of character -- the villain a failure because he deceived and embezzled. How many Alger books were sold? No one knows. Estimates range from 100 million to 300 million. We do know that his books inspired thousands of American boys from poor families to strive to do the right thing because it was right and to acquire wealth."

That was the first time I had heard of Horatio Alger, but it never occurred to me to try to find his books. Over the years, I founded Creators Syndicate, which became one of the most successful newspaper syndication companies in the world. I attribute much of our success to our positive thinking and upbeat attitude. We became a multimillion-dollar international corporation by syndicating a wide variety of journalists, celebrities and award-winning cartoonists.

As we were expanding into new businesses, e-books and audiobooks were a natural starting point because we work with so many talented writers and artists. But we also wanted to try new things. With that in mind, I remembered Mr. Stone's enthusiastic recommendation of Horatio Alger's books, and I decided to read some. Many were available as e-books, and I thoroughly enjoyed them.

I had a good feeling whenever I was transported back to New York City as it was in 1870, when trains were called "cars" and there were no automobiles. There was a constant risk of crossing the streets without streetlights or walk signs. A number of years later, the Brooklyn Dodgers, now the Los Angeles Dodgers, got their name from the treacherous dodging of horses, wagons and streetcars that was required to cross the street in the city. In those days, plumbing with hot and cold running water was not taken for granted, much less radios, televisions, computers or smartphones. Are you kidding? A smartphone in the 1860s? There wasn't even a telephone.

But what great stories Alger wrote -- one after another. I couldn't get enough of them! And it was impossible not to feel grateful for all the modern conveniences of the 21st century when immersing myself in the world of America as it was in the 1860s and '70s.

As I read book after book, I felt like a teenager all over again, excited about the future and the promise of a brighter tomorrow. It was then that I decided to go full bore into spreading the word of Horatio Alger.

One of the problems with the e-books was the lack of organization; another was the maddening number of typos, over and over and over, or the lack of illustrations or the lack of a table of contents. In fact, what was intended to be a good deed to spread Mr. Alger's message really turned out to be something of a disservice.

So I made it my mission to have professional editors edit the texts so there were no typographical or spelling errors. We found appropriate illustrations. We included detailed tables of contents for each book, and we decided to publish them in groups, when appropriate, which has never been done before. We are including commentaries and teachers guides with each e-book.

We also decided to make audiobooks of as many of these "Stories of Success" as possible. We hired a terrific actor, Ben Gillman, and his initial experience shows you how far we have to go to spread the word. Ben went to the Hollywood public library to find some Horatio Alger books, but there was none. "You'd have to go to the downtown public library, in the historical section, to find those," the librarian told him.

Remember, this is one of the best-selling American authors of all time, yet it is as if he never existed.

Part of the problem is that some of the caricatures of Horatio Alger over the years have been absolutely brutal. Even to this day, the Encyclopedia Britannica, from which we expect objective reporting, calls Alger's dialogue and plots "outrageously bad." Come again? The encyclopedia is supposed to provide broad knowledge on specific subjects, not offer the biased literary criticism of a handful of editors. Talk about being unfair -- and just plain wrong!

How do you answer a cheap shot like that? Really, it is nothing more than an incredibly snooty opinion; in fact, it is an "outrageously bad" opinion. Remember, the Horatio Alger books were intended to be not great literature but rather inspirational stories to motivate young boys to achieve a better life. If the dialogue and plots were not lively and believable, the books would not have sold in the millions. The fact that Horatio Alger helped form the American character shows that an incredible number of boys ate up his books as thrilling and believable.

The brilliant writer Stefan Kanfer wrote an extensive review of Horatio Alger's works in 2000 for City Journal magazine, a publication of the prestigious Manhattan Institute. He started off believing the critics, but when he actually read some of Horatio Alger's books, he drew a totally different conclusion. "I began reading the novels aloud to my children," he wrote. "We found them well-plotted, entertaining, and instructive, not at all the righteous antiquities that I had been led to believe. Almost every chapter ends with a cliff-hanger, and all of us could hardly wait for the next night to find out what happened. The conclusions never failed to produce an emotional satisfaction and a feeling that what the author was selling -- independence, forbearance, square dealing -- was well worth buying."

We can only speculate about why the critics have been so harsh on Horatio Alger, but no doubt some it stems from their being turned off by precisely the character traits that Mr. Kanfer identifies. Like it or not, there is a mindset that scoffs at individual achievement through hard work, a positive attitude and generosity -- living every day with an "attitude of gratitude," which is the essence of Horatio Alger's message.

W. Clement Stone was routinely mocked for starting the day by saying, "I feel healthy! I feel happy! I feel terrific!" He encouraged his employees to do the same. In fact, he encouraged everyone to demonstrate outward enthusiasm and PMA, which stood for a positive mental attitude. His critics thought he was ridiculous, but Mr. Stone got the last laugh, living to age 100, which he had set as his goal, and accumulating hundreds of millions of dollars.

Roswell Crawford is an important character in Ragged Dick and Fame and Fortune because he oozes the world-owes-me-a-living attitude that is so common today. "Roswell was troubled with a large share of pride," Alger writes, "though it might have troubled himself to explain what he had to be proud of."

Roswell never understands the importance of integrity and its relationship to earning one's living. In fact, he once says that he would be happy to be paid $10 a week for nothing. "Well, if I get it, I don't care if I don't earn it," he says. In fact, Roswell is ashamed to be seen in the streets carrying a large bundle as part of a delivery for his job. Before being fired, his boss tells him, "You appear to think yourself of too great consequence to discharge properly the duties of your position."

Contrast that with Richard Hunter's attitude toward his entry-level job when he first starts working at the firm. "I'm ready to do anything that is required of me. I want to make myself useful," he says.

I have the impression that was the same attitude that Horatio Alger had as he approached his goal of becoming a successful writer who could change the world -- or at least the world of the thousands of homeless street urchins in the big city. It is difficult to imagine how bad their plight was. For instance, in 1874, which was seven years after Ragged Dick was first published, there was a little girl named Mary Ellen Wilson, who was beaten unmercifully by her stepmother. She was sent out into the streets ill-clothed in winter. There were other abuses, and they were horrible.

So a social worker named Etta Angel Wheeler wanted to intervene, to help get the child out of that environment. But there were no laws to protect children in such situations. Etta was desperate -- and clever. She enlisted the help of the American Society for the Prevention of Cruelty to Animals because animals were protected by law. Her attorneys argued that Mary Ellen, "as a member of the animal kingdom, deserved the same protection as abused animals." This led to new legislation and various child protective services.

Horatio Alger was at the forefront of this movement. He wanted to help the poor kids in the inner city, and he wound up not only helping them but inspiring millions of other young readers across the country. Many of them transformed their lives as a direct result of the inspiration of the "Stories of Success" that Horatio Alger managed to tell in one exciting setting after another.

It is not surprising that Ernest Hemingway's sister said that her brother could not get enough of Horatio Alger or that Walter Brennan, a famous actor for much of the 20th century, devoured his books. As the legendary Groucho Marx said: "Horatio Alger's books conveyed a powerful message to me and to many of my young friends -- that if you worked hard at your trade, the big chance would eventually come. As a child, I didn't regard it as a myth, and as an old man, I think of it as the story of my life."

Groucho was speaking for millions of Americans in the past and, we hope, millions more in the future.

Rick Newcombe is the founder and CEO of Creators Syndicate, Creators Publishing and Sumner Books.

PREVIEW OF ANOTHER ADVENTURE IN THE HORATIO ALGER "STORIES OF SUCCESS" SERIES

RAGGED DICK

By Horatio Alger, Jr.

"Wake up there, youngster," said a rough voice.

Ragged Dick opened his eyes slowly, and stared stupidly in the face of the speaker, but did not offer to get up.

"Wake up, you young vagabond!" said the man a little impatiently;

"I suppose you'd lay there all day, if I hadn't called you."

"What time is it?" asked Dick.

"Seven o'clock."

"Seven o'clock! I oughter've been up an hour ago. I know what 'twas made me so precious sleepy. I went to the Old Bowery last night, and didn't turn in till past twelve."

"You went to the Old Bowery? Where'd you get your money?" asked the man, who was a porter in the employ of a firm doing business on Spruce Street. "Made it by shines, in course. My guardian don't allow me no money for theatres, so I have to earn it."

"Some boys get it easier than that," said the porter significantly.

"You don't catch me stealin', if that's what you mean," said Dick.

"Don't you ever steal, then?"

"No, and I wouldn't. Lots of boys does it, but I wouldn't."

"Well, I'm glad to hear you say that. I believe there's some good in you, Dick, after all."

"Oh, I'm a rough customer!" said Dick. "But I wouldn't steal. It's mean."

"I'm glad you think so, Dick," and the rough voice sounded gentler than at first. "Have you got any money to buy your breakfast?"

"No, but I'll soon get some."

363

While this conversation had been going on, Dick had got up. His bedchamber had been a wooden box half full of straw, on which the young boot-black had reposed his weary limbs, and slept as soundly as if it had been a bed of down. He dumped down into the straw without taking the trouble of undressing.

A bootblack working in New York City.

Getting up too was an equally short process. He jumped out of the box, shook himself, picked out one or two straws that had found their way into rents in his clothes, and, drawing a well-worn cap over his uncombed locks, he was all ready for the business of the day.

Dick's appearance as he stood beside the box was rather peculiar. His pants were torn in several places, and had apparently belonged in the first instance to a boy two sizes larger than himself. He wore a vest, all the buttons of which were gone except two, out of which peeped a shirt which looked as if it had been worn a month. To complete his costume he wore a coat too long for him, dating back, if one might judge from its general appearance, to a remote antiquity.

Washing the face and hands is usually considered proper in commencing the day, but Dick was above such refinement. He had no particular dislike to dirt, and did not think it necessary to remove several dark streaks on his face and hands. But in spite of his dirt and rags there was something about Dick that was attractive. It was easy to see that if he had been clean and well dressed he would have been decidedly good-looking. Some of his companions were sly, and their faces inspired distrust; but Dick had a frank, straight-forward manner that made him a favorite.

Dick's business hours had commenced. He had no office to open. His little blacking-box was ready for use, and he looked sharply in the faces of all who passed, addressing each with, "Shine yer boots, sir?"

"How much?" asked a gentleman on his way to his office.

"Ten cents," said Dick, dropping his box, and sinking upon his knees on the sidewalk, flourishing his brush with the air of one skilled in his profession.

"Ten cents! Isn't that a little steep?"

"Well, you know 'taint all clear profit," said Dick, who had already set to work. "There's the blacking costs something, and I have to get a new brush pretty often."

"And you have a large rent too," said the gentleman quizzically, with a glance at a large hole in Dick's coat.

"Yes, sir," said Dick, always ready to joke; "I have to pay such a big rent for my manshun up on Fifth Avenoo, that I can't afford to take less than ten cents a shine. I'll give you a bully shine, sir."

"Be quick about it, for I am in a hurry. So your house is on Fifth Avenue, is it?"

"It isn't anywhere else," said Dick, and Dick spoke the truth there.

"What tailor do you patronize?" asked the gentleman, surveying Dick's attire.

"Would you like to go to the same one?" asked Dick, shrewdly.

"Well, no; it strikes me that he didn't give you a very good fit."

"This coat once belonged to General Washington," said Dick, comically. "He wore it all through the Revolution, and it got torn some, 'cause he fit so hard. When he died he told his widder to give it to some smart young feller that hadn't got none of his own; so she gave it to me. But if you'd like it, sir, to remember General Washington by, I'll let you have it reasonable."

"Thank you, but I wouldn't want to deprive you of it. And did your pants come from General Washington too?"

"No, they was a gift from Lewis Napoleon. Lewis had outgrown 'em and sent 'em to me—he's bigger than me, and that's why they don't fit."

"It seems you have distinguished friends. Now, my lad, I suppose you would like your money."

"I shouldn't have any objection," said Dick.

"I believe," said the gentleman, examining his wallet, "I haven't got anything short of twenty-five cents. Have you got any change?"

"Not a cent," said Dick. "All my money's invested in the Erie Railroad."

"That's unfortunate."

"Shall I get the money changed, sir?"

"I can't wait; I've got to meet an appointment immediately. I'll hand you twenty-five cents, and you can leave the change at my office any time during the day."
"All right, sir. Where is it?"

"No. 125 Fulton Street. Shall you remember?"

"Yes, sir. What name?"

"Greyson—office on second floor."

"All right, sir; I'll bring it."

"I wonder whether the little scamp will prove honest," said Mr. Greyson to himself, as he walked away. "If he does, I'll give him my custom regularly. If he don't as is most likely, I shan't mind the loss of fifteen cents."

Dick always jokes about having Erie Railroad shares, but doesn't actually have them. This is what they would look like if he did have them.

Mr. Greyson didn't understand Dick. Our ragged hero wasn't a model boy in all respects. I am afraid he swore sometimes, and now and then he played tricks upon unsophisticated boys from the country, or gave a wrong direction to honest old gentlemen unused to the city. A clergyman in search of the Cooper Institute he once directed to the Tombs Prison, and, following him unobserved, was highly delighted when the unsuspicious stranger walked up the front steps of the great stone building on Centre Street, and tried to obtain admission.

"I guess he wouldn't want to stay long if he did get in," thought Ragged Dick, hitching up his pants. "Leastways I shouldn't. They're so precious glad to see you that they won't let you go, but board you gratooitous, and never send in no bills."

Another of Dick's faults was his extravagance. Being always wide-awake and ready for business, he earned enough to have supported him comfortably and respectably. There were not a few young clerks who employed Dick from time to time in his professional capacity, who scarcely earned as much as he, greatly as their style and dress exceeded his. But Dick was careless of his earnings. Where they went he could hardly have told himself. However much he managed to earn during the day, all was generally spent before morning. He was fond of going to the Old Bowery Theatre, and to Tony Pastor's, and if he had any money left afterwards, he would invite some of his friends in somewhere to have an oyster-stew; so it seldom happened that he commenced the day with a penny.

The Bowery Theater, which is one of the places where Dick would spend his money.

Then I am sorry to add that Dick had formed the habit of smoking. This cost him considerable, for Dick was rather fastidious about his cigars, and wouldn't smoke the cheapest. Besides, having a liberal nature, he was generally ready to treat his companions. But of course the expense was the smallest objection. No boy of fourteen can smoke without being affected injuriously. Men are frequently injured by smoking, and boys always. But large numbers of the newsboys and boot-blacks form the habit. Exposed to the cold and wet they find that it warms them up, and the self-indulgence grows upon them. It is not uncommon to see a little boy, too young to be out of his mother's sight, smoking with all the apparent satisfaction of a veteran smoker.

There was another way in which Dick sometimes lost money. There was a noted gambling-house on Baxter Street, which in the evening was sometimes crowded with these juvenile gamesters, who staked their hard earnings, generally losing of course, and refreshing themselves from time to time with a vile mixture of liquor at two cents a glass. Sometimes Dick strayed in here, and played with the rest.

I have mentioned Dick's faults and defects, because I want it understood, to begin with, that I don't consider him a model boy. But there were some good points about him nevertheless. He was above doing anything mean or dishonorable. He would not steal, or cheat, or impose upon younger boys, but was frank and straight-forward, manly and self-reliant. His nature was a noble one, and had saved him from all mean faults. I hope my young readers will like him as I do, without being blind to his faults. Perhaps, although he was only a boot-black, they may find something in him to imitate.

And now, having fairly introduced Ragged Dick to my young readers,

I must refer them to the next chapter for his further adventures.